THE
EMOTIONAL WOUND
THESAURUS:

A Writer's Guide to Psychological Trauma

ANGELA ACKERMAN

BECCA PUGLISI

First print edition, October 2017
ISBN-13: 978-0-9897725-9-4
ISBN-10: 0-9897725-9-4

Edited by C. S. Lakin (www.livewritethrive.com) and Michael Dunne (www.michael-dunne.com/)

Book cover design by The Book Design House (www.thebookdesignhouse.com)
Book formatting by Polgarus Studio (www.polgarusstudio.com)

MORE WRITERS HELPING WRITERS® BOOKS

The Emotion Thesaurus: A Writer's Guide to Character Expression (Second Edition)

Emotion Amplifiers: A Companion to The Emotion Thesaurus

The Positive Trait Thesaurus: A Writer's Guide to Character Attributes

The Negative Trait Thesaurus: A Writer's Guide to Character Flaws

The Urban Setting Thesaurus: A Writer's Guide to City Spaces

The Rural Setting Thesaurus: A Writer's Guide to Personal and Natural Places

The Occupation Thesaurus: A Writer's Guide to Jobs, Vocations, and Careers

TABLE OF CONTENTS

FOREWORD

Forewords are a bit like prologues in that there's a temptation to skip them and get to the meat and potatoes of the book. We hope that, in our case, you'll indulge us for a very quick yet important word about the content you'll find within.

The purpose of this book is to provide useful information about wounding events and how they impact characters—not only the hero but any member of the story's cast. Mentors, sidekicks, love interests, and villains are all affected similarly by trauma, which will determine the motivations that drive them toward their chosen goals. So as you read, think about each important character and how past wounds may create damage and cause personality shifts, biases, and changes in behavior and attitude.

Please also note that while we have done our best to respect these wounds by researching them thoroughly, neither of us are psychologists. The content here is not meant for real-world application and should only be used to better understand the deeper layers of our characters and how past traumas can drive their choices.

Finally, despite this content being for writing purposes, trauma is, sadly, not fictional. It is a very real, damaging thing, and reading about it can sometimes be triggering, as we have all experienced emotional pain in one form or another. We urge you to take this into account as you explore the darker aspects of your characters' wounds. If necessary, consider putting safeguards in place for yourself. To this end, we've included the following section on self-care should any entries in this book hit you particularly hard.

SELF-CARE FOR WRITERS

Use This Book in a Safe Place. Many authors like to work in a busy coffee shop, a library, or even at a group writing event. But if you are exploring a character's wound that touches something from your own past, it isn't uncommon for a rush of unpleasant emotions to hit. If this happens, it is much better to be in a place where you can take a few moments to privately process whatever comes.

Incorporate a Time Buffer. Writing about a difficult moment in a character's life isn't easy, especially if some of it feels personal to you. As such, it may be better to not tackle painful content right before a scheduled appointment or over the lunch hour. When writing an emotionally taxing scene, give yourself ample time to get back into a balanced mentality before returning to your responsibilities in the real world.

Take as Many Breaks as You Need. If you feel overwhelmed, go for a walk, cuddle with your cat, or indulge in a special treat. Lighting a scented candle at the start of the session and blowing it out when you're ready to stop is also a great way to signal your mind that it's time to back away emotionally and turn to something else.

Have Someone You Trust on Standby. If you'll be working on a scene that is especially personal or difficult, having a friend in the loop can be helpful. Let them know when you'll be writing it and that you may need to call on them for a bit of support or encouragement. You might also ask them to check on you through text, email, or social media messaging. This can help with any feelings of isolation that may hit as you write.

THE MIRROR OF FICTION:
A REFLECTION OF LIFE AND OUR DEEPER SELVES

If there's a universal truth in life, it is that people are spellbound by story. Deep down, each of us craves a view into other worlds and is fascinated by the unspooling of a reality that is different from our own. We solve mysteries, fight battles, visit fantastical places, discover (or rediscover) romance, and follow the stepping-stones of a character's journey that may or may not be similar to our own. A great story becomes a unique threshold, offering us an opportunity to cross over and experience the life of another person.

On the outside, it may seem that fiction is solely about escaping the dullness or stress of the real world, yet entertainment is only one reason people are drawn to it. Throughout the ages, story has been used to guide and teach, allowing us to pass on important information, ideas, and beliefs in many different forms.

This storytelling tradition continues today. We might tell a half-true tale to friends about our crazy weekend in Vegas or relay to co-workers an eye-rolling anecdote about What My Moronic Neighbor Did This Week. Often, however, a story comes from a more meaningful place, giving us the chance to share our raw feelings, hopes, and desires with others. Either way, as writers, if we approach the page only planning to entertain, our stories will lack depth. To ensure that our writing connects with readers, we need to acknowledge that storytelling resonates deepest when it provides them with something they are always searching for: context.

Why is context so important? Because life doesn't come with a user's manual (oh, how some days we wish it did!). As people, we spend a lot of time pretending that we've got it together and know exactly what we're doing, but, in reality, most of us don't. Obstacles, challenges, and opportunities come along in life and prompt difficult questions: *How do I deal with this? What should I do? What will it say about me if I fail?*

Unfortunately, fear, self-doubt, and insecurity are all part of the human baggage we lug around each day. Because we don't want to seem weak, most of us won't share our uncertainty openly; instead, we manage situations the best we can and look around for examples—context—of how to behave, move forward, and hopefully become more experienced and capable people.

This universal need to grow provides writers with a special opportunity to create a mirror of the real world through fiction, allowing readers a safe way to probe their own deeper layers. After all, as characters face tough choices, painful consequences, and hard-won achievements, readers can't help but be reminded of their own journeys. By sharing a character's experiences, they get an intimate glimpse into how others wrestle with difficult situations, moral dilemmas, and the disruptive nature of change. And whether readers are consciously aware of it or not, this exposure provides the context they seek, offering information that may help them better navigate their lives.

Above all else, the fictional character's internal journey from brokenness to wholeness is one everyone can identify with because, deep down, each of us is a bit damaged. We've all suffered emotional hurts and are looking to heal. And stronger still are the deeper motivations to find our purpose in this world, to belong, and become better people. To accomplish these things, like the hero or heroine of a story, we need to cast aside that which holds us back: our own fears and emotional pain—the root of our insecurities.

Connecting readers with complex characters who remind them of themselves results in story magic—achievable, but magic all the same. And creating true-to-life mirrors with our fiction is the key to drawing readers in. Human desires, needs, beliefs, and emotions are all areas to explore, but one of the most potent real-life reflections that should steer a story from start to finish is the character's emotional wound.

WHAT IS AN EMOTIONAL WOUND?

Growing up, do you remember something happening that you didn't expect, something that surprised you—and not in a good way? Maybe you came home with a third-place Science Fair ribbon, and rather than wrap you up in a breath-stealing hug and fawn over the yellow slip, your mother barely gave it a glance, declaring that you should have tried harder. Now, fast-forward to junior year. You auditioned for the lead in the school musical, but the part went to someone else. How did that feel, especially when you had to deliver the news to dear old mom? What about when you missed the cut for a university program that, as she likes to remind you, your brother got into with no problem, or the time you were passed over for a promotion and had to sit through an agonizing family dinner where your sibling was lauded for his accomplishments?

Chances are, this wounded past doesn't match your own. But if it did, at what point would resentment set in over your mother's love being withdrawn each time you failed to meet her unrealistic expectations? How long until you stopped talking about your goals or—even worse—refused to try at all because you believed you would only fail?

Unfortunately, life is painful, and not all the lessons we learn are positive ones. As with you and me, the characters in our stories have suffered emotional trauma that cannot easily be dispelled or forgotten. We call this type of trauma an **emotional wound**: a negative experience (or set of experiences) that causes pain on a deep psychological level. It is a lasting hurt that often involves someone close: a family member, lover, mentor, friend, or other trusted individual. Wounds may be tied to a specific event, arise upon learning a difficult truth about the world, or result from a physical limitation, condition, or challenge.

Whatever form they take, most wounding experiences happen unexpectedly, meaning, characters have little or no time to raise their emotional defenses. The resulting pain is brutal and immediate, and the fallout of this trauma has lasting repercussions that will change the character in significant (often negative) ways. As with us, characters experience many different painful events over a lifetime, including ones in their formative years. These wounds are not only the most difficult to move past, they often create a domino effect for other hurts that follow.

Now, you might ask why we should care about what happens to our characters before page one. After all, isn't it what they do during the story that matters? Yes, and no. People are products of their pasts, and if we want our characters to come across as authentic and believable to readers, we need to understand their **backstories** too. How a character was raised, the people in her life, and the events and world conditions she was exposed to months or years ago will have direct bearing on her behavior and motives within the story. Backstory wounds are especially powerful and can alter who our characters are, what they believe, and what they fear most. Understanding the pain they've experienced is necessary to creating fully formed and compelling characters.

When we think of emotional trauma, we often imagine it as a specific moment that forever alters the character's reality, but wounds can present in a variety of ways. It's true that one may develop from a **single traumatic event**, such as witnessing a murder, getting caught in an avalanche, or experiencing the death of one's child. But it can also come about from **repeated episodes of trauma**, like a series of humiliations at the hand of a workplace bully or a string of toxic relationships. Wounds may also result from a **detrimental ongoing situation**, such as living in poverty, childhood neglect caused by addicted parents, or growing up in a violent cult.

However they form, these moments leave a mark, albeit a psychological one, just as a physical injury does. Wounds damage our characters' self-worth, change how they view the world, cause trust issues, and dictate how they will interact with other people. All of this can make it harder for them to achieve certain goals, which is why we should dig deep into their backstories and unearth the traumas they may have been exposed to. This is especially important because within each individual wound there is a darkness that has the power to not only lock the character's mind in the past so he can't move forward but also embed an untruth that will sabotage his happiness and leave him feeling deeply unfulfilled.

THE WOUND'S DARK PASSENGER: THE LIE

Emotional trauma is terrible to experience, but in a cruel twist of fate, the trauma itself is not always the worst part . . . it's what hides within a wound: **the lie** (also known as a *false belief* or *misbelief*). The lie is a conclusion reached through flawed logic. Caught in a vulnerable state, the character tries to understand or rationalize his painful experience, only to falsely conclude that fault somehow lies within.

It might sound melodramatic, but this situation is not unique to fiction; it is a familiar reflection of how people process painful events in real life. Think about it—when something bad happens, something we don't understand, it's human nature for us to try to make sense of it. In doing so, we often turn our questions inward: *Why didn't I see this coming? Why didn't I act sooner?* Or perhaps in the case of disillusionment: *Why did the system (or government, society, God, etc.) fail me?* This usually leads to a form of self-blame or the belief that had we been more worthy, chosen differently, trusted someone else, paid more attention, or better safeguarded ourselves, a different outcome would have resulted.

Because the lie is tied to **disempowering beliefs** (that the character is unworthy, incompetent, naïve, defective, or lacks value), a path of destruction is left in its wake. The lie affects his level of self-worth and how he views both the world and himself. It causes him to hold back, making it difficult for him to love fully, trust deeply, or live life without reservation.

Imagine a character (let's call him Paul) who discovers five years into his marriage that his wife is gay. They have a home, debt, kids—the whole matrimonial package. Perhaps she sits Paul down to reveal her secret after finally coming to terms with it herself. Or maybe he discovers that she's been exploring her sexual identity with someone else. Either way, it's a devastating blow when he realizes that the person he married is not who he believed her to be, and it throws Paul's road map for the future into chaos.

In the immediate aftermath, Paul will feel betrayed, hurt, and angry. But as the shock settles, he will also look back and search his memory for signs that he missed, details that slipped past him that would have prevented this painful rejection: *If I'd been more observant at the start of our relationship, I would have saved myself this heartache. But no, I was too stupid to see it.*

Once Paul starts down this track of self-blame, his doubts and insecurities will flare, feeding the fire: *If I'd been a better partner, a better lover, this probably wouldn't have happened. She would have been happy. Then our life would be all we imagined and hoped for when we each said "I do."*

Thanks to our objective viewpoints, you and I recognize that Paul could not have stopped this devastating situation from coming to pass. But all he sees are his shortcomings: the warning signs he missed, things he didn't do right, his failures as a husband. In his mind, he starts to believe that this was partly his doing. Internalizing the wound then leads to a false conclusion that an inner deficiency must be to blame, making Paul question his own worth: *There's something wrong with me. I'm not good enough to build a life with.*

And then the lie emerges: *Defective people just aren't marriage material.*

Once a lie forms, it's like a fungus releasing toxic spores. This false belief seeds itself deep into the character, damaging his self-esteem, sabotaging his confidence, and creating the fear that if he tries to get into a relationship again, he won't measure up, and sooner or later, his partner will leave.

While most lies center on a perceived personal failing due to self-doubt or guilt, not all of them do. In cases where a wound isn't as deeply internalized, the person may become disillusioned in another way. Using Paul's situation as an example, he might apply his pain to the world at large by adopting a jaded outlook on life: *Everyone lies. No one is who they claim to be.* Or even: *Love doesn't last. Sooner or later, people always find an excuse to leave.*

This type of lie becomes a critical judgment about how the world works, because, in the eyes of the character, it's true: Paul's wife *wasn't* who she said she was. She *did* lie, and she *did* leave. His conclusions may be skewed, but these "facts" will cause Paul to hold back, limiting how deeply he connects with other people. His fear of abandonment and rejection will grow rather than diminish, since—thanks to the negative lessons his wounding experience taught him—he'll always be expecting the other shoe to drop.

Born of insecurity and fear, the lie is a destructive force, and until it can be reversed, it will continue to hamper happiness, fulfillment, and inner growth. Within the character arc, this lie will often clash with a protagonist's efforts to achieve his goal because deep down he may feel unworthy of it and the happiness it will bring. Only when he is able to shatter this false belief will he truly feel that he deserves the prize he seeks.

FEAR THAT GOES BONE DEEP

Some writers argue that a truly fearless character shouldn't be held back by emotional wounds. If so, this deviates from real-world experiences, because the unfortunate reality is that no one is immune to the pain of psychological trauma. What holds true for people should extend to characters as well, meaning, no matter how strong or brave a protagonist might be, wounds are the great equalizer. It might take losing a loved one to a random act of violence, becoming disfigured, or just failing to do the right thing when it really matters; in the end, the debilitating pain of a wound will awaken a **fear** unlike anything the character has encountered. This fear is so strong that it burrows into the character's mind with a single purpose: do whatever it takes to ensure the painful emotional experience never happens again.

None of us are strangers to fear. Whether it's rational or not, we feel the niggling pressure of it in our everyday lives. *If I walk down that alley, will I be mugged? If I let the kids play in the backyard alone, will they be safe?* Fear is part of our survival instinct, alerting us to possible danger.

The fear surrounding an emotional wound is a different creature, though. Rather than dissipate when the crisis has passed, it endures and grows, feeding on insecurity and self-doubt.

Because characters are rendered utterly vulnerable when emotional trauma strikes, they become convinced that they are doomed to reexperience the agony caused by these negative emotions if they do not protect themselves. Nothing motivates quite like the psychological fear of emotional pain, and the certainty that this prophecy will come to pass becomes all-consuming. As with a colonel clearing his desk to roll out a map before battle, whatever mattered to the character before no longer does, or the importance of it lessens in the face of this new threat. Prevention becomes the prime directive.

One of the most significant (and damaging) results of this type of fear taking the driver's seat is the construction of **emotional shielding**, which the character erects as a barrier between him and the people or situations that could lead to more hurt. Hollywood story expert Michael Hauge calls this shielding "emotional armor" that the character dons to keep further painful experiences at bay.

What makes this shielding so damaging is that it consists of character flaws, self-limiting attitudes, skewed beliefs, and dysfunctional behaviors—all of which the character eagerly adopts to block anyone who might wish to hurt him. It also helps him avoid the negative emotions that were present during his wounding experience.

Fear is all about avoidance, and that's why a character's emotional shielding locks into place. Understanding the exact fears associated with a wound will help you see all the ways your character dodges uncomfortable situations and problems. A fear of intimacy might turn your character into a self-made outcast because this allows him to maintain distanced relationships or bypass them altogether. Or it might send him on a dark pursuit of power and control, creating a hardened and ruthless persona that will keep others at arm's length.

However, as in real life, using avoidance to solve problems will result in blowback. To the character, this shielding seems like a protective layer, but in reality it encases him in his fear. Always kept close and never forgotten, a spotlight stays trained on what he's afraid of, and it becomes a constant sore spot, a reminder of what will happen if he drops his guard or lets people get too close. Not only that, the flaws and negative attitudes he adopts to keep people at a safe distance are the very ones that hold him back time and again in life. Because the wound is never allowed to heal, fear of what could happen again steers the character's actions and choices each moment.

Being motivated by fear rather than the desire for fulfillment leads to all sorts of fallout for the character—from relationship problems, to his deeper needs being neglected, to a gnawing dissatisfaction that life is not all he hoped for and dreamed of.

WOUND FALLOUT: HOW PAINFUL EVENTS RESHAPE CHARACTERS

Because life is a painful teacher, a character will enter the story wearing some form of emotional armor. These flaws, biases, and bad habits are very often the result of the profound difficult moments he has experienced; as authors, it's important for us to explore those. We should especially have a clear picture of the unresolved trauma the protagonist needs to face and move past, such as Paul's own wounding event.

Wounds and the lies tied to them can influence the core aspects of a character, which in turn will dictate how he'll behave in your story, so let's take a closer look at the changes these negative experiences can produce.

How They View Themselves

Because the lie within a wound is the great saboteur of self-worth, it becomes the noxious root of your character's thoughts, actions, and decisions. If a self-taught musician believes she is stupid and lacks true talent, she will fear ridicule and avoid situations that might showcase her skills. This could cause her to miss out on an opportunity to follow her passion. She may also allow others to tell her what she's good at and should do because she has no faith in herself.

The lie a character believes is critical to her arc because it dictates what she must learn in order to achieve a balanced, healthy view of herself and the world. When a character changes how she views herself, she gains new insight. This not only encourages self-growth but can also underscore the theme of your story.

Personality Shifts

All people have a personality blueprint: traits, beliefs, values, and other qualities that make them unique and interesting. This blueprint becomes the bedrock of who they are, setting them apart from everyone else. But when emotional trauma enters the picture, the psychological side of a person engages to figure out what caused the hurt. As mentioned earlier, if fear is in charge, a hypercritical lens will focus on whatever might have led to this moment of exposure and vulnerability so emotional shielding can be slapped into place. One of the first things on its hit list is personality.

In light of a wounding event, certain positive attributes may be labeled as weaknesses, such as being too friendly, too kind, or too trusting. When emotional shielding goes up, these traits are replaced by others (flaws) that will do a better job of keeping people and the pain they can cause at a distance.

For example, a character who fell victim to fraud may discard her helpful, friendly ways and instead embrace mistrust, miserliness, and apathy so she doesn't get suckered again. Ironically, these negative traits become a blind spot because she doesn't view them as flaws at all. Instead, she rationalizes that they are strengths, keeping her alert to scams and scammers alike. It is only when these flaws start to mess up her life later on that she begins to see their true nature.

It's important to note that not all personality changes resulting from a wound will be negative. Lessons are learned during any good or bad experience, and they can lead to the character also embracing helpful traits. Perhaps this character used to jump into situations recklessly, going with her intuition rather than thinking things through. As a result of being the victim of fraud, now she's more cautious and takes time to investigate before making decisions, especially financial ones.

Positive attributes also form when the character is coping with the wound in a healthy way, so if you want to incorporate them, pay attention to where you are in the story. For instance, when your character is in a dysfunctional state due to the trauma, her flawed behaviors should come to the forefront. But if she's starting to move past the wound through change and growth, the emergence of these positive attributes can be a strong signal to readers that her mind-set is shifting and she's on the path to recovery.

What They View as Important

When a character experiences a trauma, she refocuses. Things that used to matter may lose significance because of the character's defensive state; she assesses possible vulnerabilities and gives up goals that could lead to further hurt (which creates unmet needs, discussed in a later section). She also may cling to certain people or activities because she is terrified of losing them.

Imagine a character who is investing all her time and money into getting her dream of a pottery business off the ground. Then, her eldest son is killed in a fall on a hiking trip, and everything changes. In her grief, she feels responsible for not having been there to protect him, and the terror that this could happen to her surviving daughter pushes her to sell her business and return to her previous career in accounting. This job is stable and allows her to be home more to keep tabs on her child, but it's soul-crushing work, providing no joy or satisfaction. She sacrifices her own happiness to ensure she is always there to keep her daughter safe.

To uncover what's most important to your character in the story, examine the past wounding event. Was there someone or something your character was trying to protect during that terrible time? What did she lose that cut her so deeply she would rather go without it than risk having it stolen from her again? What is she sacrificing that is now leaving her unfulfilled?

Understanding the answers to these questions will lead to rounded characters with real desires and longings. This in turn will help us brainstorm a strong, compelling story goal that will correlate with what the character needs and wants most.

Relationships, Communication, and Connection

Because an emotional wound often involves people closest to the character and creates insecurity and mistrust, it will affect how she communicates with others and how close she lets people get. Perhaps she is unable to talk to people without offending them, or maybe she has a difficult time communicating clearly, having to explain to make herself understood. She might always seem to be getting involved with toxic people, or she is one herself. Or maybe she's perfectly healthy in her interactions—except with this one person or group. The dysfunctional relationships in her life, along with the unhealthy ways in which she connects with others, can be a direct result of her wounding experience.

Emotional Sensitivities

One thing we see in top-notch fiction is that no two characters express their feelings the same way. Likewise, characters will become emotionally activated (in good ways and bad) by different things based on the pain they've encountered. Of all backstory experiences, few are as defining as an emotionally traumatic one. Depending on how your character was hurt (Did it crumble her confidence? Shake her beliefs about family? Make her question her identity?), she will be sensitive to certain feelings.

Emotional shielding doesn't just keep people and hurtful situations at a distance, it also protects a character from the specific emotions she does not want to feel. If your character was betrayed by a parent—say, by her mother walking out when she was barely a teen—she may be sensitive to the typical feel-good emotions that accompany loving family bonds. As such, if she attends a friend's wedding and is exposed to acceptance and unconditional love, she may react with skepticism, jealousy, or anger. Nurturing parents may be like a knife in the back, a painful reminder of what she never had. How she expresses these negative emotions at such a happy event will speak volumes about what she's feeling and why.

The added benefit of knowing a character's emotional sensitivities is that not only can you write her responses authentically—that is, her thoughts, visceral sensations, body language, dialogue, and actions—you will also know what buttons to press when you're looking for a juiced-up emotional reaction.

Their Moral Code

Every person (excepting sociopaths and other unhinged individuals) has a deeply ingrained set of moral beliefs. Provided our characters don't fit into the unbalanced category, they will each have a code that they abide by, a line in the sand they will not cross. How and by whom a character was raised will primarily shape their morals, but a wounding event can alter this blueprint. When something bad happens, such as a character being victimized by his own government, tortured, persecuted, or abandoned, it can taint his beliefs about people and the world, causing morals to shift.

Even the kindest, most loving parent can become a monster under the right circumstances. Imagine a boy who accidentally scratched someone's car with his bike and was beaten to death by the enraged owner. If the boy's father discovered that police had bungled the evidence and the perpetrator was about to be set free, what actions might be spawned from his grief, anger, and need for justice?

Your character's moral beliefs are part of his inner core and will dictate what he is willing to do (and not do) to achieve the story goal. Having his actions reflect his morals, even if they have shifted, adds credibility to the story as long as you have carefully connected the cause-and-effect dots for readers.

WOUND FALLOUT: A CASE STUDY

As you can see, a wounding event has the power to influence core aspects of a character as well as change the trajectory of his life. The repercussions of carrying a false belief will also cause him to become "stuck" in many ways, so the importance of taking the time to understand the fundamental shifts within a character can't be understated.

Let's return to Paul and his dying marriage to observe how his wound has reshaped him. As you'll recall, following his wife's devastating confession, Paul played the blame game and emerged with the flawed idea that she had sought love elsewhere in part because Paul wasn't good enough and therefore wasn't worth loving (the *lie*).

Put yourself in Paul's shoes for a moment. Imagine the pain of believing deep down that there is something vitally wrong with you, and because of it, you'll never find true love and acceptance. Your belief in yourself is shaken. Your self-esteem plummets. You torture yourself by visiting that ugly place within—the Well of Insecurity—where you draw up bucket after bucket of personal deficiencies, shortcomings, and memories of the stupid things you've done.

This is Paul's mind-set. Suffering rejection in this way has cut him to the core, and now he's trapped in an awful reality he never saw coming.

Suddenly in the midst of this pain, a terrifying realization hits: if this emotionally disemboweling experience could happen once, it could happen again. Fear sends Paul into a panicked scramble to do whatever it takes to ensure that this type of rejection and the pain associated with it won't be repeated.

Here's what that might look like, and how Paul's life will be different in the days ahead.

Emotional Fortifications, or "Raising the Psychological Drawbridge"

When Paul's fear kicked into overdrive, he immediately started erecting emotional shielding, leading to shifts in his personality, attitudes, and behavior. Perhaps before the event he was a friendly guy, always willing to listen, with an optimistic outlook on life. Now he's aloof and skeptical, never accepting what people say at face value. If he senses a co-worker knows more than she claims, he becomes angry and will grill her, using manipulation or even intimidation to find out what was held back. Others in the office have noticed this, and Paul has been reprimanded by his manager twice.

Distanced Relationships

It should be no surprise that Paul holds back when it comes to people, and his standoffishness keeps relationships on the surface, not letting them deepen. He is slow to warm to newcomers and has a difficult time opening up even about small things. When he's with established friends, he's a bit better but often finds himself reading into what they say and do or questioning their motives. Overall, he assumes most people are not being fully genuine, and this outlook justifies his determination to never fully trust anyone.

When it comes to romance, Paul stays away from commitment; most of his relationships with the opposite sex are shallow and transactional or contain safeguards to ensure a certain distance. He chooses sexually aggressive women who are clear about which team they play for. The one time Paul started to grow close to someone, he broke it off because, in his mind, ending it early was better than becoming the jilted lover again once she realized he wasn't worth the effort.

Viewing the World Through a Filter of Fear, Not Hope

Believing that one's emotional pain will reoccur is like expecting that every dog one meets will bite. As Paul navigates his life moving forward, every action and decision is steered by his fear of rejection and abandonment. Trusting people, taking them at their word, letting them in—all these things contributed to his past hurtful experience, so now he places limits on certain activities and interactions. To avoid situations that aggravate his wound or challenge his misbelief, Paul also underachieves, because trying for a big goal (such as chasing a promotion at work) will reveal his shortcomings if he fails, reminding everyone that he's defective.

Because he's always avoiding ways to be hurt by playing it safe emotionally, he doesn't feel as deeply about things, and this limits his opportunities for true happiness and fulfillment. By holding on to fear rather than facing it, Paul is also denying inner growth, something that would be not only personally satisfying but necessary for him to achieve important goals. His fear makes him unwilling to take certain risks even though this results in him living a half-life of discontent and stagnation.

Paul's bright spot is his kids, and he tries to spend as much time with them as he can. However, in the back of his mind sits the fear that if he doesn't build a strong relationship with them now, they too will one day leave him. As a result, he caters to them, and is starting to notice that if they don't get their way, they act out.

A Hole Within that Grows

After his marriage ended, the last thing Paul wanted was another failed relationship, so he's careful to not let things get serious with anyone. He dates to satisfy his carnal needs but is ignoring a deeper one: love and belonging. And while he finds satisfaction in his relationship with his children and enjoys hanging out with friends, as time goes on, he feels as if something is missing. In fact, as much as he hates to admit it, a part of him yearns for the very thing he's sworn off having: a committed, loving relationship. He tries to satisfy himself with other things, such as buying a new motorbike, taking trips to exotic locations, and indulging in rich food and alcohol, but the dissatisfaction caused by this hole refuses to yield.

THE TRIGGER FOR CHANGE: UNMET NEEDS

When emotional shielding goes up, it transforms a character, creating damage that must be undone for him to find his way back to a life of balance, happiness, and fulfillment. Unfortunately, the effects of emotional trauma run deep, and the fear it generates can send a character off-grid for years until a deeper urgency emerges that prompts a course correction. The accompanying sense of something being amiss will cause its own pain that needs to be addressed. But when such a deeply embedded fear of psychological pain is driving the bus, how can the character get back on course?

Several things can cause him or her to act: regret, anger, guilt, or even a moral belief, such as fairness or honor. But above all, the primary motivators in life are fear and need. Fear, as discussed, can cause a lot of fallout and hold a character back in life. But unmet needs have the power to direct behavior above all else, meaning, if the urgency is strong enough, needs can push characters to act even if their deepest, most debilitating fears are telling them not to.

The Hierarchy of Human Needs is a theory created by psychologist Abraham Maslow that looks specifically at human behavior and the drivers that compel a person to act. Separated into five categories, it begins with needs that are the most pressing to satisfy (physiological) and ends with needs centered on personal fulfillment (self-actualization). The pyramid representation of Maslow's original hierarchy makes a great visualization tool for writers as they seek to understand what motivates their characters.

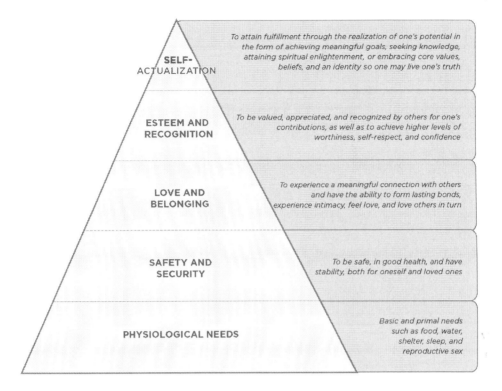

Physiological: the most basic and primal needs, such as food, water, shelter, sleep, and reproductive sex.

Safety and Security: the need to be safe, in good health, and have stability, both for oneself and loved ones.

Love and Belonging: tied to human connection and the ability to form lasting bonds, experience intimacy, feel love, and love others in turn.

Esteem and Recognition: the need to be valued, appreciated, and recognized by others for one's contributions, as well as to achieve higher levels of worthiness, self-respect, and confidence.

Self-Actualization: the need to attain fulfillment through the realization of one's potential. This might come in the form of pursuing and achieving meaningful goals, seeking knowledge, attaining spiritual enlightenment, or embracing core values, beliefs, and an identity so one may live one's truth.

The categories of needs are arranged by importance. So food, water, and other primal physiological needs are the most critical to fill since they are based on survival. Next in line is the need to be safe, then to be loved, to be respected, and, finally, to reach one's potential. These needs, when met, create balance and satisfaction within a person or character. But if one or more is absent, it creates a hole, a feeling that something is missing. As this lack builds in intensity, the psychological pressure will grow until finally it pushes the character to seek a way to fill the void.

When a human need is diminished or missing to the point of disrupting the character's life, it becomes a motivator. For example, a person can skip lunch and only experience minor discomfort until the next meal. But if it's been a week since he last ate, his discomfort becomes a gnawing void that demands to be filled, an obsession he must pursue. He might cross moral lines to steal food or resort to personally humiliating actions, such as begging or digging in a dumpster. He may even take foolish risks, such as eating food that has spoiled, because his singular focus is on that unmet need. Everything else—pride, fear, self-esteem, even safety—becomes secondary.

Sacrificing one need to satisfy others happens often, which is why there's a hierarchy. If a character must choose between a job where he's universally admired (*esteem*) or financially stable (*safety*), he'll choose the latter. Or his goal to become a doctor (*self-actualization*) may be set aside if his wife is diagnosed with a terminal disease and he must leave school to care for her (*love*). Just like that skipped meal, placing one need before others usually isn't a problem in the short term, but the longer a need goes unmet, the more disruptive it becomes until it eventually hits a breaking point. Unhappy marriages end in divorce when the pain reaches an unbearable level. An employee quits a job when workplace esteem levels bottom out or mistreatment escalates. Everyone has a "final straw" moment, after which they can take no more. How quickly it's reached will depend on the individual and the reasons he has for being in the situation in the first place.

These "need" categories help us imagine our characters' layers and the wholeness they seek. Some unmet needs can be ignored longer than others, but they all end up at the same tipping point: once that hole grows big enough, the character will act, despite the presence of fear.

For our character Paul, despite his terror of being rejected, the void of not having a partner to share his life with creates a longing that becomes hard to ignore. At the same time, his emotional shielding is making it difficult for him to get along with people at work, and he's struggling with the spoiled behavior of his children. Add this to his loneliness and the dissatisfaction caused by underachieving, and he's growing increasingly unhappy and frustrated.

Eventually one of two things will happen: Paul's unmet needs will grow until his day-to-day existence seems intolerable. Deep down he will know something is missing and feel compelled to figure out what it is and fix it. His unmet need takes over and will push him to look inward to see what's holding him back. As urgency increases, it will eventually force him to reshape his behavior so changes can come about.

The second possibility is in the form of a new goal that causes Paul to question his current path. Maybe he meets a woman who is single, fun, and has no interest in a committed relationship. On the outside, this seems perfect to Paul . . . until he starts to develop feelings for her, something that hasn't happened in a long time. This leaves Paul with a choice: pursue the challenge of this new goal (find love), or give it up because his fear is still too great (and break things off as he's done in the past). He can't have both. And, of course, he also can't find love if his deepest internal belief is that he's not worthy of it. So to move forward and meet that need, his lie must also be unmasked.

Change isn't easy. In fact, it is often painful, and it takes great courage to step into the unknown. The temptation is always there for a character to stay in the safe but dysfunctional comfort zone: to settle for less while trying to ignore the hole created by an unmet need.

At the end of the day, the choice is up to the character, and, by default, it's up to you as the author. The journey of change (character arc) is at the heart of most stories, which we'll discuss in the next section.

CHARACTER ARC:
AN INTERNAL SHIFT TO EMBRACE CHANGE

In movies, the crazy explosions, car chases, and *Mr.-&-Mrs.-Smith*-type trysts often get the glory. That's all fine, but there's so much more to a great piece of fiction than squealing tires and things blowing up. Beyond the *what* of any story lies the *why*: Why should readers care, why should they invest, and, most of all, why is the protagonist driven to act?

Every narrative has a series of events that provide a framework for the character's journey throughout the novel. This is the **outer story**. Most works of fiction also contain an **inner story**: the character's arc, which is the transformation he undergoes from start to finish. It is this internal element that really draws readers in, reminding them of their own personal struggles and providing the context they seek to better understand their experiences in the real world.

This inner story, or character arc, comes in three forms.

THE CHANGE ARC

This arc is the most common one. Typically, during the course of the story, the protagonist undergoes a much-needed internal evolution that allows him to free himself from the fears, biases, emotional wounds (and resulting lies) of his past. Without this baggage clouding his perspective and steering his actions, the hero is able to view his situation with clarity and act from a position of strength—not fear—which leads to goal achievement and fulfillment.

THE STATIC ARC

Some stories contain high action or are intensely plot-driven, meaning, there is less emphasis on the character's internal growth and more on him achieving a specific goal. While these protagonists may not evolve too much, they will be challenged heavily and so must hone their skills, gain knowledge, or apply learned techniques to overcome the forces that stand against them.

THE FAILED ARC

Not all stories end with a happily ever after. Sometimes the protagonist fails, and the story ends in tragedy. This results from a failed arc, where the character was working toward internal growth but was unable to complete the necessary transformation. His fear was too great, and the hero was either unable to change or couldn't change enough to attain the desired outcome. Often, failed arcs leave the protagonist in a worse position than he started from because salvation was within reach but he lacked the courage to shuck off his emotional shielding and free himself from fear. This is the path taken by many antiheroes.

When it comes to character arcs that involve internal change, emotional trauma becomes especially important. One of two things usually happens within this type of arc: the character starts the story lacking something, feeling an emptiness within that leaves him yearning for something more. This is the unmet need, and the rest of the story becomes about the pursuit of that need by the character chasing a tangible goal that will fill it. Take our character Paul, whose perfect life was ripped apart when his wife left him. His story may include needing to find love again (*love and belonging*), achieving an important accolade at work (*esteem and recognition*), or both.

Other times, the character starts the story feeling satisfied and complete, with his needs fully intact. Almost immediately there is a great upheaval, and something is taken from him. The story then becomes about the character regaining what was lost. This could occur with a family vacationing in a foreign country, but civil war breaks out and they must risk a dangerous border crossing to find sanctuary (*safety and security*). Whatever the circumstance, in a change arc, the protagonist will struggle until he masters his fears, faces his past wounds, and sees the lie for what it really is. This change in his outlook and renewed belief in himself marks the internal growth needed for him to move forward from a position of strength, putting him on the path to reach his goal.

In most works of fiction, the same four dinner guests have a seat at the storytelling table:

- An unmet or missing need that creates a deep longing or sense of urgency (**Inner Motivation**)
- A tangible goal that represents the fulfillment of this need (**Outer Motivation**)
- People or forces that oppose the character's mission (**Outer Conflict**)
- Any fears, flaws, wounds, or misbeliefs that block personal growth and diminish the character's self-worth (**Inner Conflict**)

These four pieces make up the core of storytelling. Take one away and what remains is diminished, or the story as a whole may fail to work. The possible exception is a story containing a static arc; in this situation the inner motivation isn't clearly linked to a specific missing need, and the inner conflict may consist of a weakness that hampers success and must be overcome. Still, at the heart of such stories is a problem to be solved, and the protagonist is driven to solve it.

Understanding the moving pieces of the character arc and the tug-of-war that ensues within the protagonist is often difficult for writers. (For a visual representation of these elements and how they work together in a change arc, see Appendix B.) There are many different ways to approach this, but the following is an example of the successful psychological journey a character might take when moving from dysfunction, sabotaged esteem, and fear to a mind-set of growth, renewed belief in his own worthiness, and hope.

THE JOURNEY OF LETTING GO

At the start of a story, the character is seeking to obtain his goal (*outer motivation*), which he may be pursuing to either avoid something undesirable or to satisfy a yearning (*inner motivation*). The pursuit of this objective is difficult or maybe seems impossible. There might be roadblocks in the way and people or forces standing against the character (*outer conflict*), but the unmet need continues to drive him toward his goal.

As the story progresses, he gradually gains small insights into the things that are holding him back (*inner conflict*), what he fears and why (the *wound* and the *lie*), and how his habits and biases (*emotional shielding*) are probably not helping. With these baby steps of self-growth, he learns and matures, adapting to his environment and achieving minor successes that increase his confidence. These successes may be akin to false positives, though, because he hasn't fully rejected the fear and false beliefs that are causing him damage. Still fearful of emotional pain, a lot of his armor remains in place. He also continues to embrace the lie; he doubts whether he really deserves the goal but is cautiously hopeful things will work out.

A point will come when he hits an impasse or suffers a significant setback. This is the black moment, his rock bottom. He sees that he can't win going forward as he has been—that if he wants success, he must examine his position honestly and take a closer look at some of his internal issues. This means he must confront his emotional pain and challenge the lie he believes.

Depending on the nature of the wounding event, gaining insight can be painful, but it has to be done. The character must eventually awaken to two things. First, he must see his wound in a new light, admitting that it has held him back and kept him from being happy and fulfilled. Then he must view himself differently, in a kinder light, and believe he is worthy of something better and is deserving of happiness.

This self-awareness will change his view of himself, allowing him to replace his disempowering beliefs of unworthiness with **empowering beliefs** (that he is worthy, has value, and is capable of achieving change). This new, balanced perspective frees him from any feelings of blame, responsibility, and unworthiness, shattering the lie and replacing it with the truth.

Refuting the lie and putting the wounding event into perspective enables him to forgive himself (if necessary) and be free of the fear that has steered his actions. It also changes his misconceptions about the world and how it operates. He is no longer held prisoner by fear; instead, he has hope and is infused with determination. Complete, centered, and embracing his true self, he does what is needed to achieve the goal, even if it means making personal sacrifices.

Let's return to Paul one last time. His awakening to the truth that he wasn't to blame for his wife's rejection frees him on many levels. He no longer feels he must protect himself from the intimacy and depth of loving connections. Recognizing that it is unfair to color every relationship with the fear of rejection and abandonment, he decides to open himself to the possibility of finding love again, believing he deserves the happiness that the right partner will bring.

Paul also sees that the love between him and his children is unconditional and he needn't fear losing them when he doesn't give in to their every whim. Life at work has changed too. He's able to see people more honestly instead of misreading their motives and actions. As a result, morale and productivity in the office have skyrocketed. Now believing that he's capable of more, Paul stretches himself to take on new challenges, making him feel fulfilled and actualized.

Even if the character in your story is able to move past the wound like Paul, he will still feel fear because he will be stepping out over an abyss of the unknown. But because he believes in himself, the character knows what he must do, and he embraces the challenges ahead. Despite the forces that stand between him and his goal, he is ready to move forward by shedding the negative qualities that are holding him back and either adopting new, positive traits or honing forgotten ones. He may in fact be tested by encountering a situation similar to the wounding event. This will trigger the same fear, but his newfound strength and belief in himself allow him to master it instead of being mastered by it.

Provided your protagonist successfully navigates the change arc and achieves his goal, the wounds of the past won't disappear. That pain will always sting. The difference is that the character, embracing empowering beliefs, has an inner strength he lacked before that will keep him from allowing the hurt to fester. Moving forward in the face of adversity, he will deploy healthy coping strategies and harness positive qualities to stay centered and on the path to wholeness.

POSITIVE COPING PRACTICES THAT FACILITATE HEALING

As you can see, before behavior can shift, a character must want things to be different. Emotional healing begins when a character can change his perspective and see his own value. This is how he starts the process of refuting the lie he has embraced, rejecting disempowering beliefs, and accepting himself for who he is—a work in progress (thereby achieving self-acceptance).

Once this level of awareness comes about, accountability should follow. The character must recognize how bad habits, poor coping methods, and emotional reactiveness have led to heartache and failure. This shift from negative to positive practices doesn't happen overnight, and the process will vary from one character to another. Here are some of the ways he or she can vanquish self-defeating behaviors and attitudes to move into the healing portion of the character arc.

Step 1: Taking Ownership and Envisioning a New Reality

A critical first step toward positive change involves the character's willingness to acknowledge that her coping methods to date have done more harm than good. Taking ownership in this way marks a shift in her mind-set, triggering the courage to look within and objectively identify unhealthy patterns that must change. Knowing what problems to target helps lighten the emotional burden so she is able to imagine a future devoid of the pain she currently feels. Visualizing how life can be better helps her chart a course toward a goal that will fill the longing within. Rather than dwell on the negative or be bogged down by past setbacks, the character should instead answer this question: *What can I do differently moving forward to bring about this reality?*

Step 2: Creating Small, Achievable Goals

Failure can lead to bitter disappointment, and fear is often what keeps people from trying again. Once the character is fully on the path of change, her newfound awareness and shifted outlook allow her to resist the lure of fear and, instead, feel hope. But the ground of this new perspective is shaky. To avoid a relapse when disappointment or failure hits, the character should set smaller, achievable goals that lead her toward a larger one. Each victory will increase her self-esteem, empowering her, and even if she encounters minor setbacks, she should be able to power through them. A chain of small successes will help reinforce that this new, happier future and the goals associated with it are possible.

Step 3: Adopting Good Habits

Depending on your character's emotional state and layers of shielding, there may be many bad habits to break. A big part of committing to a new course of action is recognizing these problem areas and making an active choice to replace bad habits with good ones. Showing your character taking better care of her health (by eating properly, getting more sleep, improving her hygiene, and exercising) will let readers know she's actively trying to improve. A character can also move away from toxic friends and influences to make room for loved ones. Another positive change may involve joining a group, connecting with nature, reading, journaling, or pursuing a creative outlet. Seeking education and other forms of self-improvement are also good signs that a shift is taking place in the character's mind.

Step 4: Packing an Emotional Parachute

Despite your character's newfound attitude and determination to achieve better results, setbacks may happen. If she isn't ready for these, it could be easy for her to fall back into the emotional traps of denial or avoidance. Unless you're intending to show only a temporary improvement, you don't want her to revert to past negative coping strategies, such as drinking too much, playing the blame game, or becoming emotionally reactive. And unless your story requires a failed arc, she can't develop a defeatist attitude and give up. When your character does suffer a disappointment, use one of the following **setback survival techniques** to show her creating some emotional distance to gain perspective:

Identify the Downward Spiral. Patterns are hard to break, so when disappointment comes, your character's self-esteem and self-worth are likely to be impacted. This can quickly turn into a hopeless whirlpool that will drag her emotions into a dark place. If your character recognizes what's happening before the train of negativity goes too far, she can make an active decision to take back control.

Focus on the Positive. Instead of your character only dwelling on what went wrong in a situation, show her also looking for what went right. Small successes can be embraced and celebrated, offering perspective. Plus, no matter how awful a setback is, it's never as bad as it could have been. A character able to recognize that things could have been worse can remain balanced when disappointment comes.

Take a Time-Out. The character can go for a walk, spend time with a friend or loved one, listen to music, meditate, or participate in a hobby that helps her de-stress and change her outlook. If you choose this strategy, just make sure it doesn't interfere with the story's forward momentum. Pacing should always be thoughtfully considered, and every scene should contribute to the forward motion of the story.

Give Back. If your character is pessimistic about what happened and there's a risk of her spiraling into old habits, give her an opportunity to do something nice for someone else, such as holding a ladder for a fixer-upper neighbor, helping a little brother with homework, or giving someone a ride. Assisting others or doing a good turn can provide the mental boost that's needed to get the character back into a positive frame of mind.

Confide. Sometimes your character just needs a listening ear or a supportive shoulder. Having her reach out instead of shutting down is another way to show she's dealing with disappointment or failure in a healthy way. Talking with someone about an issue, even if it won't solve the problem, relieves stress all by itself, because the burden has been shared and the character is no longer bearing it alone.

Adopt Humor. Another method of coping with adversity and struggle is to keep a sense of humor. Joking about a situation or making light of one's role in it may diffuse some of the character's frustration and can promote camaraderie with other members of the story's cast.

Step 5. Make a Plan of Action (And Stick to It)

The character will need to navigate certain steps or stages to best position herself to achieve the overall goal. Have her identify what needs to be done, anticipate potential problems and ways to circumvent them, and then follow through with her plan, even when it gets tough. This commitment will show that she has the goal solidly in her sights. It will also provide her with the ability to make any sacrifices that are necessary to reach her goal.

THE VILLAIN'S JOURNEY

As we've mentioned, this journey from brokenness to wholeness is common for people in real life and can be applied to any character in your story. But there's one cast member for whom the process is especially important.

As the primary source of opposition for the protagonist, the villain (if your story has one) plays a crucial role. He's the main source of conflict, making the hero's success that much more difficult to achieve. Sadly, when it comes to character arc, bad guys tend to draw the short straw. How they start the story is often how they end it, with little or no change. Backstory information can be scant or nonexistent; without a clear explanation for his actions, readers are mistakenly led to believe that the villain is simply evil for evil's sake.

While revealing little background detail can occasionally result in a truly nightmarish villain (Dolores Umbridge, anyone?), the most compelling and fascinating antagonist usually has an equally compelling and fascinating past. So if a villain figures largely into your story, it's important, as the author, to unearth those formative backstory moments so you can relay this information in a myriad of ways. Even if you choose to only hint at those details through behavior and action rather than reveal them outright, just knowing them will enable you to create an antagonist who is unique and authentic.

It's important to note that even if it is not visible, the villain's character arc will follow the same pattern as the protagonist's: the wounding event begets an irrational fear that leads to the formation of emotional armor that results in an unmet need, leaving him unfulfilled. However, the process differs for villains in a few critical ways.

Living with Unmet Needs

The first big distinction is that while the protagonist eventually reaches a tipping point where he's no longer willing to live without his unmet need, the villain doesn't always get to this place. Why is that?

One common possibility is that the antagonist once made an attempt to face his wounding experience and that attempt was unsuccessful, reinforcing the same pain he first felt. As a result, he became hardened and unwilling to risk that kind of hurt again.

Another likelihood is that the villain has never tried to deal with his excruciating trauma; he may recognize that a need is missing, but to him, living without it is better than facing his past pain or risking experiencing it again. So he muffles the gnawing void by pursuing whatever temporarily eases the hurt. This may result in him rejecting his emotions so he feels nothing for himself or anyone else, thereby enabling him to seek revenge (Howard Payne, *Speed*) or do truly horrific things without remorse (Jigsaw, *Saw* franchise).

A final possibility is that the villain's dysfunctional behavior is personally satisfying to the extent that he's not willing to give it up. Vices are ultimately destructive, but on a base level they're enjoyable; for someone who is in denial or is mentally imbalanced, these activities can act as motivators that make it difficult to sacrifice them in favor of lifelong changes for the better.

Self-Blame

As we've discussed, self-blame is a natural result of the majority of wounding events, even if the character was in no way at fault. The process of working through self-blame is part of the healing journey. It is also the crucible that turns many heroes into villains.

In the aftermath of trauma, some characters either don't struggle with guilt or they turn it outward. Whether it's warranted or not, they blame someone else for what happened, be that an individual, organization, or existing system. Their goal becomes getting back at the responsible party, no matter what it takes.

Alternatively, many villains start out as good guys trying to come to grips with their pasts, but they're never able to see the circumstances realistically; they just can't forgive themselves or accept that they weren't to blame. Unable to break the lie that binds them, they fall deeper into self-loathing, self-centeredness, and darkness. Their morals shift to accommodate this view of themselves, and they end up pursuing a motivation that won't fulfill their need.

Pursuing the Wrong Motivation

The fulfillment of the unmet need is at the heart of the character's story goal; he believes that achieving that outer motivation will fill the void, which is why he has chosen to pursue it. In fiction we do see instances of both protagonists and antagonists initially pursuing a false goal, but their paths differ in that protagonists will recognize their mistake and correct their course while antagonists do not.

Two characters could suffer the same devastating circumstance—say, one of their children dying in a hit-and-run accident. Though they end up with the same missing need of safety and security, depending on the character's personality, support system, mental state, and a slew of other factors, they could go about filling this need in different ways. One character might pursue a career in law enforcement, seek to change the law regarding drunk-driving offenses, or open a rehab center to make it easier for alcoholics to receive treatment. Goals like these are inherently positive pursuits and make sense for a protagonist seeking security.

Another character could go a completely different direction: stalking and ultimately murdering his child's killer or going on an arson spree and burning down bars around town. He thinks that eradicating the responsible person or establishments from his neighborhood will make the world safer. But because the character refuses to work through grief and instead allows fear to dictate his behavior, these goals are ultimately dissatisfying, leading him to commit bigger offenses in a desperate effort to find peace.

The character's steps for achieving the story goal are tied to his personal moral code because there are only certain things he's willing to do. This is often the biggest difference between protagonists and villains; while the hero will stop short when something really challenges his morals, the villain keeps right on charging. His do-not-cross line, if he has one at all, is set much farther back than the protagonist's, enabling him to do unthinkable things to get what he wants. And the more he wanders from his moral center, the harder it is to find his way back, which virtually ensures that he will never be truly fulfilled and will remain stuck.

The State of Their Character Arc

Another big difference between the hero and the villain is that the antagonist's character arc doesn't typically play out during the course of the story. By the time your story begins, the villain is typically uninterested in examining or dealing with his past. He may be ignoring or denying his wound, with no intention of ever doing anything about it. Some villains actually embrace their past; they take the attitude that their wounds have made them stronger, more capable individuals, and they tell themselves that they prefer who they are now to the weak and vulnerable people they used to be.

In other cases, the villain attempted at one point to overcome the wounding event but failed. This character is no longer interested in addressing the pains of his past to become a better person and is now moving ahead as a wounded, deeply dissatisfied individual—still pursuing goals that he thinks will fulfill him in some way.

Redemption Is Nigh

Exceptions to the above come when the villain's arc is featured within the main storyline. Mostly, this happens in a tale of redemption. While the protagonist is undergoing his own transformation, an event occurs that causes the antagonist to examine his trajectory and reconsider his path, resulting in him returning to his arc. Whatever form this catalyst takes, it will trigger deep and unexpected emotions that lead to a change of heart. The villain sees a future in which the long-suppressed need can at last be met or redemption is possible. Another option is that his eyes are opened to a cause that is greater than himself and justifies the sacrifice of personal desires. The villain either turns back to the light or fails to defeat his demons.

For a villain choosing redemption, the process is often condensed, and like a switch being flipped, he turns away from darkness in the final pages of the story. This type of reversal usually requires self-sacrifice and may end with the villain's own death.

Regardless of how the story finishes for them, characters like Darth Vader (*Star Wars*) and Benjamin Linus (*LOST*) prove that recovery through the character arc is as much a possibility for the bad guy as it is for the hero.

Villains are products of their past, just like everyone else. Genetics and anomalies can play a part, but the overwhelming majority of deranged individuals are that way because of the negative people and events they were exposed to. This is why it's so important for you, the author, to understand your villain's history and consider his arc, even if it doesn't figure into the story. Knowing what's driving him and why he's chosen his particular goal helps you to portray a villain who is credible. Again, most of those backstory details won't be shared with readers, but the more you know, the better you'll be able to write them so their actions, though reprehensible, will ring true.

BRAINSTORMING YOUR CHARACTER'S WOUND

Because wounds are invasive, shaking even the strongest character's foundation, choosing the right one is no small (or easy) task. While some authors prefer to let a protagonist's fears and wounds emerge as they write, spending some time up front to dig around in her backstory can save countless hours of revision.

Many writers fear the word *backstory* because of generalized advice telling them that it should be avoided. These unfortunate statements fail to acknowledge the different types of backstory. The kind discussed here—character brainstorming—is one of the most vital parts of writing. No matter what your genre, characters should come across as well rounded and authentic, with clear motivations. Everything they do, say, and decide should result from whatever is driving them, be it a fear, unmet need, or other catalyst. What your character wants (*outer motivation*) and why she wants it (*inner motivation*) will both be rooted in her past.

Unless your character introduces herself to you fully formed and ready to go, you'll need to poke around in her darker places to uncover the emotional trauma she has experienced. As you brainstorm, rather than dredging up every hurtful situation, look for sore spots and a pattern of events that follow a theme. For example, if a character's past was speckled with sibling rivalry, a need to be the best, and achievement confused with parental acceptance, it may point to a wound involving conditional love in her early years.

Not all characters will need the same amount of backstory research; depending on who they are and the role they play, you'll have to decide how much is necessary to write them accurately. When it comes to brainstorming backstory, think of it as an island that can be reached by a variety of routes, including the ones that follow.

PAST INFLUENCERS

It's unfortunately true that those closest to us are in a position to inflict the most pain. In this way, the people our characters interacted with prior to the start of the story are often tied to their wounding events. Caregivers top the list, with their maltreatment birthing deep fears, generating irrational beliefs or biases, creating a legacy of abuse, or even causing unintentional parental failings to be passed through the generations.

For example, imagine a girl who helplessly watched her four-year-old sibling choke and die. She, in turn, could become a controlling mother, her fear causing her to hover over her own child to keep him safe. She may choose his friends and make most of his decisions for him because she believes she knows what's best. And her son, growing up in this tightly monitored environment, will likely have lower self-esteem because he doesn't trust his ability to make good decisions. Place this young man into your story as the main character and you have someone who struggles to be independent, obsesses about what others think, is hypersensitive to criticism, and avoids responsibility because he thinks he'll screw up.

The ability to inflict pain is not just reserved for parents and caregivers or even family in general. Think about people who left a negative mark on your character, perhaps restricting her growth, sabotaging her self-worth, inflicting a humiliation, or undermining her self-confidence. Mentors, past lovers, ex-friends, and people in positions of power may have imparted negative life lessons or acted as bad role models, which could have led to a wound. To prompt ideas about possible influencers, look for the answer to this question: Whom from your character's past would she never want to run into again and why?

UNPLEASANT MEMORIES

Wounds hide within negative past experiences, such as a particular time of hardship, an event that cannot be forgotten, or a moment your character wishes she could utterly erase. Don't be afraid to interview her about difficult situations she's endured. Every person's past is littered with mistakes, failures, disappointments, feelings of inferiority, and fear, so try your best to learn about these painful memories.

PERSONALITY FLAWS

Some writers find that as they brainstorm a character, personality is the first thing to emerge. Maybe she has an amazing sense of humor, loves to learn, and is the most unmaterialistic person you might meet. But along with these qualities, she's incredibly temperamental, going from hot to cold in a flash and taking offense when none was meant. Do some digging to uncover the *why* behind this flaw. What causes that reactiveness and hypersensitivity? Why is she so quick to see enemies where none exist? Identifying the situations that lead to this knee-jerk response will help you spot the emotions the character doesn't want to feel, which will help you brainstorm the wounds that could be the cause of her emotional armor. This can also be a helpful exercise to determine a character's fatal flaw, the lynchpin in her emotional shielding that holds her back more than anything else—the one problematic aspect of herself that she must overcome in order to have a chance at achieving her goal.

FEARS

Fear is something most people hate, or at the very least are reluctant to experience, because while it can push us to strive harder for what we want, it also comes with a host of uncomfortable emotions. Clearly, your character will have a deep fear sitting at the heart of the defining wound that must be faced, but other fears and worries can also be markers of a wounding event. If during the character brainstorming process you realize that your protagonist is afraid of water, why is this? If she tenses every time she encounters a stranger on the sidewalk, or her heart rate picks up when her sister calls, delve into that response for more information. Fears don't manifest by themselves, so search for their underlying reasons.

UNMET NEEDS

A quick flip back to Maslow's pyramid can reveal what's missing from your character's life, which can be a signpost for an emotional wound. If you know what need is going unmet, think about why that is. Is it being sacrificed for another need, or is it merely absent? If the character is avoiding a need (such as *love and belonging*), there's a reason she's convinced herself she's better off without it.

If you're beginning to get to know your character and don't see a missing need right away, ask yourself what might be causing her to feel dissatisfaction. Is there an aspect of her life that she dislikes, avoids, or even dreads? Chances are this touches on an unmet need, which can help guide you to the type of wound she may bear. When ferreting out a character's missing need, it can also be helpful to first identify the outer motivation. If you know what she's overtly pursuing, you can then figure out *why* she's pursuing it, which will point to the lack she's seeking to fill.

SECRETS

One thing experience teaches us is that everyone keeps secrets. It's second nature to hide the things that embarrass us, cause shame and guilt, or leave us feeling exposed and vulnerable. Often a character's secret will mask her wound, so ask yourself what your character is hiding. What information does she guard closely and would never want others to discover? This most likely touches on a shard of emotional trauma that she wishes to keep buried in the past.

INSECURITIES

Self-doubt is, to some degree, a problem for everyone. Worrying about not measuring up, making a mistake that impacts others, and disappointing loved ones can eat away at our self-worth. If your character is insecure about fitting in and being accepted, why is that? In which situations is she reluctant to make decisions or take risks? Thinking about her doubts and worries will create a starting point for brainstorming the negative experiences and influencers who left her feeling this way.

BIASES OR A JADED OUTLOOK

Even the most optimistic and open-minded individual can't display tolerance and patience all the time. Most likely, she'll have a few built-in prejudices. Some characters have an entire closet of biases and negative beliefs based on their past experiences and observations. Think about what skewed viewpoints your character may have, the types of people she has no patience for, and the situations that cause her to disengage. Every effect has a cause, so follow these trails and find the negative experience or exposure that encouraged this dark outlook to form.

OVERCOMPENSATION

Another way to unearth painful backstory elements is to look for ways your character overcompensates. Does she work hard to please a certain person, putting more time and energy into the relationship than the other party? Does she make excuses for someone, shrugging off bad behavior or "rescuing" them by continually solving their problems and fighting their battles? Overcompensation can come in other varieties, too, such as falling over backward to be generous, working extra hard to fit in, or doing anything to win the approval of someone important. If your character overcompensates, look for the why to see if self-blame or fear is at the heart of her actions.

DYSFUNCTION

No one has a perfect life, least of all our characters, and thanks to their dysfunctional emotional shielding, they are often the source of their own problems. Think about the areas of friction in your character's life. Is she bad with money? Does she have problems with authority that get her into trouble at work? Does she drink too much? Does she lie about trivial things without understanding why she does it? Negative behaviors and friction points aren't the result of some random cosmic machine; it starts and ends with the character. Look at how she gets in her own way, and follow this string to a past moment that created her reflexive responses or negative coping mechanisms.

EXPLORING WOUND CATEGORIES

A sad fact of the human experience is that there are seemingly innumerable ways for people to inflict emotional pain on one another and themselves. The wounds we profile in this book are by no means exhaustive and can play out in endless variations to suit a character's backstory. They've been grouped into categories of universally painful themes, so if you're struggling to choose a particular wound for your character, it can help to understand the common areas of psychological damage.

Disabilities and Disfigurements

This kind of wound centers on a condition outside of the perceived societal norm that the character believes puts him at a disadvantage. It may be physical, cognitive, or a mixture of both and can result from an accident, a birth defect, a condition or disease, or an act of violence. A character with this type of wound often feels "less" or different and questions his self-worth, especially if the disability is not something he's always had.

This wound's impact will depend on the individual trials the character faces in the story, how old he was when it happened, and the severity of the disfigurement or disability. Many people with these types of wounds feel a sense of shame and try to hide the extent of their impairment. They fear being labeled, ridiculed, and rejected, and have the added burden of needing to function in a world that isn't always accommodating to their particular challenges.

Injustice and Hardship

These emotional traumas shine a light on inequities and differences, making the character feel targeted. This impacts his self-worth, and because he suffers in ways others do not, it causes him to question the moral fiber of humanity, can challenge his religious faith (if it exists), and in some cases may damage his ability to empathize with others. These wounds usually lead to disillusionment and bitterness rather than self-blame, since the fault lies with others and is beyond the individual's control.

If the character's loved ones suffer collateral damage due to this wound, or the injustice or hardship stretches into a long-term circumstance, the distress will increase, creating an unmet need that must be filled more quickly. Because imbalance is not a natural state, the character will be driven to do something to right the situation, even if it is only to sacrifice one need for another.

Failures and Mistakes

Wounds that involve a personal failing are common and are often deeply internalized, since most characters are their own worst critics. Self-esteem is impacted, as these wounds can quickly evolve from "I made a mistake" to "I am a mistake," leading the character to feel deficient or defective. This can spawn the belief that he deserves to be punished, resulting in various forms of self-castigation, impacting core needs, and keeping the character from finding happiness and fulfillment.

The significance of this backstory wound will depend on the kind of mistake, how personal it was, and whom it affected. The character may shy away from future responsibilities out of fear or overcompensate through perfectionistic tendencies to try to atone for what happened. Often, a strong catalyst will be needed to push him to risk failure again, especially in situations in which other people may pay the price.

Misplaced Trust and Betrayals

These are caused by the people closest to the character who exploited his love and vulnerability. Trust-based wounds can be especially difficult to move past because the character is no longer able to rely on his intuition about people, believing his judgment to be flawed. Due to their innate sense of connectedness as maternal nurturers, women can be more deeply affected by these wounds than men.

This type of trauma often results in the character becoming overly sensitive to real or perceived betrayals. Small offenses tend to take on more meaning and reinforce the need for him to protect himself and hold back. The character finds it nearly impossible to give people the benefit of the doubt, and forgiveness becomes a mountain to climb. The closer and more personal the relationship was that involved the betrayal, the more bitterness and resentment will set up camp, and the harder it will be for the character to move on.

Crime and Victimization

Wounds of this nature awaken fears of death or pain, leave a character feeling violated, and shake his faith in people and the world at large. While he might blame the perpetrator (say, a drug addict who stole his car), the character sometimes ends up finding fault with something greater, such as the government, an established social system, or humanity in general. This can lead to fear and resentment directed at multiple sources, along with a high level of disillusionment. In this case, the character feels let down and unprotected by a world that should care and do more to keep people safe.

Victims of crime also may blame themselves unfairly; a woman who was raped may believe that her flirting was a contributing factor, or a man whose home was robbed might blame himself for leaving the door unlocked. In this circumstance, the underserved and self-directed blame is very often (if not always) part of the lie the character believes to be true.

Traumatic Events

Traumatic events have an element of randomness, making them almost impossible to prepare for or protect against. In real life, a wound like this reveals a person's inner core of strength or weakness, and while we all hope to respond well in these situations, we often don't. For our characters, the shock of the experience can leave raw emotional gouges that are slow to heal.

A wound that is sudden and shocking often deprives a person of closure, leaving him with only questions: *Why did this happen? Why me? How can the world be so cruel?* Not only will a character be shaken by the experience, he may also question his own reactions and assign himself blame for not ensuring a better outcome. This self-blame is usually irrational, damages self-worth, and creates guilt (including survivor's guilt, in some cases). A traumatic event leaves a person especially changed and perhaps jaded. His fear of something similar happening again can lead to extreme shifts in personality and behavior, especially when it comes to safety and security. It is also the category most likely to lead to a character suffering from post-traumatic stress disorder (PTSD).

PTSD is a recognized disorder affecting some people who have experienced a significantly frightening or dangerous event. Someone suffering from PTSD may relive what happened via dissociative episodes that can last for moments, hours, or days. The character might also be triggered by reminders of the event, avoid emotions or thoughts associated with the trauma, have nightmares and difficulty sleeping, and be tense and on edge due to a chronic state of hypervigilance. Emotional volatility (including self-blame and guilt) is common, along with negative self-thoughts and depression-like symptoms such as isolation and losing interest in passions or hobbies.

While it's normal for victims to experience a range of these responses following a trauma, those suffering from PTSD have symptoms that linger for a longer period of time (even indefinitely) and are severe enough to impact their daily lives. If they have difficulty obtaining the help they need, more fallout can occur in the form of broken marriages, job losses, violence, homelessness, and drug or alcohol abuse—all of which compound the problem and further degrade the character's ability to cope with the condition. It's important to note that children also fall victim to PTSD and may respond differently than adults. As with any mental disorder, it's critical for authors to research it and the circumstances that create it thoroughly. How PTSD will manifest is highly individual, requiring writers to have a deep understanding of the character so they can convey this condition accurately in the story.

Specific Childhood Wounds

Of all the wounds, childhood-specific ones can do the most damage, since the younger the victim is, the fewer emotional barriers are in place for protection. Children don't typically have the experience or maturity to understand what they're seeing and experiencing, and this leads to dysfunctional rather than healthy coping mechanisms. There is a physiological aspect as well, as some traumatic wounds affect the structure of the brain itself, which is still developing even into a person's twenties. This cognitive rewiring hampers the ability to cope.

Childhood wounds may contain deep elements of betrayal that sometimes aren't felt until later, when the character realizes that he should have been protected by caregivers and society in general (if the culture embraces the idea that children are innocent and must be protected). This betrayal burrows even deeper if a caregiver or close family member inflicted the wound, and it will greatly impact how the character bonds with others as an adult. Childhood traumas also have the most time to fester, meaning there will be more layers of emotional shielding that will be harder to undo.

While these groupings can be helpful in categorizing possible traumas for your character, one fact remains true for all of them: backstory wounds are much more than painful memories. Real damage is done, and the fallout will seep into many aspects of a character's life moving forward. Inside each incident is a seed of doubt: *Is this somehow my fault? Am I to blame?* This doubt blossoms, eroding self-worth, and while time can be a great healer, it doesn't always work this way. If another moment of similar emotional pain comes along, it can reinforce the original fear and false belief. Only by gaining perspective through self-growth and self-acceptance can the deeper pain of a wound be finally put to rest.

Remember that while a character's past will likely contain a minefield of negative experiences, for story planning purposes, the reader will need to be clear on which pain the character will have to confront and overcome. To achieve this, it can be helpful to focus on creating a single backstory wound that represents the bottleneck of hurt and pain your character feels. Charting this event or series of related events will also help you understand which false belief will emerge to attack your character's self-worth or alter his perceptions, leaving him with a jaded worldview. For more help on planning this part of your character's past, see Appendix D.

PAIN RUNS DEEP:
FACTORS THAT WILL IMPACT THE WOUND

We know that a wounding event can greatly change a character. But how much impact will it really have? In truth, the effects of these incidents vary due to the character's unique history; an event may be devastating for one person while leaving no lasting mark on another. However, in a story that follows a change arc, the backstory wound should always be debilitating. The havoc it wreaks should hamstring the character in a way that makes it impossible for her to get what she desperately wants and needs unless she changes and sheds her **fatal flaw**—a key negative trait, bias, or intrinsic modus operandi that can only be overcome through self-growth and rejection of her false belief. To choose a wound that will be a truly crippling force within the story, take the following factors into account and apply them as needed.

PERSONALITY

One vital component to understanding the impact of emotional trauma is knowing who the character was before the wound sent her life off course. Core personality traits make all the difference in a crisis. For instance, an innocent or naïve character could be hit hard by a wound involving injustice, resulting in disillusionment and the formation of emotional shielding that causes her to pull away from others. Yet someone more worldly and experienced may react differently, perhaps seeking a way to balance the scales, even if she must sacrifice her moral code to do so.

Each character's unique makeup of traits affects her handling of stress and strain, and knowing her pre-wound personality makes it easier to predict the exact type of shielding that will go up in the aftermath of a painful event.

PHYSICAL PROXIMITY

While all wounding events have the potential to be torturous, characters who experience one directly are likely to be more affected than those who are farther removed from it. Take, for example, a group of people involved in a school shooting. A student who is critically wounded by the assailant will experience much more trauma than a classmate who hears the gunshots but does not encounter the shooter. And dealing with the event will be more challenging for both of these characters than it will be for a teacher who was absent that day.

Everyone involved in a tragedy will be impacted on some level, but those closer to it will have the most difficulty moving past it.

RESPONSIBILITY

As we've discussed, wounding events are traumatic, in part, because the victims almost always blame themselves. So one way to construct a truly invasive experience is to make sure the character feels responsible. A mother whose child drowns could be entirely free of wrongdoing but might still blame herself because she didn't react quickly enough, never signed up for that CPR class, or let her phone's battery die so there was no way to call for help. Following this train of thought, a victim who truly is culpable on some level may have an even harder time recovering from the blow.

One thing to remember when assigning true blame to your victim is that it can affect the reader's ability to empathize. Few people will hold the death of the aforementioned child against the mother, despite her perceived guilt. But if the child drowned because the mother was shooting up in the bathroom? Readers will have much less sympathy for her and may distance themselves from such a protagonist. Granted, a character's responsibility for a horrible event can do good things for your story by adding tension that may be missing from a true accident, and lessened empathy can be overcome in other ways as events play out. But it's something to bear in mind.

SUPPORT

A large part of resiliency has to do with the amount and kind of support that's available for a person when tragedy strikes. A character buoyed by loved ones who share the stress burden and infuse positivity into her life may bounce back more easily when bad things happen. Likewise, a strong faith that remains unshaken through difficult circumstances can keep a person grounded in the aftermath. On the other hand, a person with little support or whose faith is crushed by traumatic events will have a harder time getting back on her feet.

RECURRENCE

Any tragic event can be traumatic. Being sexually or physically abused, failing others, or being rejected by a parent are all horrible experiences with long-lasting effects. But when the same occurrence happens repeatedly, those wounds dig deep, making healing and recovery more challenging.

COMPOUNDING EVENTS

While the wound itself is life changing, it can be worsened when the victim also has to deal with hardships that follow, such as getting divorced or being fired. Mental and emotional complications (panic attacks, depression, or incapacitating fears, for example) can follow a traumatic event, giving the character other challenges that must be faced. And, of course, any recurring reminders, like physical scars, nightmares, or stimuli triggers, will make healing that much more elusive.

INVASIVENESS

Another factor that can make a wounding event even worse is how personal it is. Attacks on the body and mind are incredibly intimate and can produce a heavier burden than something more random. Being specifically targeted (as in a case of bullying) can be harder to deal with than an arbitrary incident, such as being one of a dozen people whose identities were stolen.

EMOTIONAL PROXIMITY

In a similar fashion, the person's emotional closeness to the assailant can affect how intimate the victimization is. Imagine a character who told the truth about a heinous crime but wasn't believed. If the person dismissing the character is just an acquaintance, such as a school counselor or police officer, the betrayal may not have much of an emotional effect. But when it happens with a parent or sibling, it can be particularly detrimental.

EMOTIONAL STATE

What is the character's emotional state when the trauma occurs? Is she coming off a success that has left her feeling confident and capable? Or is she already struggling with issues that have worn her down? The event will be harrowing no matter what the extenuating circumstances, but a person who is feeling good about herself and life in general may have more resiliency than someone who's struggling with other issues or is already recovering from a heavy blow.

JUSTICE

Humans are infused with a natural sense of fairness. When we've been victimized, we want the guilty party to be held responsible, and the bigger the crime, the bigger the punishment should be. Part of closure is knowing that justice has been served, reparations will be made, and the person at fault won't be able to strike again. It's hard for a character to move on when she knows that the person to blame for her pain hasn't been punished or is still out there, an unseen threat.

These are some of the factors that can compound an already awful situation and make it even more injurious. So if you're interested in making things more desperate for your protagonist—or creating the desired degree of separation for a secondary character—keep these aspects of a wounding event in mind when planning one for your story.

REVEALING THE WOUND THROUGH BEHAVIOR

Once you've determined which wounding event has molded your character into who he is in your current story, you must begin the tricky process of revealing it to readers. This is important to do for a number of reasons. First, it gives readers information that ties the character's present to his past; in effect, it lets them know what's driving him, and why he is the way he is now. It's also critical for readers to identify the wounding event because it sets up exactly what the protagonist will have to face and conquer by the end of the story for him to succeed. And acknowledging the wound can lead to increased empathy, which plays a pivotal role in readers being engaged in the character's journey.

Keep in mind that if you choose a static arc, it may not include much inner growth, nor a reconciliation with the past. But using behavior to hint at old trauma is still important. Characters should always have complexity and depth, even if it isn't fully realized through a transformative change arc.

So how do we convey this vital piece of backstory to readers? This is where the importance of showing instead of telling comes in.

As with any vital story element, showing is almost always preferred because it allows the reader to share the experience of what's happening rather than be spoon-fed data. It's the difference between painting someone a picture and giving a factual report; the former evokes emotion, provides texture, and engages the viewer, while the latter is simply a means of relaying information. Whether you're describing a character's emotional state, revealing his personality, or establishing the mood in a given scene, showing is typically better because it draws readers deeper into the character's experience. The same is true when you're revealing the wounding event. This important moment from the past can be shown two ways, and both can be effective in proving just how broken the character is.

THE BIG REVEAL

Sometimes it's best to reveal the wound in its entirety through a flashback, a memory, or a conversation with another character. Disclosing this event all at once can be impactful because the reader is able to see it in one poignant scene, giving it a much more active feel. This is the most dramatic method, enabling readers to experience what happened along with the character, heightening that emotional connection. We see this in the first scene of the

Harry Potter series. Through a conversation between Dumbledore, Professor McGonagall, and Hagrid, readers are shown the tragic incident that Harry will spend the next seven books coming to grips with.

The Big Reveal is effective because it makes the wounding event very obvious. Readers see immediately that the violent loss of Harry's parents is going to cause issues he'll have to address in order to become whole. What we don't know is what those issues will be. The lie, the flaws that develop, the unmet need Harry will be driven to regain—all these are doled out in bits and pieces throughout the course of his story. While readers already know what the wounding incident is, it's through this careful showing of what happens *afterward* that they'll understand how it has changed him and why he must face it.

Normally this type of reveal comes later in the story as a final puzzle piece for readers. If it occurs at the very start and there's a jump in time before the next scene (as in the *Harry Potter* example), you likely are dealing with a prologue. Prologues are notoriously tricky because they're often not necessary; many times, the information can be conveyed much more effectively by sharing it *later*, once readers have fallen in love with the character and have been prepped with hints and clues about this important backstory moment. Prologues can also be problematic when they're written poorly—with a big info dump or large passages of telling that slow the pace and keep readers at a distance. For these reasons, starting your story in this way is often discouraged. So if you've decided that you absolutely must reveal the wounding event with a prologue, plan it carefully. Familiarize yourself with what methods work and which ones don't. Tips on how to write both prologues and flashbacks can be found in the Problems to Avoid section.

THE BIG TEASE

With this method, the audience is kept in the dark about precisely what happened to the character. Through dropped hints and teasing tidbits, readers see glimpses of the past but don't fully identify the wounding incident until they've collected and put together all the pieces; they may come to the conclusion on their own or the dropped hints may be capped off with a final reveal by the author. That *aha!* moment can happen at any point in the story but typically is saved until well into the second half.

In the movie *The Cutting Edge*, the audience sees a lot of clues as to what makes Kate tick, but the wounding event from her past is never overtly stated. It's hinted at mostly through her personality and actions: she's perfectionistic, extremely competitive, and impossible to get along with. These clues, combined with a meaningful scene with her father toward the story's end, give us a clear picture of her wound: growing up with a parent whose conditional love was based on her ability to perform. This structure keeps readers guessing about the wounding event, but its aftereffects and how it is hindering the character are obvious from the start.

THE BREADCRUMB TRAIL: LEADING READERS TO THE WOUNDING EVENT

Regardless of whether the wound is overtly shown or merely hinted at, it will always be necessary to reference the event in smaller ways throughout the story because it's a piece of the character's past that holds vital significance. Someone who's endured the loss of a loved one, physical torture, or a messy divorce can't simply forget it—especially if it hasn't been dealt with. It will haunt her, and others will see its effects. So you'll still need to master the art of obliquely referencing what has happened in a way that reads naturally. Mixing and matching the following by-products and vehicles is a great way to feed information about this event to readers without using info dumps or giving the whole thing away.

Fear

As we know, wounding events beget fear as the character seeks to avoid a repeat of what she's suffered through. Building scenarios into your story that showcase her avoidance will provide clues as to what might have befallen her in the past.

For instance, let's say your character experienced a failure, one that resulted in major fallout for a lot of people. As a result, this character —we'll call her Jess—may avoid being in charge because she doesn't want to risk repeating that experience. You can hint at this by creating situations that show her shunning responsibility. At work, she might be offered a chance to lead an all-star team in a bid to bag a wealthy client. To the reader, the decision seems like a no-brainer. But Jess cites lame reasons and declines, or she accepts, then fabricates an excuse to back out. This avoidance raises questions. Why would she pass up such an amazing opportunity? What is she afraid of? And why has she chosen a career that affords opportunities like these if she's going to sidestep them when they come along?

Avoidance is great for referencing, in a roundabout way, a character's fear; when this by-product is combined with other clues, readers can figure out what's haunting her. It's also good for the character arc. In the case of our irresponsible lead, she is allowing her fear to keep her from true happiness, and she won't be whole until she faces and overcomes it.

In a well-structured story, this won't happen immediately. She'll need many chances to triumph (and fail) before she realizes that her fear is holding her back. Building these scenarios into the plotline will provide the chances she needs to move along that character arc toward eventual success.

Self-Doubt

Characters, like real people, are complex. No matter how popular, attractive, or accomplished they are, they will still experience self-doubt and uncertainty. And these areas of insecurity often relate back to the wounding event.

Look at Jess. She might be confident and self-assured most of the time but feels insecure in certain situations: when she has to lead, when people are depending on her, or when an important decision needs to be made. Her self-doubt may also be tied to specific circumstances surrounding her past failure. For instance, if she goofed up in a TV interview, she may become a nervous wreck in a public forum or anytime she has to go on the record.

Once you've decided on your character's wounding incident, ask yourself some questions to better understand her insecurities relating to it. When does she doubt herself? In what scenario does she not trust her intuition? When does a simple decision paralyze or turn her into a second-guessing mess? The answers to these questions will let you know where her uncertainties lie; you can then show the contrast between her normal self and the circumstances where her personality changes. Done consistently, this can shine a spotlight on your character's doubts, hinting at her wounding event and showing how it's impacting her even now.

Overreactions and Underreactions

When you know your character well, you're able to write her consistently. Readers get to know her and what to expect from her in the various situations that arise. If she reacts in a way that's either understated or overly dramatic, it's like a red flag for readers, telling them that something isn't quite right.

Let's imagine that Jess is typically an outgoing, bigger-than-life kind of girl. She's always up for a party, so when her company throws a celebratory bash, she's there in all her extroverted glory—until she's asked to field questions from the local news crew. We'd expect a person like Jess to respond with exuberance at the chance to ham it up for the cameras. Instead, the animation leaves her face. Her body goes still, and the pitch of her voice drops. With a stricken smile, she declines, suggests someone else as a replacement, and excuses herself.

This response is way too subdued for the Jess we've come to know. It's a sign that something about this interview scenario is freaking her out. We'd be similarly alerted in a situation in which a run-of-the-mill response was expected but she went ballistic.

If you've laid the foundation for your character's personality and have remained true to her emotional range throughout the story, contrary reactions will warn readers that something is wrong while allowing you to hint at trouble from the past.

Triggers

A trigger is something that reminds your character so strongly of the wounding event that it brings on the emotions, fears, and negative responses related to it. A trigger can be something sensory, such as a smell, color, taste, or sound. It might be a person, object, situation, or setting that reminds her of what happened. It could even be a strong emotion she was prone to feeling during that time. When the character encounters one of these things, it brings her back to that hurtful moment, feeling the same negative emotions and fight-or-flight responses she's been trying to forget about all these years.

Imagine Emily, who was a victim of human trafficking as a teen and was forced to work as a prostitute by her captors. As an adult, she is free, and for the most part her life is normal. But periodically she'll encounter something that awakens those negative associations. Cheap motel rooms, the jingle of change in a trouser pocket, the taste of orange soda, or a certain kind of cologne might send her into panic mode. Her body tenses, and breaths rasp in and out of her throat. Her initial impulse is to run, and she must focus all her energy on quelling the terror and convincing herself that the danger isn't real, that she's safe.

This is an extreme response to a mundane thing like the scent of cologne. Readers may not know about Emily's wounding event, but when they see her repeatedly responding in such a way to the same trigger, they'll know it's associated with something personally awful. And when they eventually learn what the trauma is, everything will fall into place.

Denied Emotions

You may have a character who is quite comfortable with her feelings—except for the one that reminds her of how she felt when that horrible thing happened to her. In Emily's case, shame is the touchstone emotion of her wounding event. Though she was forced into the situation and wasn't in any way to blame, the choices she had to make to survive were appalling, and shame was her constant companion.

As an adult, the likelihood of this exact trauma recurring is virtually nil, but whenever she feels—or is made to feel—shame, it takes her back to that horrible time. It's as if she never left, as if she's stuck in her memories and will never be free of them. So she adopts new habits that will excise that emotion from her life. She holds herself to the highest moral standard, following a series of rules that, when adhered to, keep her free from any remorse. Or she may do the opposite—throwing morality to the wind so every decision she makes will be a shame-free one.

Emotional health involves being able to experience and exhibit all our emotions in a natural manner. Avoidance and denial of our emotions is a sign of trouble. When you can show your character consistently sidestepping certain feelings, it will hint at past pain. This is one of the more subtle by-products you can use to indicate the type of wound your character has, but when enough clues are dropped, it all will make sense to readers.

Obsessions

On the flip side of denial, there's obsession. When someone has suffered trauma, while they naturally avoid certain things, they also become hyperaware of others. In Emily's case, after years of being mistreated, she has become infatuated with personal safety. Her apartment has an expensive alarm system, and she sleeps in a locked bedroom with the dog for company. Whether she goes to the gym for a self-defense class or out to dinner with friends, her purse holds a concealed carry permit and a handgun. And wherever she is, she's noting the exits and analyzing the people around her to determine their threat level.

What a character is obsessed with can be telling in regard to past traumas. Readers may not be able to identify the exact wounding experience from such overcompensations, but they'll recognize that these sensitivities are related to it.

Dialogue and Other Characters

Characters are hopelessly clueless as to the impact of their own wounding events; as such, they're not the best or most reliable sources. Other characters, though—particularly those closest to the victim—are often aware of what has happened and how it has changed this person. Even when they're walking on eggshells, the supporting cast can be a great source of information, and what they know can easily be imparted to readers through dialogue.

In *The Patriot*, Benjamin Martin is haunted by something from his past that he refuses to discuss. But because so many other people bring it up, its significance is clear. His son asks him what happened at Fort Wilderness, and Benjamin turns away. An opponent mentions Benjamin's fury during the Wilderness campaign, causing him to clam up. A fellow soldier references what Benjamin did to the French at Fort Wilderness, and he underreacts and just goes on giving orders.

Dialogue—even when it's one-sided—is a natural way to hint at a wound, so maximize this vehicle for sharing bits and pieces of that important event when it makes sense to do so.

Setting Interactions

The setting may not seem like an obvious vehicle for revealing information about a wounding experience, but it actually works well. This event is part of who the character is; try as he might to distance himself from it, he's never completely successful. There will often be people or objects in the current setting—or the setting itself—that remind him of what happened.

Returning to *The Patriot*, Benjamin Martin has a hatchet that he keeps in a trunk. The mere sight of it brings anguish to his face, and he clearly wants nothing to do with it. We get a bigger glimpse into why this is when he's forced to use it to keep one of his sons from being killed. He's skilled in its use and becomes a different person when he's wielding it: violent, vengeful, monstrous.

This one prop is a huge clue to his wounding event. Combined with the references to Fort Wilderness and the knowledge that he was once a soldier, the hatchet allows readers to put together a framework of what is haunting Benjamin Martin.

Think about your own character's wounding incident. What items might have played a part in it or simply been present at the time? Which people or kinds of people could remind your character of what happened? What symbols, locations, weather phenomena, or seasons would naturally tie into it? Include these elements in the setting, and your character's response to them will give readers another missing piece to the puzzle.

Defense Mechanisms

Defense mechanisms are a powerful form of emotional shielding that help protect the character from painful wounds. In the real world, when we see signs of a possible recurrence of a traumatic event or the negative emotions related to it, these mechanisms kick into gear to protect us. They may not be good for us or our characters, but because they're subconscious, we aren't usually aware of them. If even a hurtful defense mechanism is pointed out to the protagonist, she'll cling to it because she believes it's shielding her from harm.

When readers see the character repeatedly employing one of these shielding techniques, they'll recognize when she's being triggered and that the circumstance could point to a painful occurrence. The following is a list of common defense mechanisms and how you can add them to your character's behavior profile.

Denial occurs when the character refuses to believe or admit that the wounding event happened. It may begin with a verbal denial, but when pressure is increased, she'll become more agitated. Depending on her personality, her behavior may progress to aggression or violence in an effort to stop the offending person from pursuing the frightening topic. Denial can be shown through the character's response when the topic is brought up, as she either disengages and flees from the conversation or becomes confrontational in a short period of time.

Rationalization happens when the character tries to convince herself and others that what happened wasn't so bad. An incest victim might claim that she and the offender had a special bond no one would understand. The victim may also rationalize the behavior of the perpetrator. This can happen when someone abused by her boyfriend makes excuses for him: *He's only like this when he drinks*, or *I should've called to tell him I'd be late*.

A benefit of this mechanism is that it makes the wounding incident obvious. Then, when the character begins to try to normalize it, readers will see her unhealthy response and recognize that it's altering her psyche in an alarming way.

Acting Out is often written off as undesirable attention-seeking behavior, but it's really an extreme way of expressing desires or releasing emotions the person is incapable of communicating in a healthy manner. Children are described as acting out when they become angry and throw a temper tantrum because they simply don't know how to convey what they're feeling.

As it relates to a wounding event, you can show this mechanism by putting the character into a situation in which a certain response is expected, then have her react in an overblown or unexpected way. For instance, a woman in a relationship with a controlling partner may desperately desire control herself but doesn't feel comfortable asking for it. So when she's feeling particularly oppressed, she steals things—things she doesn't even need but is compelled to take. Other examples of acting-out behaviors in this context include self-harming, violence against others, bullying, fits of rage, irresponsibility (not showing up to work, deliberately not finishing a school project, etc.), substance and food abuse, and sexual promiscuity.

Showing your character acting in these uncharacteristic ways can reveal the depth to which the trauma has affected her; if the behavior continues, readers may even begin to see the wound changing her before their very eyes.

Regression is a common coping mechanism that involves someone reverting to a previous level of development during times of stress. This can occur specifically when something reminds the character of past trauma, such as a grown man losing control of his bladder when a trigger appears. Showing this change and always associating it with the same trigger can start the gears turning for readers, who will want to know what frightening event is causing this response.

This mechanism can also manifest when the character reverts for extended periods of time. This can be seen when an adult woman regresses by dressing the way she did as a young girl, such as when she was in college or even elementary school. In this situation, the behavior itself is so obviously abnormal that it points to something serious at the root of her problem.

Dissociation is a state of feeling disconnected from one's body, emotions, or the world at large. This separation is a means of protecting oneself from unwanted feelings or triggers that are associated with a wounding event. In severe cases, the person exists in a constant state of dissociation, which can be especially bad because she's living in an ongoing rejection of what's real.

For storytelling purposes, it can be helpful to show the character dissociating—disengaging mentally or emotionally, even to the point of feeling as if she's floating outside of her body and watching things happen—in the presence of certain triggers or circumstances. Someone who was raped may dissociate when having sex, pulling away from what should be a desirable act because she wants to avoid the emotions and memories it unearths.

Another way to show this mechanism is through memory loss; if your character can't recall certain periods of time from the past, this can indicate that she's protecting herself from a painful memory or event.

Projection occurs when a character attributes undesirable traits, attitudes, or motives to someone else. This mechanism allows the character to avoid or deny the things about herself that she doesn't like. For instance, a teenager who was verbally abused by a caregiver may turn those hurtful slurs on a friend, calling her stupid, ugly, slutty, or weak. By applying these labels to someone else, the character separates them from herself. The truth or falsehood of the accusations are inconsequential. If she convinces herself that these labels are accurate for her friend, she can feel better in comparison.

It's important to remember that, to some degree, most people project. This doesn't mean they have a problem that needs addressing. In the case of your character, you'll want to show her doing this with triggers directly related to the wounding event; with consistency, readers will see that something isn't quite right. Be careful, though, not to make the character's projection so strong as to turn readers off. Balance it with other elements that will generate reader empathy.

Displacement is the act of someone turning their emotions or responses away from the person they're directed at and putting them onto someone else. Consider a character who witnessed his sibling being physically abused as a child. Growing up in such a household, he might have had trouble expressing feelings of anger toward his dad because he was afraid of retribution. Even as an adult, when he feels rage building for his father, he might take his anger out on someone "safer," such as a co-worker, spouse, child, or even the family pet. When readers see a character consistently redirecting certain feelings away from one person, they'll know that dysfunction exists between the two, and something significant is at the root of it.

Repression occurs when someone subconsciously rejects certain actions, thoughts, or feelings (as was explored in the earlier section on Denied Emotions). They refuse to entertain or even acknowledge that whatever they wish to avoid exists. In severe cases, whole memories may be repressed or changed to reflect something other than the truth. By showing your character constantly avoiding mentions of certain moments from the past or remembering things differently than everyone else, you can reveal, little by little, that this event is at the crux of their issues.

Compensation is the act of striving to prove to others and oneself that a real or perceived weakness doesn't exist. In relation to wounds, it's used to make up for a deficiency the character believes he exhibited during the event or to regain something he lost because of it. This is usually accomplished by overemphasizing certain qualities, abilities, or physical characteristics to prove strength in the less-than-perfect area. For example, a boy who was bullied for being weak may grow up with a fierce desire to prove his physical prowess—living at the gym, entering bodybuilding competitions, competing in combat sports, or taking steroids.

As with most mechanisms, this can only work if you're able to show readers the change that has occurred. Even if your character is this way at the start of the story, you can show his former self through flashbacks, memories, dialogue, old pictures, and other clues. Readers will either recognize how the wound has affected him or wonder what could have happened to bring about such a change.

The human psyche is the original mama bear, sniffing out potential threats and using a variety of methods to protect the mind, body, and spirit. Additional defense mechanisms exist, but for purposes of length, we chose to focus on the most common ones that are the easiest to write into a story. What's important to remember is that most people use a healthy combination of these responses in everyday life. But in relation to wounding events, especially ones the character hasn't fully come to grips with, the mechanisms outlined here can be used to show his blind spots, what frightens him, and how the trauma (even if it has not yet been revealed) impacts him. To keep things clear for readers, it's best to pick one of these reactions and show your character utilizing it consistently. Applying it to the event or the person associated with it will tie everything together, helping the reader to connect the dots.

Showing the incident through your character's behavior is important because it allows you to reveal it a bit at a time in a way that appeals to readers. It also emphasizes the wound's stifling weight, as readers see the impact it continues to have regardless of how much time has elapsed. As the story progresses, the character's fears, triggers, avoidances, defense mechanisms, and other responses will reinforce to readers that this isn't simply an isolated event from the past; it's a debilitating memory that continues to haunt the character years later, into the present.

PROBLEMS TO AVOID

Every aspect of storytelling has its problem areas, and the writing of emotional wounds is no exception. As you work through your character's past trauma, keep an eye out for the following pitfalls and use the advice here to avoid them.

PROBLEM #1: INFO DUMPS

An info dump occurs when the author interrupts the flow of the story to impart information via a chunk of narrative or exposition. This trap is particularly common when the author believes it's necessary to reveal backstory, especially in the opening pages. But large passages of exposition are undesirable on a number of levels. Info dumps are a form of telling because readers are forced into the passive role of listening to the author relate what has happened instead of being able to experience it along with the protagonist. Not only does this create distance between the reader and the character—with empathy being sacrificed as a result—it kills the pace.

Every author falls into the info dump trap at some point. The good news is that evading it becomes easier with time and practice. In the case of your character's wound, if you find yourself using an info dump to describe it, rewrite the passage using the following techniques.

Narrow It Down

One thing to keep in mind about the protagonist's (and possibly the antagonist's) wounding experience is that while it's necessary for your reader to know, it's still backstory. Showing this event in its entirety can be risky because you're either using a flashback and pulling readers out of the world they've become invested in, or you're slowing the pace with a lengthy passage of dialogue or inner reflection.

To keep readers engaged, take a good look at the entire event and figure out how you can shrink it down to its essence. Though you may know every possible thing about it, not all those details need to be shared. Ask yourself: What does my reader absolutely need to know about this? Which details are going to have the most impact? If you can weed out data that isn't critical, you can reduce the word count so the episode doesn't drag on and stop the story in its tracks.

Vary Your Techniques

Too much of a good thing typically *isn't* a good thing. For this reason, using a variety of techniques to share information about the wounding event is an effective way to keep your storytelling fresh. Utilizing a trigger and the overwhelming emotions that follow can break up a passage of dialogue that could easily become stagnant. Consistently showing a character's obsession or preferred defense mechanism is another way of painting the overall picture without always falling back on conversations or memories.

As an example of how to bring multiple techniques together, consider the following passage.

Sara poured sugar in her coffee and stirred, the clink of the spoon melodic against the cozy murmur of voices from neighboring tables. Sunlit, with a breeze coming off the water, the outdoor café was so peaceful this time of day—before the high school kids took it over.

"I like this place," Mom said, blowing on her tea. "It reminds me of where I used to go as a girl."

Sara smiled and leaned back, the wooden seat slats warming her skin. "The place with the éclairs?"

"Mmmm. That's the one." Mom took a sip, then her eyebrows shot up. "Oh, a friend of yours showed up at Mass on Sunday. Annemarie? Marybeth?" She shook her head. "Something with two names."

Sara jerked, dousing her hand in hot coffee. She set the cup down with a clatter and shrugged. *Don't know who you mean.*

"My memory these days—I swear." Mom sighed. "She said you two worked together last summer during your internship."

Sara met her mother's gaze, which showed curiosity instead of the horror that would be there if she knew the truth.

"Doesn't ring a bell." Sara grabbed the check. "I'll get this. Hey, how's your yoga class going?"

Here we see various methods being employed to show (rather than tell) the haunting event from Sara's past. Dialogue is used to impart information about the mysterious girl. Her name acts as a trigger, elevating Sara's emotions and eliciting a flight response as she prematurely wraps up her outing. We also see avoidance through the way she clams up then changes the subject. Lastly, not everything is revealed at once; a tiny piece of the puzzle is shown here—one that will be added to others as the story goes on until the full picture is realized.

This is an example of how you might disclose details about the wounding event in a compelling way without hindering the pace. Not only are these tips helpful for educating the reader about what has happened, they're good for "showing" in general, regardless of what you need to get across.

PROBLEM #2: POORLY STAGED FLASHBACKS

A flashback can be very effective at revealing the wounding situation because the reader sees it play out as if it's happening in real time, even when it's not. But proper placement of this device is key, because while a flashback is an active scene, it still is pulling the reader out of the current timeline and into one that has already passed.

Problems also arise if a flashback comes too soon in the story; readers have only started to become invested in the character's narrative, and if the focus suddenly shifts to the past it may be an unwelcome disruption, as they want to get back to the tale they've become immersed in.

Where, then, should a flashback occur so it's best received by your audience? Ideally, you want a landing spot that ties in with a critical scene and affects the character's emotional state. When the flashback relates to what's happening now, it feels like less of an interruption because the current action and the past event are clearly connected. If it also impacts the character's feelings, it has a greater chance of engaging the reader's emotions, which will keep them more involved.

In *Minority Report*, John Anderton is a drug-addicted cop whose marriage has recently fallen apart. We know from clues and bits of dialogue that he once had a son, but we're not clear on what happened to him. After being accused of a crime and going on the run, Anderton undergoes a risky surgery that will help him escape detection long enough to prove his innocence. It is during his recovery, when he's alone, his eyes are bandaged shut, and he's in a drug-induced stupor that the wounding moment is finally revealed: his son's abduction from a public pool while in Anderton's care.

This is an example of how poignant the reveal can be when it's shown through a well-placed flashback. Anderton's wound is disclosed when he is at his most vulnerable; when we think he's at his weakest, we see how truly broken he is. It's tied in with his current narrative in a way that keeps readers interested because the authorities are closing in, yet Anderton is oblivious as he relives this haunting moment from the past. Thoughtfully placing a flashback in this way makes the reveal seamless and puts readers in a position of being eager to know what will come next.

Whenever a wounding event is shown in its entirety, it's also important to keep in mind the effect it could have on your audience. Traumas that are intensely personal or violent have a greater chance of triggering readers who have experienced them. One way to minimize this possibility is to provide clues early on; this will hint at what's coming, and when the event is disclosed, readers will be prepared and can skip ahead or skim through it, if necessary. The scene can also be written from a limited or more distant viewpoint (rather than a deep point of view that pulls readers in super-close), which allows them to stand farther back from what's happening and feel as if they're viewing it from a safer place.

PROBLEM #3: MISUSED PROLOGUES

Prologues are second-class citizens in the literary world—mostly because they're overused or done poorly. To make yours the best it can be, take the following advice into consideration.

Make Sure It's Necessary

The prologue's purpose is almost always to convey information of some kind: the history of a people or region, the rise to power of a person who will influence the cast, a cataclysmic event that sets the stage for the current-day story, or—for the purpose of this discussion—a character's wounding event. Doing this at the very start of the story can create issues for readers who don't want to be fed a bunch of information up front; they just want to jump into the story and get to know the cast of characters they'll be spending the bulk of their time with. So the first order of business if you're considering using a prologue to reveal your character's wound is to be certain that it's needed. Ask yourself: Can the wounding event be shown later in the story? Why does the reader need to know this information right now? Pushing the reveal to a later point allows you to jump right into your character's current story—the one the reader wants to dive into.

Build Empathy Quickly

As with any story opening, the prologue has to hook readers. And don't make the mistake of thinking that your character's traumatic past will be enough to pull them in. Empathy isn't formed by a wounding event; it's formed when the reader cares about *who* the event is happening to. Building that bond takes time. The reader needs to be fully on the character's side before anything major happens, and with a prologue, you have significantly fewer pages to bring that about.

One way to speed up the process is to focus on things that build empathy: your character's likable or admirable traits, vulnerability, and positive actions. When you can bring out these aspects right away, the empathy bond is encouraged, so when that horrible thing happens a few pages later, readers will be engaged. A solid bond can be pivotal in carrying the audience through the transition from the prologue to the next chapter.

Avoid Clunky Temporal Shifts

Because readers don't always pay attention to chapter headings, they may not notice they're starting with a prologue. They become deeply invested in the main players and what's happening in that scene, and when there's an unexpected lurch into the next chapter, it's jarring. One way to inform readers of the change is to start the first chapter by announcing the new date or proclaiming how much time has passed: *Fifteen Years Later*. This shows the jump in time, but it isn't smooth; it shouts to readers that the next passage is going to be vastly different than the one they've just finished.

On its own, an abrupt shift in time won't kill a prologue, but it can contribute to it not being well received. A subtle smoothing of this transition can greatly improve the reader's experience. Author Ruta Sepetys does this beautifully at the end of her *Out Of the Easy* prologue by referencing *within the story* how much time will pass before the next chapter. Mentioning the passage of time in this way gives authors the opportunity to build interest and make readers want to turn that page.

Here are some examples of how the change in time can be slipped into the story as the prologue comes to a close:

> They said that with therapy I'd be walking again in three months. But by the close of 2020, I was still stuck in that chair.

> It would be fifteen years before their paths would cross again.

> I was sure Jack would forgive me, but it took forty-three long years before my second chance came.

Another way to smooth the transition between the prologue and what follows is to stick with the same setting for both scenes. The location will connect the two, acting as a bridge for readers. There will be changes, and referencing those differences will show a jump in time, but it will be less jarring if the background is familiar.

PROBLEM #4: WOUNDS THAT AREN'T CREDIBLE

Sometimes even a well-researched wound falls flat when it's revealed. The reader can't buy into it or doesn't respond favorably to it. To make sure your character's wounding event has maximum impact, confirm that it meets the following criteria.

It's Connected to the Character's Fatal Flaw

When the wounding event is revealed, we want to hear a virtual *aaaaaah* from readers. They should feel a sense of satisfaction, recognizing that this piece of backstory aligns exactly with the character they've come to know in the present. Remember that in a change arc the wounding incident will result in the emergence of a fatal flaw that will keep the character from achieving her overall goal. Once the wound is revealed, readers will see why she's having trouble overcoming this particular weakness. If the issues your character must address aren't ones that would naturally flow out of the painful past event you've chosen, get back to the drawing board and find another traumatic situation that better fits your character and will tie more precisely into the story.

It Motivates the Character

A wounding event should be a haunting experience. If the character's choices aren't being driven by what happened, it usually means you haven't fully examined the wound and its impact on her. Set aside some time to really explore this wound and its effects. Identify the resulting fear that will begin to determine your character's decisions. Figure out the lie she will embrace and how her behavior will change based on this new belief. Pinpoint which flaws would likely develop and how they will impede her progress. Once you know these important elements related to the wounding event, you'll have a much better idea of how she's going to act and respond to stimuli—in effect, what's driving her. Knowing this will enable you to write the character and her past trauma in a way that will ring true with readers.

It's All-Consuming

By definition, a wound is traumatizing. If your character is able to bounce back without it consuming and significantly diminishing her, there's something seriously wrong. Again, it's possible that you need to find a different trauma, one that will affect her more severely. Or maybe you need to make your chosen event or painful circumstance more personal via the previously discussed section on factors that impact the wound.

Another possibility is that your incident just isn't invasive enough. The character's fear-driven choices and emotional shielding should create disruption. Flaws especially will sow dysfunction in every area of life—sabotaging the character's relationships, undermining her professionally, ravaging her perception of herself, and keeping her from moving forward. If the wound isn't a destructive force for your protagonist, explore the important areas of her life to see how they should be impacted by the trauma.

PROBLEM #5: WOUNDS THAT RESOLVE ABRUPTLY

Facing and overcoming an emotional wound doesn't happen overnight. For writing purposes, it takes the course of an entire story for the character to navigate his arc and complete this process. So if it happens abruptly—if he faces the wound and triumphs in quick fashion—it's deeply dissatisfying to readers. When things resolve too swiftly, this often signifies a problem with structure.

It can be tough to design a story so events happen at the right times and the pace remains rigorous. But mastering this part of the process is pivotal. Information must be spread out evenly over the course of the story, building intrigue and enticing readers as the character traverses his arc, moving inexorably toward that moment when he achieves the goal and his journey is complete.

If you need help in this area, the One Stop for Writers® website offers a comprehensive structure mapping tool that can help you plan your story and character's arc. Other options can be found on the Recommended Reading page at the end of this book.

FINAL WORDS FROM THE AUTHORS

Emotional trauma comes in endless variations. While we've tried to create a strong range of possible wounds to kick-start the brainstorming process, these entries are by no means comprehensive. We urge you to really explore your character's past to better understand the unique factors that helped mold him into who he is at the start of your story. Don't be afraid to go off the map and customize the wounds outlined here.

If you have a wound in mind but are unable to find the exact scenario you need, we suggest reading through the other entries in the same category, as these will all share a common theme and may spark ideas on how you could adapt an existing entry to fit a particular character's situation. For authenticity, we also recommend doing further research on the wound you've chosen and tailor it according to the options in the Factors That Will Impact the Wound section.

You will notice as you peruse entries that the bulk of the listed behaviors are negative. This is by design, as backstory wounds are disruptive and will create aftershocks leading to further harm until good coping strategies are adopted. For specific information on the healing part of your character's process, please see the section on Positive Coping Practices. You can choose the ones that feel right for your character's situation and use them to awaken their desire to heal, lead them to accept what can't be changed, and help them achieve internal growth and greater self-worth.

Another thing to keep in mind when reading through the entries is that you will notice some conflicting behaviors. For example, a character who loses a limb may isolate herself by withdrawing from those around her, or she may do the opposite and become completely dependent on others. Because each character is unique, with her own traits and histories, she will respond differently to her trauma than someone else may. To this end, we have tried to cover a large range of reactions. When sourcing these entries for ideas, always ask yourself if the suggestion you'd like to use fits the character. This will ensure that her actions in the story line up with her personality and will seem credible to readers.

When unearthing the lie your character believes to be true, use the examples in the entries as a starting point, since these are purposely general in nature. Every wounding event is distinct, and the peripheral people involved, along with the character's specific history with them, will influence the exact lie that emerges. For instance, the death of a sibling who was always cared for and protected by the character will generate a different lie than if the relationship was a distant one. Characters are complex, layered beings, and their wounding events and the embedded lies should fit them like custom-tailored clothing.

It is our hope that this book will help you discover and flesh out the possible wounds for many future characters. Events like these are incredibly formative. Inspecting them carefully and considering them from many different angles should enable you to choose ones that fit perfectly, resulting in layered and well-rounded characters your readers will respond to.

THE EMOTIONAL WOUND THESAURUS

Crime and Victimization

A CARJACKING

EXAMPLES:
Being forced out of one's car and it being stolen and driven away
Being forced to drive one's car to an isolated location under threat of violence by the carjacker

BASIC NEEDS OFTEN COMPROMISED BY THIS WOUND: Safety and security, esteem and recognition

FALSE BELIEFS THAT COULD BE EMBRACED
I was targeted because I was weak.
I froze in the moment; I can't be depended upon in an emergency.
I can't be truly safe.
I can't keep my family safe.
Acquiring material items is pointless since they'll only be taken from me.
Trying to look for the good in this world is naïve.
The police are impotent and can't protect anyone.
The only way to combat violence is with violence.

THE CHARACTER MAY FEAR…
Being victimized again in another way
Having another prized possession forcibly taken away
Owning nice things, since they will make the character a target
A random act of violence ending badly for them or a loved one
The kind of person who carried out the carjacking
Being attacked at home (due to the carjacker finding personal information in the vehicle)

POSSIBLE RESPONSES AND RESULTS
Purposely buying things that aren't quite as nice in the hopes one won't be targeted for them
Becoming tighter with money to recoup the loss
Hounding the police to make sure the perpetrator is caught
Avoiding the area where the carjacking occurred
Patrolling the area of the attack, looking to confront the carjacker and reclaim one's power
Becoming confrontational with strangers perceived to be a threat
Being paranoid
Embracing vigilantism due to the belief that the police are unable to adequately protect the public
Buying pepper spray or a weapon and keeping it in one's new car
Increasing security for one's car and home
Growing pessimistic; viewing the world through a negative filter
Taking safer routes, even if it means adding time to one's commute
Turning down opportunities that would require one to drive alone to get somewhere
Not allowing teenaged children to drive alone

Insisting that family members call when they get to where they're going

Being unable to sleep or relax until all family members are home

Becoming hyperalert when driving

Heightened anxiety if someone approaches one's vehicle on foot

Refusing to be a Good Samaritan (not stopping to help if someone's car has broken down, etc.)

Mistrusting people in general

Developing a panic disorder

Being possessive with one's things; not being willing to "hand things over" again

Developing control issues

Staying home rather than going out

Thinking and acting prejudicially against people similar to the carjacker

Seeking reforms at the municipal level in an effort to make the streets safer

Becoming less materialistic; needing less stuff

Seeing this near miss as an opportunity for a do-over in life

Expressing love and showing affection more freely with loved ones

Reordering one's priorities (putting family first, spending less time at work, not worrying so much about money, etc.)

PERSONALITY TRAITS THAT MAY FORM

Attributes: Affectionate, alert, analytical, appreciative, bold, centered, diplomatic, focused, generous, independent, introverted, just, meticulous, observant, organized, persistent, protective, responsible, simple

Flaws: Addictive, apathetic, confrontational, judgmental, macho, morbid, nervous, paranoid, pushy, resentful, rowdy, vindictive

TRIGGERS THAT MIGHT AGGRAVATE THIS WOUND

Someone approaching one's car at a stoplight or in a parking lot

Seeing a car on the road exactly like the one that was stolen

A child or spouse being out later than they're supposed to be

Being victimized in a smaller way, like a friend being manipulative or a boss using a guilt trip

Being followed for a period of time by another car, turn for turn

Someone tapping a knuckle against the car window

Hearing the song that was playing on the radio at the time of the attack

Driving in similar conditions (late at night, in the same area of town, through a traffic tunnel, etc.)

OPPORTUNITIES TO FACE OR OVERCOME THIS WOUND

A chance to do something one really wants, but it means driving in the same area where the carjacking occurred

Noticing that one's lifestyle of fear and paranoia is affecting one's children

Being too afraid to drive and realizing it is impacting one's happiness through its limitations

Being forced to interact with someone similar to the carjacker and becoming aware of prejudice that has developed since the event

A HOME INVASION

EXAMPLES: Having one's living space broken into while one is there, either alone or with family, and then being forced through the ordeal of being robbed, victimized, assaulted (physically, mentally or sexually), and possibly even kidnapped.

BASIC NEEDS OFTEN COMPROMISED BY THIS WOUND: Physiological needs, safety and security, love and belonging, esteem and recognition, self-actualization

FALSE BELIEFS THAT COULD BE EMBRACED
Strangers should be feared.
Anyone I don't know is a potential threat.
I wasn't safe in my own home, so I'm not safe anywhere.
Sympathy (empathy, kindness, etc.) is a sign of weakness.
I can't keep my loved ones safe.
I am to blame for what happened (for not having proper home security, not locking the door, not being strong enough, etc.).
The police are inept and can't protect me.
The world is full of evil people.
Control is only an illusion.

THE CHARACTER MAY FEAR...
Trusting the wrong person
Being alone and vulnerable
Having their control taken away
Another break-in
Criminals and addicts, or people similar to the perpetrators in some way (race, appearance, etc.)
Intimacy and sex (if they were sexually assaulted)
Particular elements associated with the ordeal (e.g., enclosed spaces, if they were hiding in a closet)

POSSIBLE RESPONSES AND RESULTS
Being obsessive about home safety (checking locks repeatedly, installing floodlights, setting up a security system, etc.)
Heightened alertness (noticing noises one would have dismissed in the past, tracking movements all the time, marking the exits, etc.)
Becoming withdrawn or secretive
Struggling when one is alone, even suffering panic attacks and paranoia
Insomnia or difficulty sleeping; experiencing vivid nightmares
Waking with a racing heartbeat
Feeling uncomfortable around certain items used in the attack (kitchen tools, leather gloves, duct tape, etc.)

Creating a safe room within one's home fortified with locks and home protection

Difficulty concentrating

Being unresponsive in conversations

Jumping at loud noises

Anxiety flaring up when one must open the door, even when company is expected

Feeling followed or watched

Feeling unsafe in one's home but being too fearful to leave it

Reliving what happened over and over

Having a difficult time enjoying the little things (visits with friends, smiling, laughing, etc.)

Needing to know where one's children are at all times

Needing to have control over everything (possibly damaging relationships in the process)

Buying a weapon for home protection or joining a self-defense class

Being grateful for the things and people that survived

Being less concerned with material things

Seeking therapy

PERSONALITY TRAITS THAT MAY FORM

Attributes: Alert, analytical, cautious, independent, introverted, mature, meticulous, observant, perceptive, private, protective, responsible, sentimental, wise

Flaws: Compulsive, defensive, humorless, inflexible, insecure, irrational, materialistic, nervous, obsessive, paranoid, pessimistic, prejudiced, suspicious, timid, uncommunicative, withdrawn

TRIGGERS THAT MIGHT AGGRAVATE THIS WOUND

Sensory stimuli associated with the event, like the smell of blood or pain of a carpet burn

Hearing about a break-in within one's neighborhood

Being left home alone

The doorbell chiming when one was not expecting visitors

A stranger asking for help (if this ruse was used by the perpetrator to get inside the house)

An event that leaves one feeling exposed (a power outage, losing one's cell phone and having no way to call the police, etc.)

Leaving one's teenager home alone and her not answering the phone when one calls

OPPORTUNITIES TO FACE OR OVERCOME THIS WOUND

Saving an important heirloom from being stolen only to lose it in some way later

Obsessing over keeping one's home safe only for a family member to be attacked elsewhere

Experiencing marital friction due to one's inability to move past the event

Becoming so over-protective as a parent that one's child rebels and ends up in danger

Experiencing a disaster (a flood, a house fire, etc.) and being welcomed into a stranger's home and shown kindness

A PHYSICAL ASSAULT

EXAMPLES

Getting beaten up by unknown assailants (e.g., jumped by a gang, a hate group, or peers at school)

Being hit or physically harmed by a family member

Being mugged

Being attacked by a single person (in a bar fight, for looking at someone's girlfriend, etc.)

Interceding to protect another and becoming targeted

BASIC NEEDS OFTEN COMPROMISED BY THIS WOUND: Safety and security, esteem and recognition, self-actualization

FALSE BELIEFS THAT COULD BE EMBRACED

I'm weak—an easy target.

Only constant vigilance will keep me safe.

Violence must be met with violence.

I can't trust people of that gender (or race, ethnicity, etc.).

The authorities aren't able to protect anyone.

Getting involved is never worth the pain. People can solve their own problems.

I can't be responsible for the welfare of others because I'll only let them down.

THE CHARACTER MAY FEAR…

Becoming a victim again

Victimization becoming part of their identity, a role they can't escape

Never being able to reclaim their power

Vulnerability

That something similar will befall their loved ones

Being attacked and/or killed

That others will think poorly of them because of the beating

POSSIBLE RESPONSES AND RESULTS

Not venturing out after dark

Never going anywhere alone

Avoiding the place where the assault occurred

Frequent panic or anxiety attacks

Becoming overprotective with loved ones

Working out excessively in an effort to become stronger

Hiding whatever it was that made one a target (one's beliefs, religion, ethnicity, orientation, etc.)

Becoming more cautious with one's words to avoid provoking others

Always being on alert

Suspecting all strangers of ill will

Needing to win in every situation so one won't be considered weak

Avoiding responsibility out of a fear of failure or being proven unworthy of trust

Turning a blind eye to injustice (if getting involved in someone else's fight caused the assault)

Becoming prejudiced against one's attacker

Emotional volatility; being prone to overreactions

Resentment toward the police (if one blames them in part for the attack)

Drinking or using drugs

Taking self-defense classes

Finding a confidante to vent to and help one gain perspective

Being grateful that the assault didn't result in even greater harm

Viewing violence in a new light and trying to resolve differences another way

Appreciating one's blessings more; feeling like one was given a second chance

Not sweating the small stuff

Avoiding behaviors that could be intimidating so others won't experience the same fear one endured

Becoming a pacifist

PERSONALITY TRAITS THAT MAY FORM

Attributes: Alert, appreciative, bold, cautious, courteous, diplomatic, disciplined, observant, private, proactive

Flaws: Abrasive, addictive, callous, confrontational, hostile, inhibited, irrational, martyr, needy, nervous, paranoid, reckless, suspicious, temperamental, uncommunicative, violent, volatile, weak-willed, withdrawn

TRIGGERS THAT MIGHT AGGRAVATE THIS WOUND

Seeing someone physically similar to one's attacker

Running into one's attacker

Being in an area where a fight breaks out

Having to go to the hospital (for tests, to visit a sick friend, etc.)

Sensory stimuli that cause a flashback (a shoe kicking loose gravel, the smell of wet pavement, etc.)

News reports of muggings and assaults

A loved one being roughed up on a smaller scale (e.g., being shoved or tripped at school)

Being awakened in the night by a strange noise

Being in a place similar to where the attack happened

OPPORTUNITIES TO FACE OR OVERCOME THIS WOUND

A romantic relationship that turns abusive

Overreacting and embarrassing oneself in response to a perceived attack that turns out to be nothing

Exacting vengeance against one's attacker and discovering that it didn't take away the emotional pain of the event

When the choice to not get involved in another's problems leads to the person being victimized, it forces one to face one's own cowardice

BEING HELD CAPTIVE

EXAMPLES: Being kidnapped…
And held for ransom
And kept captive for an extended period of time
And sold into slavery
By one's biological parent or other relative to start a new life elsewhere

BASIC NEEDS OFTEN COMPROMISED BY THIS WOUND: Safety and security, love and belonging, esteem and recognition, self-actualization

FALSE BELIEFS THAT COULD BE EMBRACED
I'm an easy mark, a target. People will always try to victimize me.
I will never be the same, never be whole.
The others didn't make it out; I shouldn't have either. (Survivor's guilt)
My captor wasn't all bad. (Stockholm syndrome)
My judgment is faulty and can't be trusted. (If one believes one was at fault somehow)
The only person I can trust or count on is me.
Specific beliefs caused by a captor's brainwashing: *No one loves me, I deserve to be punished*, etc.

THE CHARACTER MAY FEAR…
Having their power and freedom stolen again
Trusting the wrong person
Not being able to achieve their dreams
Not being able to adjust to the real world after escaping
Someone they love being taken and suffering the same ordeal
That the things endured during captivity will cause loved ones to reject them
Men or women (depending on the captor's gender), especially ones with a close physical resemblance
Being assaulted, trapped, captured again, or killed

POSSIBLE RESPONSES AND RESULTS
Becoming cautious almost to the point of paranoia
Hyperawareness of one's surroundings
Sensitivity to trigger stimuli, such as being in an enclosed space or having one's movements restricted
Withdrawing from friends and loved ones
Difficulty trusting others
Fatigue due to nightmares
Becoming security-obsessed (taking self-defense classes, turning a home into a fortress, etc.)
Depression and anxiety
Losing interest in hobbies or the activities one used to enjoy

Being overprotective of one's children

Difficulty adjusting to changes in the world since one's abduction (if it lasted a long time)

Being evasive or dishonest out of a desire to protect one's privacy

Self-medicating to cope

Thoughts or attempts of suicide

Flying under everyone's radar so as not to draw attention to oneself

Feeling empathy for one's kidnapper followed by feelings of guilt (Stockholm syndrome)

Self-loathing over things that happened or one's inability to escape

Post-traumatic stress disorder (PTSD) symptoms, such as flashbacks, paranoia, and anxiety jitters

Becoming extremely subservient; losing one's will

Impaired concentration, focus, and memory

Feeling powerless, fearful, and anxious

Taking steps to leave the past behind (changing one's name, moving, switching jobs, etc.)

Feeling as if one has been given a second chance

Believing that one escaped for a purpose and living to fulfill that purpose

Believing a debt of gratitude is owed to one's rescuer, and living that out

Finding a therapist or support group

PERSONALITY TRAITS THAT MAY FORM

Attributes: Alert, appreciative, bold, cautious, disciplined, empathetic, industrious, meticulous, nurturing, observant, patient, persistent, private, proactive, protective, resourceful, socially aware, wise

Flaws: Addictive, compulsive, evasive, hostile, inhibited, insecure, irrational, morbid, needy, nervous, obsessive, paranoid, self-destructive, subservient, suspicious, timid, uncommunicative, uncooperative, withdrawn

TRIGGERS THAT MIGHT AGGRAVATE THIS WOUND

Specific smells, sounds, tastes, or objects associated with one's captor

Places that act as reminders of one's captivity, such as a basement or a barn

Hearing that one's captor is up for parole or has been released from prison

A child moving away (going to college, attending summer camp, renting an apartment, etc.)

Flashbacks that cause one to relive the event

Seeing a stranger that resembles one's captor

Watching movies or shows that portray a situation similar to what one went through

OPPORTUNITIES TO FACE OR OVERCOME THIS WOUND

Feeling like one is being watched or stalked (even when one isn't) and recognizing that seeking help is the only way to be free of this delusion

Discovering that one's child was detained to keep them safe (like being locked in a storage closet during a mall robbery)

Recognizing that one's fears caused by the kidnapping are driving loved ones away

Realizing that one's quality of life and ability to connect with people is being ruined by PTSD, and deciding to seek help

BEING SEXUALLY VIOLATED

NOTES: While there is a huge difference between being raped and receiving unwanted text images, the sense of sexual violation is the same. For this reason, we have included all kinds and levels of sexual harassment, violation, and assault in this entry.

EXAMPLES

Rape or attempted rape (by a stranger, acquaintance, family member, or partner)
Being forced or coerced to perform sexual acts, such as oral or anal sex
Being prostituted
Fondling or unwanted sexual touching
Incest
Being rubbed up against in a crowd
Being forced to watch pornography
Being forced to pose for pictures or participate in videos
Being flashed
Receiving unwanted sexual texts, photos, or messages

BASIC NEEDS OFTEN COMPROMISED BY THIS WOUND: Safety and security, love and belonging, esteem and recognition, self-actualization

FALSE BELIEFS THAT COULD BE EMBRACED

If I tell, people will think I'm lying or I encouraged it.
It's my fault. I brought this on myself.
My judgment is flawed for not seeing what was right in front of me.
The people closest to you always cause the deepest hurt.
No one will want to be with me now.
Nothing can keep me safe from predators, including myself.
Trusting people means getting hurt.

THE CHARACTER MAY FEAR…

Sex and intimacy
Letting people get close
Misreading a situation and putting themselves or a loved one at risk
Men or women, depending on who the perpetrator was
Being attacked or held against their will
Telling the truth and not being believed (by police, family, friends, the media, etc.)
Getting pregnant or contracting a sexually-transmitted disease
Being rejected or abandoned by a loved one because of what happened

POSSIBLE RESPONSES AND RESULTS

Doing everything possible to hide what happened, due to shame or fear of retribution
PTSD symptoms, such as flashbacks, nightmares, etc.

Abusing drugs or alcohol as a means of coping

The development of phobias or an eating disorder

Difficulty focusing at work or school

Not taking care of oneself (having poor hygiene, etc.) due to depression

Becoming uncommunicative

Pulling away from family and friends

Giving up hobbies and interests

Questioning one's sexual orientation

Decreased libido or an increased and unhealthy interest in sex

Confusion over one's feelings toward the abuser (if the abuser was a friend or family member)

Negative feelings or thoughts about one's body

Suicidal thoughts and behaviors (making plans, writing a note, attempting suicide, etc.)

Emotional volatility

Acting out as a form of rebellion

Mistrusting those in authority (if the abuser held a role of power)

Difficulty being naked in front of others; covering up with layers of clothing

Startling when one is touched by others

Becoming very controlling

Difficulty trusting others

Difficulty standing up for oneself

Maintaining platonic relationships where sex is not a possibility

Becoming overly protective of loved ones and the vulnerable people in one's life

Telling a therapist, trusted friend, or loved one about the assault

Trying to affect change by telling one's story, donating time or money, or lobbying

PERSONALITY TRAITS THAT MAY FORM

Attributes: Alert, cautious, courageous, disciplined, discreet, empathetic, gentle, independent, meticulous, nurturing, obedient, observant,

Flaws: Addictive, antisocial, callous, childish, controlling, dishonest, disrespectful, hostile, inhibited, insecure, reckless, resentful, rowdy

TRIGGERS THAT MIGHT AGGRAVATE THIS WOUND

Seeing a TV show or movie that depicts a sexual assault

Experiencing a sensory stimulus that triggers memories of the assault

Meeting the perpetrator unexpectedly at a social event like a reunion, party, or charity event

Seeing the perpetrator with a child or person who could potentially be a victim

Being approached from behind unexpectedly

OPPORTUNITIES TO FACE OR OVERCOME THIS WOUND

Unintentionally driving away a desired lover or spouse, then realizing one's mistake

Wanting a romantic relationship to move forward, but to do so, one must open up about what happened and face possible rejection

Hearing about a friend's sexual assault and gaining the courage to speak up or seek help

BEING STALKED

EXAMPLES: Stalkers are typically obsessed with their subjects, either out of a romantic interest, from the belief that the subjects have rejected or slighted them in some way, or another reason they themselves may not completely know or understand. Stalkers come in many forms, including…

A fan whose mail went unanswered

A former business partner

A student whose scholarship application was denied

An artist whose work failed to win a contest or received a poor review

An ex-lover

An acquaintance whose romantic advances were rejected

An unstable employee overlooked for a promotion

Someone suffering delusions of unrequited love

A serial killer or rapist

A deranged individual who develops an inexplicable fascination with a certain person

BASIC NEEDS OFTEN COMPROMISED BY THIS WOUND: Safety and security, love and belonging, self-actualization

FALSE BELIEFS THAT COULD BE EMBRACED

If I hadn't been so friendly (or turned her down for a date, etc.) this wouldn't be happening to me.

People know I am weak and will always try to hurt me.

My judgment is flawed; I should have seen this person as a threat from the beginning.

No place or person is truly safe.

The authorities are powerless to help me.

Trusting the good in people is naïve and dangerous.

THE CHARACTER MAY FEAR…

For their life

That the stalker will get out of jail and seek revenge

That the stalking will never end (if it is ongoing)

Trusting the wrong person

Letting anyone get close in case they too become obsessed

That innocent family members or loved ones may be victimized by association

POSSIBLE RESPONSES AND RESULTS

Insomnia and fatigue

Loss of appetite

Isolating oneself; avoiding unnecessary social interactions

Avoiding social media or shutting down one's accounts

Clinging to those one knows is safe

Relying on loved ones to make decisions due to doubting one's discernment and judgment

Becoming overprotective of loved ones and pets

Becoming overly suspicious and paranoid

Developing a mental disorder like agoraphobia or depression

PTSD symptoms (nightmares, flashbacks, startling easily, irritability, etc.)

Making changes to throw off a stalker (moving, changing one's name or appearance, etc.)

Becoming very concerned with personal safety

Self-medicating through food, alcohol, or drugs

Bouts of irrational self-blame

Engaging in critical self-assessment to discern what caused the attention

Shedding attributes one believes caused the stalking (e.g., trading friendliness for hostility)

Hypertension, gastrointestinal issues, sexual dysfunction, and other stress-related physical symptoms

Performing poorly at work or school

Giving up hobbies and activities that take one out of the home

Difficulty trusting others

Not talking to people or responding to casual friendliness

Avoiding romantic relationships

Weight gain or weight loss as a result of stress

Being unable to enjoy life fully or let go of worry

Being more alert and aware of one's surroundings

Making safer choices and taking necessary precautions

Joining a self-defense class

Being more community-minded; extending security efforts to include everyone in one's apartment building or neighborhood

PERSONALITY TRAITS THAT MAY FORM

Attributes: Alert, appreciative, cautious, disciplined, discreet, empathetic, focused, independent, nurturing, observant, private, proactive

Flaws: Addictive, controlling, defensive, hostile, humorless, inhibited, insecure, irrational, needy, nervous, paranoid, suspicious, temperamental

TRIGGERS THAT MIGHT AGGRAVATE THIS WOUND

Having one's picture taken

Seeing someone who looks like the stalker

A sensory trigger tied to one's stalker (a certain song being hummed, the scent of roses, etc.)

Milestones (a holiday, an annual work party, etc.) that occurred at the time of the stalking

OPPORTUNITIES TO FACE OR OVERCOME THIS WOUND

Being put into the same situation that created one's stalker in the first place (having to promote someone within the company, being asked out on a date and wanting to decline, etc.)

Learning that one's stalker has been freed from jail

Getting into a relationship with someone who begins to exhibit possessiveness or jealousy

Discovering that a love interest has a history of domestic violence or emotional instability

BEING TREATED AS PROPERTY

EXAMPLES
Being prostituted
Being enslaved
Being sold to another person
Having one's marriage arranged against one's will
Being given to traffickers
Being raised as a donor (organs, marrow, etc.) for a family member
Being forced to do things one doesn't want to do in order to benefit others
One's value being determined by how much money, power, or prestige a special quality such as beauty, strength, or virtue may bring

BASIC NEEDS OFTEN COMPROMISED BY THIS WOUND: Physiological needs, safety and security, love and belonging, esteem and recognition, self-actualization

FALSE BELIEFS THAT COULD BE EMBRACED
I have no value.
I exist merely to benefit others.
What I want doesn't matter.
This must be what love looks like.
I'll never be free.
My will is not my own.
I'm no better than an animal.
I'll only be free in death.

THE CHARACTER MAY FEAR…
Being sold or given away to someone worse
Becoming attached to someone and then having to leave them
Being used by others
Never escaping the culture of abuse
Being killed because their value is no longer the same
Never experiencing unconditional love

POSSIBLE RESPONSES AND RESULTS
Becoming highly obedient in hopes of winning a handler's favor and avoiding punishment
Losing one's will or identity; associating solely with one's captors
Being cowed by anyone in authority
Doing one's best to fly under the radar and not attract attention
Having little or no self-esteem
Being unable to feel or express certain emotions
Engaging in detachment or dissociation to get through the abuse
Going through the motions, keeping to oneself, and doing what one is told

Focusing on activities that will please one's keepers and help achieve their goals

Rebelling in small ways (by hoarding items, obeying in action but not in attitude, etc.)

Considering suicide as the only way to escape

Privately honing a skill that could help one eventually succeed

Privately practicing a forbidden talent in an effort to hold onto something of one's own

Secretly stockpiling items for a future escape attempt

Subtly reaching out for help (e.g., passing a note to someone considered to be sympathetic)

Running away and possibly turning to drugs or alcohol to cope with one's past

Having frequent thoughts of suicide or possible suicide attempts

Not trusting people

Not planning too far into the future

Underachieving; thinking small

Viewing the world with apathy

Showing disrespect for anyone in authority

Exerting control over those considered to be weaker (animals, siblings, schoolmates, etc.)

Distractibility; being unable to focus

Seeking familiarity through toxic relationships

Reluctance to build relationships (to avoid abandonment and loss)

Feeling empty but wanting to change and feel as others do

Appreciating small things that others take for granted

Slowly opening up and seeking help (through therapy, confiding in someone who is safe, etc.)

PERSONALITY TRAITS THAT MAY FORM

Attributes: Alert, cautious, cooperative, courageous, courteous, discreet, easygoing, empathetic, friendly, gentle, humble, kind, loyal, nurturing

Flaws: Addictive, apathetic, callous, cynical, devious, dishonest, flaky, humorless, ignorant, inhibited, insecure, nervous, rebellious

TRIGGERS THAT MIGHT AGGRAVATE THIS WOUND

Promises that are broken

Being left in the company of unfamiliar people, like a babysitter or an aid worker

Being given a compliment or gift one used to receive from the abuser

Perceiving that one is being used by a friend or family member for their own personal gain

Sensory triggers tied to one's abuse (the clink of a chain, the sound of mattress springs, etc.)

OPPORTUNITIES TO FACE OR OVERCOME THIS WOUND

Escaping and getting a taste of freedom only to be caught and returned to one's "owner"

After escaping, meeting a person one suspects is being mistreated and wanting to help them

Recognizing that one is repeating the cycle by treating one's own children as property on some level

After escaping, going through a string of toxic relationships and realizing one hasn't healed

BEING VICTIMIZED BY A PERPETRATOR
WHO WAS NEVER CAUGHT

EXAMPLES: When one is victimized or attacked in some way, the apprehension and punishment of the perpetrator is often part of the injured party's healing process. When the offender remains at large, the victim continues to feel vulnerable. This is true for the victims of many atrocities, including…

Rape or sexual assault

The murder of a loved one

A home invasion

A mugging or physical assault

Domestic abuse

Kidnapping

Stalking

Carjacking

Bullying

Identity theft or money fraud

BASIC NEEDS OFTEN COMPROMISED BY THIS WOUND: Safety and security, self-actualization

FALSE BELIEFS THAT COULD BE EMBRACED

I will never be safe as long as he or she remains free.

You can't believe in anything or anyone.

This person has crippled me.

I can't put down roots until he or she is caught.

Since I can't protect myself, I can't be responsible for others.

When you let people in, they will always take advantage.

The system has failed me and can't keep me safe.

THE CHARACTER MAY FEAR…

The person never being caught

Being victimized again (by this person or someone else)

Loved ones being victimized by this person

Living forever in fear

Feeling stuck emotionally due to a lack of closure over what happened

Trusting the wrong person again

Letting down their guard or letting people get close

Being unable to protect loved ones

Never being able to regain their freedom and control

POSSIBLE RESPONSES AND RESULTS

Aggressively enhancing the security at one's home, turning it into a fortress
Going into hiding (changing one's name, moving, altering one's appearance, etc.)
Hounding the police for details of the case
Showing disdain for the authorities (talking negatively about the police, arranging protests, etc.)
Hiring a private investigator to find the perpetrator
Becoming overprotective with family members
Worrying excessively about the safety of loved ones
Becoming paranoid
Mental disorders arising from the perpetrator being free and from the victimization itself (depression, PTSD, anxiety disorders, phobias, etc.)
Self-medicating
Driving people away out of a desire to protect them
Avoiding new people or keeping one's guard up so they can't get close
Only leaving one's home when it's absolutely necessary
Giving up on one's dreams due to being crippled by fear
Falling into self-pity
Misreading circumstances and attributing guilt or bad intentions where there are none
Avoiding situations that would make one responsible for others
Recognizing how certain actions made one easier to victimize (like leaving a house key under an outdoor planter or not locking one's door) and resolving to avoid those actions again
Becoming more aware of one's surroundings and being cautious when dealing with others
Pursuing goals despite fear and worry because one is determined not to be further victimized

PERSONALITY TRAITS THAT MAY FORM

Attributes: Adaptable, alert, analytical, bold, cautious, courageous, disciplined, discreet, hospitable, independent, just, meticulous

Flaws: Addictive, compulsive, cowardly, defensive, forgetful, humorless, inflexible, irrational, irresponsible, martyr, nagging, nervous

TRIGGERS THAT MIGHT AGGRAVATE THIS WOUND

Being contacted by the perpetrator (through a letter, text message, phone call, etc.)
Seeing a stranger in the distance and suspecting them of being the perpetrator
Watching a movie or reading a book that mirrors one's situation of being victimized
Odd happenings (items going missing, a car window being smashed, an object being moved, etc.) which may be coincidental or not
Sensory triggers connected to the assault (the smell of cigarettes, a creaky stairwell, etc.)

OPPORTUNITIES TO FACE OR OVERCOME THIS WOUND

Meeting another survivor who is able to live a full and happy life, and wanting that for oneself
Finding the perpetrator and extracting justice, but discovering it didn't solve one's problems
When a family member is in danger, one must trust the authorities who let one down in the past
Facing a stress-related health scare and knowing one must find a way to let go and move forward

IDENTITY THEFT

EXAMPLES
A criminal obtaining personal documents and assuming one's identity
Having one's passport duplicated and used to illegally bring a criminal into the country
One's bank account or investments being drained by someone with false documents
Accruing debt when someone clones one's card
Being harassed by creditors, police, or criminals because another person has assumed one's identity
Online accounts being created in one's name for cyber-bullying purposes
A spoof online account being created by a rival who seeks to ruin one's reputation
Being billed for Medicare when one's identity is stolen, affecting one's ability to obtain insurance
A friend or family member posing as oneself and then doing something to stain one's reputation
One's fingerprints or DNA being used by someone to implicate one in a crime
Having one's image photo-shopped into compromising situations and shared online for revenge
One's personal information being used to create a fake account at an unsavory sex or predator site
One's email being hacked and used to send criminal threats or damaging information

BASIC NEEDS OFTEN COMPROMISED BY THIS WOUND: Physiological needs, safety and security, esteem and recognition

FALSE BELIEFS THAT COULD BE EMBRACED
Trying to make a better life is useless because someone will just take it from me.
I was targeted because I am weak.
People don't respect me because I am not worthy of respect.
Predators are everywhere; I can't trust my information with anyone.
Control is an illusion; what I have can be taken away at any time.
No one can help when times get tough, especially the police.
My name will never be fully cleared; I will always be limited by this.

THE CHARACTER MAY FEAR...
Being used or exploited
Losing everything they have built
A financial ruin
Making a mistake by placing their trust in the wrong person
The institutions in society that are supposed to be safe

POSSIBLE RESPONSES AND RESULTS
Avoiding technology and information-gathering processes
Stashing money in hiding places rather than using a bank
Obsessively changing one's passwords, bank accounts, and credit cards
Refusing to share personal information
Shutting down social media accounts

Overreacting when friends or co-workers ask personal questions

Mistrust that leads one to question the motivations of others

Paranoia that pushes one toward fringe conspiracy theories

Always paying in cash

Never leaving one's wallet, phone, etc. where it can be accessed

Avoiding close relationships (if the identity theft was personal or hate-motivated)

Shredding or burning mail and other paperwork that contains personal information

Keeping paper copies of everything in case one needs to prove that other information has been falsified

Mistrust bleeding over to other trustworthy institutions (insurance agencies, banks, etc.)

Instituting unreasonable internet and technology rules for those in one's care

Always reading the fine print and often refusing to sign off on standard policies (a website's Terms and Conditions, a doctor's Consent To Share Information form, etc.)

Being slow to warm to new people

Discussing one's worries and mistrust openly, passing the fears on to listening children

Educating oneself on safety protocols so the identity theft can be avoided in the future

Hoping for the best while planning for the worst

Simplifying one's life (getting rid of extra credit cards, downsizing so life is easier to monitor, etc.)

Adopting greater self-sufficiency

Becoming independent so one can live off the grid if one has to

PERSONALITY TRAITS THAT MAY FORM

Attributes: Alert, analytical, cautious, discreet, honest, organized, proactive, sensible, simple, studious, traditional

Flaws: Controlling, cynical, dishonest, evasive, hostile, insecure, obsessive, paranoid, prejudiced, uncommunicative, withdrawn

TRIGGERS THAT MIGHT AGGRAVATE THIS WOUND

Finding an odd charge on a credit card bill

Spoof emails asking for banking information, passwords, or requests for money

Friends or loved ones asking for a loan

Being contacted by the people who came after one initially (like a collection agency or bank official)

Being hacked, even harmlessly, on one's Facebook page, a Twitter profile, etc.

One's credit card being declined at the mall

Being detained (even briefly) by customs officials at an airport

OPPORTUNITIES TO FACE OR OVERCOME THIS WOUND

Having to disprove an accusation (by a financial institution or law enforcement, for instance) long after one's identity has been restored

One's paranoia leading to false accusations of another's motives that are quickly disproven, leading to the realization that one's mistrust is hurting others

Having an opportunity to make a financial difference in someone's life

Having to testify in court against those who stole one's identity

WITNESSING A MURDER

EXAMPLES
A family dispute that turns violent
Seeing a pedestrian being killed in a mugging
A classmate dying in a school shooting
One's parents being killed in a home invasion
Watching as a police officer is shot by a criminal
A friend being murdered at a party during a gang-related hit
Being kidnapped along with another victim who is murdered by one's captor

BASIC NEEDS OFTEN COMPROMISED BY THIS WOUND: Safety and security, love and belonging

FALSE BELIEFS THAT COULD BE EMBRACED
I should have done something to stop it.
I'm useless under pressure.
I can't protect the ones I love.
I should have died instead.
The world is a dangerous and unpredictable place.
People are inherently violent.
No one is ever truly safe.

THE CHARACTER MAY FEAR…
Being murdered
A family member being killed and being powerless to stop it
Freezing up when they are needed most (if this was a factor during the wounding event)
Being responsible for the welfare of others
Making decisions, especially ones that impact other people
Being in the wrong place at the wrong time
People physically or ideologically similar to the ones who committed the murder

POSSIBLE RESPONSES AND RESULTS
Beefing up the security in one's home
Taking self-defense classes
Buying a gun and training oneself in its use
Obtaining a concealed-carry permit for a weapon
Carrying pepper spray
Not venturing out after dark
Pulling away from friends and family
Reliving the event ever and over
Beating oneself up mentally for not doing more, even if it was out of one's control
Being reluctant to help people who seem to be in trouble (self-preservation)

Worrying about family members and their whereabouts
Becoming unreliable in order to avoid responsibility
Becoming ultra-responsible and controlling as a way of proving one's capabilities
Smothering children in an effort to protect them by requiring frequent check-ins, monitoring their activities, and limiting their independence
Experiencing irrational worries that cause one to avoid certain people, places, and activities
Checking the exits whenever one enters a new place
Becoming prone to anxiety and panic attacks
Difficulty sleeping
Suffering from nightmares
Becoming obsessed with identifying and finding the killer
Turning away from one's faith or embracing one's faith
Attending a vigil or seeking therapy to process the emotions from the event
Reaching out to the victim's family
Hounding police enforcement to make sure justice is served
Using social media to inform people about what happened and garner support
Being appreciative; finding joy in the little things

PERSONALITY TRAITS THAT MAY FORM

Attributes: Alert, appreciative, bold, decisive, disciplined, just, meticulous, observant, organized, private, proactive, protective, sensible, spiritual

Flaws: Callous, childish, controlling, fussy, impulsive, macho, morbid, needy, nervous, paranoid, self-destructive, superstitious, temperamental, uncommunicative, withdrawn

TRIGGERS THAT MIGHT AGGRAVATE THIS WOUND

Witnessing an escalating argument
Watching a news report or fictional police drama that covers a murder investigation
Seeing or hearing something that makes one believe one is in danger (whether it's true or not)
Sensory cues specific to the attack, such as the smell of blood or the sound of a truck backfiring
Locations or events associated with the murder (alleyways, parking lots, a family barbeque, etc.)

OPPORTUNITIES TO FACE OR OVERCOME THIS WOUND

Legislation being passed that protects the criminal rather than the innocent, encouraging one to face the traumatizing event and become actively involved in righting the wrong
Being asked to testify in the murder trial
Wrongfully lashing out at someone of the same race or religious persuasion as the murderer, and recognizing one's prejudice
A situation that puts a big responsibility on one's shoulders (being asked to care for an ailing sister's children, being the only one who can help rescue someone who was buried in an avalanche, etc.)
Having a gut response that turns out to be correct but not acting on it because one doesn't trust one's instincts

Disabilities and Disfigurements

A LEARNING DISABILITY

EXAMPLES: Suffering from a learning disability, such as dyslexia, dysgraphia, dyscalculia, slow processing, poor executive functioning, and visual or auditory processing disorders.

BASIC NEEDS OFTEN COMPROMISED BY THIS WOUND: Love and belonging, esteem and recognition, self-actualization

FALSE BELIEFS THAT COULD BE EMBRACED
I'm defective.
I'm too stupid to learn.
I will never find a partner who loves me for me.
If I engage, everyone will know how dumb I am.
When I make fun of myself people accept me.
If I worked harder or practiced more, I'd be able to succeed.
If people find out about my disability, they'll reject me.
Why try when I'll only fail?
I should attack others before they attack me.

THE CHARACTER MAY FEAR…
Failure and mistakes (especially visible ones)
Being unable to achieve their dreams or goals
Being bullied or victimized
Being called on at school or singled out for a challenging task as an adult
Letting others down
Their secret getting out
Being rejected or abandoned by loved ones
Being labeled and limited
Passing a disability on to their children

POSSIBLE RESPONSES AND RESULTS
Avoiding responsibility out of the belief that one will only let others down
Thinking small; limiting one's dreams or goals so they will be reachable
Thinking negatively about oneself and one's abilities
Withdrawing from others to avoid ridicule and teasing
Bullying others
Overcompensating
Becoming angry or volatile
Resenting people who are naturally smart or talented
Engaging in destructive or risky behaviors
Diverting attention from one's disability (e.g., acting up and getting kicked out of class before a verbal spelling competition)
Avoiding those who could help (counselors, teachers, or tutors) out of denial or a desire to

keep one's disability secret

Making fun of someone with similar disabilities to distance oneself from them

Avoiding conversations or interactions with people that may lead to revealing a limitation

Avoiding social opportunities; staying home instead

Refusing to read if doing so is a reminder of one's limitation

Studying admirable people to become more socially confident and adept (if this is a struggle)

Becoming an advocate for those with learning disabilities

Focusing on one's strengths rather than one's weaknesses

Choosing jobs, hobbies, and activities that don't utilize one's weakness

Working super hard to succeed

Learning to compensate (by developing one's memory, utilizing software, engaging a tutor, etc.)

Refusing to allow the disability to define one's identity

PERSONALITY TRAITS THAT MAY FORM

Attributes: Adaptable, cautious, charming, disciplined, empathetic, flirtatious, funny, imaginative, industrious, meticulous, pensive, persistent, private, tolerant

Flaws: Abrasive, defensive, dishonest, evasive, inhibited, insecure, oversensitive, rebellious, resentful, self-destructive, timid, uncommunicative, uncooperative, violent, volatile, withdrawn

TRIGGERS THAT MIGHT AGGRAVATE THIS WOUND

Seeing someone with a disability being bullied or mistreated

Having to ask for help

Being unable to fix something that's broken

Not understanding instructions or a concept and feeling a wave of frustration

Hearing people use certain labels (idiot, retard, etc.) that are offensive and hurtful

Watching people with learning disabilities be mocked or misrepresented on TV and in movies

Attending a school conference to discuss a child's hereditary learning disability

Seeing a learning disability negatively impact the self-esteem of a loved one

Struggling with a new task

Making a mistake due to one's disability and having one's competence questioned

Being teased for one's weakness

OPPORTUNITIES TO FACE OR OVERCOME THIS WOUND

Having to decide whether to pass up a promising opportunity due to one's disability or tackle the extra work required to succeed

One's disability becoming public despite efforts to keep it secret

Being unfairly penalized because of one's ability (scoring badly on a test one was unable to read, being rejected as an applicant right out of the gate, etc.) and wanting justice

As an adult, continuing to take shortcuts (instead of putting in the work necessary to deal with the disability) and suffering consequences for doing so

A PHYSICAL DISFIGUREMENT

EXAMPLES

Being burned by a fire or chemicals

Bearing visible scars (from knife wounds, a gunshot, an animal attack, a car accident, surgery, etc.)

Missing a body part, such as an eye, ear, nose, or finger

Having malformed limbs

Bearing a visible and disfiguring birthmark

Having a cleft lip

Bearing large goiters or tumors

Having severe skin ailments like psoriasis, acne, discoloration, pigment loss, keloids, or warts

Having out-of-proportion body parts (elephantiasis, legs that are different lengths, etc.)

Body parts becoming flaccid or paralyzed following a stroke

Having a disfigurement due to a botched plastic surgery procedure

BASIC NEEDS OFTEN COMPROMISED BY THIS WOUND: Love and belonging, esteem and recognition, self-actualization

FALSE BELIEFS THAT COULD BE EMBRACED

No one will ever love someone like me.

They're looking at me because of my disfigurement.

This is a form of punishment.

I'm not worthy of love.

Most people aren't going to give me a chance, so I can't let go of the ones who do.

It's better to be treated badly by someone who cares about me than to have no one at all.

Anyone trying to connect with me must have an ulterior motive.

People are cruel so it's better to stay away from them.

No one could understand what I'm going through.

I'll never be able to fulfill my dreams.

"Normal" people are better than me.

THE CHARACTER MAY FEAR…

Intimacy

Whatever caused the disfigurement (fire, hospitals, a deranged ex-boyfriend, etc.)

Being stared at or ridiculed in person or on social media

Losing people (through a death or a move, for instance) who have expressed love and acceptance

Intolerance and prejudice

Being rejected or abandoned

POSSIBLE RESPONSES AND RESULTS

Developing low self-esteem or self-hatred

Never leaving one's home; becoming a hermit

Wearing clothing, accessories, or makeup that minimizes the disfigurement
Gravitating toward online activities where one can create the persona one desires
Avoiding situations where new people will be encountered
Not opening up to others
Mistrusting those who express love or kindness
Maintaining shallow relationships
Making fun of one's disfigurement in an effort to minimize it
Diving into a solitary hobby or area of interest
Feeling intense jealousy of people viewed as beautiful by society's standards
Clinging to the kind and caring people in one's life
Pursuing unhealthy relationships
Lashing out at others in frustration or hurt
Pitying oneself
Developing depression or an anxiety disorder
Engaging in self-destructive behaviors, such as abusing drugs or alcohol
Avoiding cameras and recorders
Assuming that others are staring even when they aren't
Pursuing a creative outlet for one's hurt, like composing music, painting, 3D printing, or designing clothes
Seeing beauty in imperfections and appreciating the little things others overlook
Reaching out to others who have been disfigured (joining forums or chat groups, for example)

PERSONALITY TRAITS THAT MAY FORM
Attributes: Cautious, courteous, creative, discreet, empathetic, focused, gentle, imaginative, introverted, loyal, merciful, pensive, perceptive, persistent, private, proactive, spiritual, tolerant
Flaws: Abrasive, cynical, evasive, humorless, inhibited, insecure, jealous, martyr, needy, pessimistic, resentful, self-destructive, suspicious, temperamental, timid, volatile, withdrawn

TRIGGERS THAT MIGHT AGGRAVATE THIS WOUND
One's disfigurement being pointed out by a curious child or other onlooker
Seeing oneself on video and realizing anew how one looks to others
Experiencing pain related to one's disfigurement
Being exposed to online memes that make fun of a person's physical flaws
Beauty ads, commercials, and TV shows that tie beauty to personal value

OPPORTUNITIES TO FACE OR OVERCOME THIS WOUND
Being the victim of a cruel joke that focuses on one's disfigurement
Realizing a dream can be fulfilled if one finds the courage to not let the disfigurement get in the way
Bullying or ridiculing someone and realizing one has become just like those one hates the most
Learning that another painful surgery is required that may or may not improve one's appearance

A SPEECH IMPEDIMENT

EXAMPLES
Stuttering
Muteness (being unable to speak)
Speech sound disorders and lisps
Speech issues due to a damaged larynx or injuries to the mouth or throat, such as a cleft palate

BASIC NEEDS OFTEN COMPROMISED BY THIS WOUND: Love and belonging, esteem and recognition, self-actualization

FALSE BELIEFS THAT COULD BE EMBRACED
People hate listening to me speak and can't wait to get away from me.
I have nothing worth saying anyway.
I can never make a difference because of my speech.
It's better for me to keep quiet.
I'm not romantic material.
Even if I have something important to say, no one will take me seriously because of how I talk.
It's better to avoid relationships because they lead to ridicule.
I am an embarrassment to the people I'm with.
No one understands what this is like.
I can never be a leader, only a follower.

THE CHARACTER MAY FEAR…
Public ridicule
Being singled out or put in the spotlight
Public speaking
Intimacy or vulnerability
Social events

POSSIBLE RESPONSES AND RESULTS
Choosing a job that is solitary or has minimal interactions with people
Becoming a big reader or movie-watcher
Getting tongue-tied when one does have to talk
Difficulty with romantic relationships because one struggles to converse
Being less picky about partners due to low self-esteem and the belief that this is the best one can do
Taking up solitary activities, such as camping, hiking, star-gazing, drawing, or gaming
Choosing to engage with others online, interacting through chat rather than through speech
Avoiding or prematurely ducking out of social functions and family get-togethers
Blushing or sweating when one is put on the spot

Avoiding eye contact with people to dissuade them from starting a conversation

Frequent fantasizing or daydreaming

Not participating in group sports, clubs, or activities

Sitting near an exit or at the edge of the room

A tendency to write long emails and texts

Not answering the phone; letting it go to a message box so one can text a response later

Carrying a book or phone so one can look busy and avoid socializing

Not volunteering for opportunities

Gravitating toward gregarious people who will do most of the talking

Being moved by someone who shares one's weakness but has become successful despite it (like a singer, speaker, or auctioneer)

Seeking out people who share one's challenge

Identifying and focusing on one's positive qualities, such as kindness, intelligence, or a sense of humor

Connecting with others through nonverbal methods (giving gifts, being a good listener, making one's home available for get-togethers, etc.)

Getting active on social media where messages, pictures, and videos allow expression and connection

Pursuing a passion or hobby where one can excel and gain confidence

PERSONALITY TRAITS THAT MAY FORM

Attributes: Analytical, appreciative, curious, disciplined, empathetic, focused, generous, gentle, honorable, independent, kind, loyal, merciful, nurturing, philosophical, private, protective

Flaws: Antisocial, cynical, defensive, humorless, impatient, impulsive, inhibited, insecure, jealous, nervous, oversensitive, resentful, subservient, timid, uncommunicative, withdrawn

TRIGGERS THAT MIGHT AGGRAVATE THIS WOUND

Witnessing someone with a speech impediment being teased or bullied

Listening to influential people who are reckless with their words (spreading hate or misinformation)

Stressful situations that make one's speech impediment more pronounced

Being asked a direct question

Being asked to attend a meeting that will require verbal participation

OPPORTUNITIES TO FACE OR OVERCOME THIS WOUND

Seeing speech difficulties emerging for one's child

Being asked to give a presentation or lead a meeting at work and being afraid to do so

Having trouble speaking when first impressions count (at a job interview, on a first date, etc.)

Wishing to speak out against an injustice but needing to work through one's fears to do so

Wanting to raise awareness for a cause but having to step into the spotlight to do so

A TRAUMATIC BRAIN INJURY

EXAMPLES: Experiencing a traumatic brain injury caused by…
Falling and hitting one's head
A fight
A car, bike, Jet Ski, or boating accident
A sports injury, such as a concussion from playing football or kickboxing
Being kicked by a horse
Being shot
Something heavy falling on one's head
A daredevil activity or prank gone wrong

BASIC NEEDS OFTEN COMPROMISED BY THIS WOUND: Physiological needs, safety and security, esteem and recognition, self-actualization

FALSE BELIEFS THAT COULD BE EMBRACED
I'm unable to contribute in any meaningful way.
I'll never be able to live a normal life.
My dreams are out of reach now.
Life is no longer worth living.
I'm stupid.
No one would want to be with me.
I'm dysfunctional, only part of the person I was.

THE CHARACTER MAY FEAR…
Being rejected because of their condition
Supportive family members dying or falling ill (abandonment)
Scenarios like the one that caused the injury
Symptoms worsening unexpectedly
Failing in their responsibilities to others
Becoming fully reliant on others for even the most basic of needs

POSSIBLE RESPONSES AND RESULTS
Moodiness and irritability
Changes in one's sleeping pattern (insomnia, too much sleeping, or difficulty staying asleep)
Being easily distracted
Forgetfulness
Amnesia
Becoming sensitive to light or other stimuli that disturb the senses
Being prone to headaches or migraines
Difficulty with motor skills and other dexterity-related issues
Regressing on recently learned skills
Difficulty doing things one used to be able to do (talk, read, run, etc.)

Pushing oneself too hard

Lashing out at loved ones in frustration

Depression or thoughts of suicide

Self-medicating with drugs or alcohol

Trying to hide one's difficulties rather than admit them to others or seek help

Avoiding situations where one can become over-stimulated

Staying home rather than going out

Avoiding friends and social activities

Not engaging in conversation out of fear one's difficulties will be made obvious

Reluctance to try new things because one might not be able to do them well

Refusing all help

Becoming overly dependent on others

Second-guessing one's decisions

Increased empathy for those living with limitations beyond their control

Dedicating oneself to regaining lost ground (through study, physical therapy, etc.)

Compensating for one's shortcomings by honing other skills and talents

Setting realistic goals and striving to achieve them

PERSONALITY TRAITS THAT MAY FORM

Attributes: Ambitious, cautious, courageous, easygoing, efficient, empathetic, generous, industrious, loyal, pensive, persistent, private, quirky, socially aware, spontaneous, uninhibited

Flaws: Abrasive, childish, disorganized, flaky, forgetful, hostile, impatient, insecure, irrational, needy, pessimistic, scatterbrained, self-destructive, temperamental, uncooperative, volatile

TRIGGERS THAT MIGHT AGGRAVATE THIS WOUND

Hospitals and doctors

Trying something and being reminded of one's limitations

Seeing someone younger or less experienced surpass one's ability in a certain area

Reminiscing with friends and being unable to remember certain events

Seeing an old recording of one excelling in an area where one now struggles

Failing even with a compensation in place (e.g., forgetting something despite writing it down)

OPPORTUNITIES TO FACE OR OVERCOME THIS WOUND

Facing the end of a dream, one must decide between succumbing to despair or redefining success

The death or incapacitation of a caretaker that puts one in a position of having to care for oneself

Getting a chance to do something one loves even it means the possibility of failing at it

Struggling to achieve something and having to decide whether to keep trying or give up

Realizing success is attainable in an area, though it means starting over or doing things differently

BATTLING A MENTAL DISORDER

EXAMPLES
Anxiety disorders
Bipolar mood disorder
Schizophrenia
Personality disorders, such as anti-social, narcissistic, and dissociative disorder (formerly known as multiple personality disorder)
Chronic depression
Eating disorders
Impulse control disorders (kleptomania, pyromania, compulsive gambling, etc.)
Obsessive-compulsive disorder (OCD)
Post-traumatic stress disorder (PTSD)
Debilitating phobias (agoraphobia, social anxiety phobia, etc.)

BASIC NEEDS OFTEN COMPROMISED BY THIS WOUND: Physiological needs, safety and security, love and belonging, esteem and recognition, self-actualization

FALSE BELIEFS THAT COULD BE EMBRACED
I can't care for others or myself.
I'm so messed up, no one would ever love me.
Everyone is out to get me.
I don't need medication or treatment.
My dreams are out of reach now.
I am broken and beyond repair.
I'm the only person struggling in this way.
I'm just a burden to others. It would be better if I didn't exist.

THE CHARACTER MAY FEAR…
Losing their independence
Specific fears related to the disorder (crowds, germs, being touched, etc.)
Taking medication or treatments that change their personality or have negative side effects
Passing the disorder on to their children
Becoming like their parent in other ways (if the disorder is genetic)
Accidentally hurting themselves or a loved one during an episode
Being unable to support those in their care
Permanently losing their grip on reality

POSSIBLE RESPONSES AND RESULTS
Hiding one's disorder
Making excuses when one's symptoms become clear to others
Making light of one's shortcomings instead of acknowledging the disorder
Abusing drugs or alcohol; adopting self-harming behaviors to cope

Avoiding people (family, friends, or therapists) who would hold one accountable

Becoming depressed

Pessimism and negative thoughts that are difficult to turn off

Isolating oneself from others

Frequently calling in sick to work or school

Being unable to keep a job due to the specifics of one's disorder

Living life according to the short term rather than taking a long-distance viewpoint

Going off one's medication once it starts working, thinking it's no longer necessary

Emotional volatility

Suicidal thoughts or attempts

Uncontrolled thoughts and impulses

Being suspicious of people; questioning the motives of others

Engaging in compulsions that shape one's actions and routine

Difficulty coping with day-to-day problems

Feeling drained, exhausted, and hollowed out

Attending therapy; joining a support group

Adjusting one's goals to account for the disorder

Fighting to raise awareness of one's disorder

Renewed confidence as one makes progress and realizes how strong one really is

PERSONALITY TRAITS THAT MAY FORM

Attributes: Affectionate, diplomatic, discreet, empathetic, enthusiastic, friendly, generous, idealistic, independent, innocent, kind

Flaws: Childish, compulsive, devious, disorganized, forgetful, hostile, ignorant, impulsive, inattentive, irrational, needy, obsessive

TRIGGERS THAT MIGHT AGGRAVATE THIS WOUND

Seeing another mentally ill person being taken advantage of

A disappointment or loss that deals an emotional blow (like a friend moving or a pet running off)

Struggling to make an important decision due to one's disorder

A disruption to one's routine (a cousin moving in, one's doctor closing his practice, etc.)

Being rejected or abandoned because of one's condition

A change in insurance that doesn't cover one's medication or treatment options

OPPORTUNITIES TO FACE OR OVERCOME THIS WOUND

Going off meds and endangering a loved one, which leads to a decision about what one is willing to do to get better

Meeting someone special and deciding whether to do life together or go it alone

Having a passion that requires focus and commitment, and needing to choose whether or not to take on the challenge

Someone offering support, giving one the courage to fight for happiness and accept the disorder as part of who one is

BEING SO BEAUTIFUL IT'S ALL PEOPLE SEE

BASIC NEEDS OFTEN COMPROMISED BY THIS WOUND: Safety and security, love and belonging, esteem and recognition, self-actualization

FALSE BELIEFS THAT COULD BE EMBRACED
My only worth is in my looks.
I will never be respected for my hard work, brains, or skills.
People only want to be close to me because of how I look and what my beauty can do for them.
What I think or believe doesn't matter.
I can only be what others want me to be; I can't live for myself.
I must choose a career in the beauty industry because people expect me to.
Friendships always contain jealousy, so only "surface" relationships are safe.
People who want to date me only see me as eye candy.
If I open up about my fears or struggles, I'll be scorned.

THE CHARACTER MAY FEAR…
Stalking, violence, and sexual assault (especially women)
Being taken advantage of
Being trapped by their own beauty (via life choices, careers, opportunities, etc.)
Aging or losing their beauty
Illness and disease
Being unfairly judged by others because of how they look
Trusting the wrong person
Retribution or sabotage by a jealous peer
Never experiencing a relationship that has true depth

POSSIBLE RESPONSES AND RESULTS
Meticulous health and beauty regimes
Constant dieting and working out
Fighting the aging process (through plastic surgery, buying expensive products, enduring painful treatments, etc.)
Questioning and second-guessing one's choices out of a deep need for approval
Being a people pleaser
Avoiding close relationships (due to doubt over whether they're "real" or not)
Not complaining because people will react with a lack of empathy
Acting the way people expect one to act (proper, sophisticated, self-absorbed, etc.)
Acting the opposite of what people expect as a way of proving them wrong
Fighting or hiding one's low self-esteem behind smiles and forced confidence
Keeping secrets; rarely divulging one's deepest feelings and desires
Having body issues but being unable to express them
Struggling with depression and adopting behaviors to cope with it (self-medicating, choosing

to be alone, cutting one's body in areas that won't been seen, etc.)

Downplaying one's beauty (and possibly other attributes and skills) to try and fit in

Often feeling like a decoration or object when out with a partner

Working hard to be likable and negate resentful feelings from same-gender friends

Being very safety conscious; avoiding dangerous places

Practicing kindness and acceptance of others

Improving one's character so people focus on that rather than appearances

Pursuing activities one can excel in that have nothing to do with physical appearance, such as playing a sport, learning a foreign language, or getting a degree

PERSONALITY TRAITS THAT MAY FORM

Attributes: Cautious, charming, cooperative, courteous, disciplined, flirtatious, friendly, generous, kind, loyal, mature, obedient, private, protective, sensual, sophisticated, uninhibited

Flaws: Addictive, catty, cocky, cynical, extravagant, hypocritical, impulsive, inhibited, insecure, jealous, macho, materialistic, promiscuous, rebellious, self-indulgent, spoiled, vain, workaholic

TRIGGERS THAT MIGHT AGGRAVATE THIS WOUND

Being overtly hit on in an over-sexualized way

Being called a slut or whore by someone who is jealous of one's appearance

Catching someone staring with a judgmental or assuming expression

Entering a conversation and having the topic change from intellectual to superficial

Being backstabbed by a friend and knowing that the root cause is resentment over one's looks

Someone taking control of a project due to prejudice or stereotypes (assuming one is incapable of fixing something, performing manual labor, etc.)

Having people assume that one's successes are based on looks

Seeing a person use their good looks to get what they want, reinforcing the stereotype that has caused one such trouble

Aging over time and realizing that friends are taking malicious joy at the leveling of the playing field

OPPORTUNITIES TO FACE OR OVERCOME THIS WOUND

Experiencing an accident or illness that mars one's good looks

Wanting to start a family and needing to come to terms with how one's body will change

Having an opportunity to reveal one's intelligence, talent, or passion but fearing the rejection and derision one has experienced in the past

Seeing one's child use their beauty to manipulate others

Developing an eating disorder and knowing one must get help before it's too late

Losing a friend to suicide who also struggled with self-worth and lack of fulfillment

FALLING SHORT OF SOCIETY'S PHYSICAL STANDARDS

EXAMPLES
Being much shorter or taller than the perceived norm
Having skin that is marred by acne, rashes, psoriasis, pigmentation variances, or the like
Being perceived as too thin or overweight
Being hairier than most people
Being perceived as having disproportionate features (a short neck, too-long arms, etc.)
Having an unattractive feature like an oddly shaped nose, buck teeth, or cauliflower ears
Having a deformity (one leg being shorter than the other, a club foot, scoliosis of the spine, etc.)
Missing a limb
Being scarred or physically disfigured in some way

BASIC NEEDS OFTEN COMPROMISED BY THIS WOUND: Love and belonging, esteem and recognition

FALSE BELIEFS THAT COULD BE EMBRACED
When people look at me, they only see what's different.
I'll never be accepted or have what others have.
I'm not worthy of hanging with the pretty people.
No one will ever want to be with someone like me.
If someone expresses interest, they're only doing it to set me up.
People befriend me out of pity.

THE CHARACTER MAY FEAR…
Misplacing their trust in others and misreading their motives
A physical shortcoming being pointed out
Being rejected by their peers
Being made fun of, stared at, or pitied
Romantic relationships and intimacy
Being limited in life because of how they look

POSSIBLE RESPONSES AND RESULTS
Low self-esteem
Trying to hide the feature that others consider atypical or abnormal
Becoming self-deprecating to gain acceptance or avoid ridicule
Avoiding activities that place one in the limelight
Taking offense even when none is intended; being overly sensitive
Avoiding social situations
Staying on the outskirts when one is in a crowd
Not engaging with others unless they engage first
Seeking revenge against those who have made one's life difficult
Isolating oneself from others

Always focusing on one's flaws; being overly self-critical

Engaging in relationships with toxic people because of low self-worth

Pushing people away before one can be hurt by them

Downplaying one's strengths if they will make one stand out or draw unwanted attention

Taking on jobs that allow one to be more invisible

Embracing anonymous activities, like visiting online chat rooms or using personas on social media

Not touching others or wanting to be touched

Maintaining an emotional distance from others

Seeking medical help to correct or minimize the difference

Bankrupting oneself through procedures and treatments in hopes of "fixing the problem"

Taking refuge in a form of art (writing, painting, or music) to express one's feelings

Becoming very accepting of others and seeing the qualities that others may miss

Befriending other "outcasts"

Honing a skill or talent to build confidence

PERSONALITY TRAITS THAT MAY FORM

Attributes: Alert, analytical, cautious, charming, courteous, diplomatic, empathetic, funny, gentle, humble, imaginative, kind, merciful, pensive, perceptive, private, spunky, talented

Flaws: Confrontational, frivolous, hostile, insecure, jealous, melodramatic, needy, nervous, oversensitive, paranoid, resentful, temperamental, timid, uncommunicative, vindictive, volatile

TRIGGERS THAT MIGHT AGGRAVATE THIS WOUND

Overhearing someone say something unkind about one's physical differences

Visiting locations where one has been ridiculed in the past (school, a bar, etc.)

Comparing oneself to someone "perfect" and finding oneself lacking

Attending events where looks are on display (like an award ceremony or wedding)

Ads, commercials, and products that reinforce physical ideals as being the key to happiness

OPPORTUNITIES TO FACE OR OVERCOME THIS WOUND

Witnessing someone being bullied for a physical shortcoming and having to decide between remaining invisible or standing up for them

Being inspired by someone who chooses to own their differences instead of hiding them

Discovering a strength or talent that helps or inspires others and realizing one is much more than a physical body

Being in a toxic relationship where the other person belittles one's appearance, and realizing that one has value and doesn't deserve such treatment

INFERTILITY

EXAMPLES: Being unable to conceive or bear children due to…
Medical conditions (endometriosis, uterine abnormalities, ovulation disorders, etc.)
An early hysterectomy
A botched abortion
Cancer and cancer treatments
Complications from sexually transmitted diseases (STDs)
Early-onset menopause
Low sperm count
Unknown factors

BASIC NEEDS OFTEN COMPROMISED BY THIS WOUND: Love and belonging, esteem and recognition, self-actualization

FALSE BELIEFS THAT COULD BE EMBRACED
I'm less of a man or woman because of this.
It's not fair to get involved with someone because I'm defective.
This is a punishment for something I've done.
There must be a reason why I can't have kids.
God knows I would be a bad parent; that's why I can't have children.
People will pity me if they find out, so it's better to pretend I don't want kids.
Without children, I'll never be complete or fulfilled.
Why bother taking care of yourself if things like this are going to happen to you anyway?
I'm going to grow old and die alone, with no one to care for me.

THE CHARACTER MAY FEAR…
A spouse dying and leaving them alone
What others think
That they are incapable of parenting or caring for others
Other latent illnesses or conditions within their body
Never finding happiness or contentment
Holding their partner back from fulfillment because of an inability to conceive
Their partner leaving once they discover their infertility

POSSIBLE RESPONSES AND RESULTS
Becoming obsessed with conceiving a child regardless of the inconvenience or cost
Tirelessly researching and trying new or unusual fertility methods, treatments, and remedies
Saving money so one can afford fertility treatments (or going into debt to obtain them)
Changing sex from an enjoyable experience into a clinical means to an end
Becoming obsessed with one's health
Lying to others about why one hasn't had children yet
Struggling with depression

Hiding on Mother's or Father's Day
Self-medicating
Distancing oneself from couples with children
Clinging to one's spouse or parents out of fear of losing them and being alone
Avoiding children
Only building relationships with other childless couples
Indulging in material things to fill the void
Traveling often or becoming semi-nomadic to avoid putting down roots
Resenting people who have children, especially those who complain about their kids
Throwing oneself into a job in hopes of staying busy and distracting oneself
Researching alternatives (adoption or fostering, for example)
Joining support groups
Going through the grief process as one realizes one will never conceive a child

PERSONALITY TRAITS THAT MAY FORM

Attributes: Adaptable, affectionate, appreciative, discreet, empathetic, optimistic, patient, persistent, private, resourceful

Flaws: Callous, cynical, evasive, irrational, jealous, martyr, needy, obsessive, pessimistic, resentful, temperamental, ungrateful, withdrawn

TRIGGERS THAT MIGHT AGGRAVATE THIS WOUND

A close friend or relative becoming pregnant with ease
Being invited to a baby shower and having to shop for a gift
Seeing pregnant or nursing mothers
Commercials and TV shows that feature young families or expectant parents
A friend accidentally becoming pregnant and terminating the pregnancy or giving the baby up
Milestones (Mother's or Father's Day, a birthday passing as one grows older without a child, etc.)
A well-meaning loved one voicing a hurtful comment or question: *Don't wait too long to have children*, or *Why don't you want kids?*

OPPORTUNITIES TO FACE OR OVERCOME THIS WOUND

Learning that one isn't a candidate for adoption
Having to babysit for a friend in an emergency situation and re-awakening one's maternal (or paternal) instinct
Conceiving after much sacrifice and effort, then miscarrying
The death of a child (a step- or adopted child, a child conceived prior to becoming infertile, etc.)

LIVING WITH CHRONIC PAIN OR ILLNESS

EXAMPLES
Fibromyalgia
Chronic fatigue syndrome
ALS (Lou Gehrig's disease)
Alzheimer's disease
Asthma
Cancer
Chronic Obstructive Pulmonary Disease (COPD)
Cystic fibrosis
Epilepsy
Heart disease
Autoimmune diseases (multiple sclerosis, rheumatoid arthritis, lupus, diabetes, inflammatory bowel syndrome)
Chronic STDs (herpes, HIV/AIDS, hepatitis B and C)
Ongoing pain resulting from arthritis, an injury, past surgeries, nerve damage, or migraines

BASIC NEEDS OFTEN COMPROMISED BY THIS WOUND: Physiological needs, safety and security, esteem and recognition, self-actualization

FALSE BELIEFS THAT COULD BE EMBRACED
My life will never be any better than this.
I'm useless. I'd be better off dead.
The doctors are right; it's all in my head.
I'm a burden to my loved ones.
I'm being punished for something I've done.
This life isn't worth living.

THE CHARACTER MAY FEAR…
Passing on the illness to their children
Being abandoned by a caretaker (a spouse or parent)
Being a burden to loved ones
Never finding a diagnosis or cure
Degeneration and eventual death
Developing a new or additional disease
Ending up in a completely helpless or vegetative state
Being unable to afford treatment

POSSIBLE RESPONSES AND RESULTS
Isolating oneself in one's home
Falling into depression
Moodiness and being prone to anger, frustration, and bitterness

Decreasing one's physical activity due to necessity or depression
Becoming dependent on medication
Having to be convinced by others to get out of the house
Not taking care of oneself
One's home falling into disarray through not being able to care for it
Missing work or school
Decreased efficiency at work, school, clubs, and around one's home
Giving up hobbies and favorite pastimes due to fatigue or physical limitations
Doing things that distract one from the illness (watching TV, reading, sleeping, etc.)
Hiding the illness from others
Not talking about how one feels so others won't say that it's all in one's head
Sleeping odd hours
Arranging one's day around known patterns
Going through the stages of grief
Making the most of the "good" days
Researching one's illness and trying any possible treatment options
Joining a support group, either in-person or online
Seeking out doctors who specialize in one's illness
Donating to organizations dedicated to finding a cure
Excising the stress and negativity from one's life

PERSONALITY TRAITS THAT MAY FORM
    Attributes: Adaptable, appreciative, cautious, centered, cooperative, disciplined, easygoing, efficient, generous, inspirational, loyal, nurturing
    Flaws: Addictive, apathetic, callous, compulsive, controlling, cynical, forgetful, grumpy, humorless, inattentive, indecisive, irresponsible, morbid

TRIGGERS THAT MIGHT AGGRAVATE THIS WOUND
Seeing similar symptoms in one's sibling or other close relative
Being diagnosed with another serious illness or disability
Dramatic complainers who use minor ailments to shirk responsibility
Missing an important event because of one's affliction
Overhearing someone express the opinion that the illness or pain is all in one's mind

OPPORTUNITIES TO FACE OR OVERCOME THIS WOUND
Having an opportunity to pursue a dream but needing to do it more slowly and on a longer timeline
Being abandoned by one's caretaker and having to take responsibility for oneself
Encountering someone who needs care (a child, a neighbor, a dog) and having to choose to accept the challenge or run from it
A future milestone (such as a wedding, a birth, or the fulfillment of a grandchild's dream) that offers motivation, strengthening one's resolve to fight the affliction and make it to that important date
Learning that the affliction was caused by something one did (smoking, having unprotected sex, etc.)

LOSING A LIMB

EXAMPLES: Losing a limb due to…
A birth defect
A vehicular accident
A machine malfunction in a factory or workshop
Illness or disease, such as cancer, vascular disease, arterial disease, or diabetes
A farming accident
An animal attack
A bacterial infection that doesn't respond to antibiotics
Gangrene
Frostbite
An injury resulting from one's service in the military

BASIC NEEDS OFTEN COMPROMISED BY THIS WOUND: Love and belonging, esteem and recognition, self-actualization

FALSE BELIEFS THAT COULD BE EMBRACED
I will never be whole.
No one will find me attractive.
When people look at me, they only see my disfigurement.
The life I wanted is over.
I deserve what has happened (if one claims fault for the loss).
I can't take care of myself or my loved ones.
I am a burden to my family.
They'd be better off without me.

THE CHARACTER MAY FEAR…
The judgment or pity of others
Becoming a spectacle
Being unable to accomplish their dreams
Losing their independence
Being alone; never finding a loving partner
Being unable to provide for their family
Being viewed as weak or incapable by others

POSSIBLE RESPONSES AND RESULTS
Struggling with phantom limb pain
Hiding one's missing limb
Not taking chances; always making safe choices
Becoming reckless in an effort to prove one's capability
Withdrawing from others; becoming isolated
Avoiding public places and social events

Pushing others away before one can be rejected

Clinging to caregivers and family

Becoming dependent on others

Rejecting help, no matter how big one's need is

Being confrontational or defensive

Struggling with low moods and bitterness

PTSD

Impaired patience levels; growing angry or frustrated easily

Self-medicating with drugs or alcohol

Clinging to one's routines and activities, even if they're difficult or impossible to now achieve

Resentment toward those responsible for the accident or situation (if that applies)

Getting stuck in one of the stages of mourning

Becoming perfectionistic

Accentuating other body parts in an effort to draw attention away from one's missing limb

Becoming fiercely independent (moving out, refusing therapy, not following medical advice, etc.)

Gathering with other people who have experienced the same thing

Refusing to allow the loss to limit one's quality of life

Choosing careers, hobbies, and pastimes that one can reasonably accomplish

Strengthening one's body to help compensate for the loss

Becoming an advocate for others who have lost a limb (volunteering at the Paralympics, fighting for equal opportunities, seeking legislation that protects those with disabilities, etc.)

PERSONALITY TRAITS THAT MAY FORM

Attributes: Ambitious, appreciative, disciplined, independent, industrious, inspirational, kind, mature, nurturing, persistent, private, resourceful, simple

Flaws: Controlling, defensive, hostile, humorless, impatient, inhibited, insecure, needy, oversensitive, pessimistic, reckless, resentful, subservient, timid, withdrawn

TRIGGERS THAT MIGHT AGGRAVATE THIS WOUND

Experiencing an accident that could have resulted in another physical loss

Facing prejudice, persecution, or pity from others regarding one's disability

An embarrassing moment caused by one's disability (children staring, one's wheelchair tipping over a curb, dropping items that couldn't be held with one arm, etc.)

Having to return to the hospital, even for an unrelated issue

Revisiting the site where one lost one's limb

Wanting to help in a situation but being unable to because of one's disability

OPPORTUNITIES TO FACE OR OVERCOME THIS WOUND

A dream becoming achievable if one is willing to alter it to fit one's capabilities

Bypassing an opportunity to help a loved one because one's self-pity is too great, then regretting it

Being in a position to inspire others (as a Paralympian, as a singer, by using a special talent, etc.) if one can find the courage to do so

LOSING ONE OF THE FIVE SENSES

NOTES: Our senses enable us to appropriately interpret and interact with our environment and the people around us. We don't realize how much we rely upon the senses until we lose one. While many people are able to live happy and fulfilled lives after such a loss, there's always an adjustment period, the length and severity of which varies case by case. Until the person is able to come to grips with their new reality and move forward, the wound will continue to negatively impact them.

BASIC NEEDS OFTEN COMPROMISED BY THIS WOUND: Love and belonging, esteem and recognition, self-actualization

FALSE BELIEFS THAT COULD BE EMBRACED
I will never be whole.
My happiness will always be limited by this.
People look at me and only see my disability.
I'll always have to rely on others to care for me.
My dreams are now out of reach.

THE CHARACTER MAY FEAR…
Losing one of the other senses
Having to rely on others
Losing the people who support them
Being unable to find love
Being stared at, pitied, or singled out due to their loss
Isolation
Being saddled with unfair expectations if the missing sense isn't noticeable to others

POSSIBLE RESPONSES AND RESULTS
Hiding from the rest of the world
Feeling isolated and misunderstood
Choosing jobs and hobbies that one can do alone
Lowering one's expectations for what is possible
Making excuses for why one cannot do something out of a fear of failure and disappointment
Abandoning one's dreams or goals, believing them to now be impossible
Lashing out at others; becoming emotionally volatile
Taking attention wherever one can get it
Feeling sorry for oneself
Becoming depressed
Having suicidal thoughts or attempting suicide
Being ruled by fear, anxiety, and worry
Giving in to self-pity and becoming overly dependent on others
Being easily frustrated by one's difficulty at adapting

Overindulging in some area as a way of making up for the loss

Resenting those who still have the use of all five senses

Using the loss to manipulate others; getting them to do things one is capable of doing oneself

Becoming risk-averse

Trying to control others to compensate for the lack of control in one's life

Rebelling by taking unnecessary risks, flouting rules, and being disrespectful to those in authority

Allowing one's world to shrink (not going out, interacting, or enjoying nature)

Seeking therapy to come to grips with one's new situation

Finding successful people who share one's loss and looking to them as role models

Mentoring others who share one's difficulty

Familiarizing oneself with the law and standing up for one's rights and the rights of others

PERSONALITY TRAITS THAT MAY FORM

Attributes: Adaptable, ambitious, appreciative, charming, courageous, efficient, empathetic, friendly, independent, industrious, inspirational, patient, persistent, resourceful, responsible, socially aware

Flaws: Abrasive, addictive, childish, controlling, cynical, fussy, humorless, impatient, impulsive, indecisive, irresponsible, manipulative, needy, oversensitive, rebellious, resentful, self-indulgent, spoiled

TRIGGERS THAT MIGHT AGGRAVATE THIS WOUND

Witnessing someone being bullied or belittled due to their disability

A friend's choice of words unintentionally poking one's wound: *Listen to those birds,* or *You'd have to be blind not to see that!*

Facing a situation similar to the event that resulted in one's loss

Having to ask a stranger for help: *Can you help me find the elevator?*

Hearing about people doing things that one used to be able to experience firsthand

Struggling with the disability in a public place and feeling the same embarrassment and fear one experienced when the loss first occurred

Specific things associated with how one lost the sense (hospitals, planes, water, etc.)

Being in danger because of the missing sense (not hearing a fire alarm go off, not seeing a car running a red light, etc.)

OPPORTUNITIES TO FACE OR OVERCOME THIS WOUND

Seeing someone in need but being unable to help until one learns to first help oneself

Facing a situation that would be dangerous for anyone and realizing that relying on others is healthy rather than a sign of weakness

When a friend is in need, one has the choice of giving in to self-doubt (not helping) or finding unknown strength (and helping despite the difficulty)

A diagnosis that threatens one's freedom and independence even further

Discovering that experiencing life through a loved one's senses offers a new type of wonderment

SEXUAL DYSFUNCTION

EXAMPLES: Sexual dysfunction affects both men and women and can be caused by a variety of factors, including…
A medical condition like obesity, diabetes, or heart and vascular disease
Stress
Psychological factors (anxiety, depression, phobias surrounding sex, etc.)
Past sexual or physical trauma, such as genital mutilation or rape
Side effects from prescription medications
Drug and alcohol abuse
Hormonal imbalances
Body image issues

BASIC NEEDS OFTEN COMPROMISED BY THIS WOUND: Love and belonging, esteem and recognition, self-actualization

FALSE BELIEFS THAT COULD BE EMBRACED
I can't make my partner happy.
I have to hide how this makes me feel or I'll lose him.
No one will want to be with me once they know the truth.
It's better to just be alone.
If I can't pleasure a woman, I have to prove my masculinity in other ways.
Sex is just a duty that must be performed.
I can't have a meaningful romantic relationship without sex.
I will never be whole.

THE CHARACTER MAY FEAR…
Sexual intimacy with others
Emotional intimacy with others (since it often leads to sexual intimacy)
Rejection
Being a disappointment to their partner
That they will never view sex as anything but negative
Rituals that tend to lead to sex (a back rub, romantic dinners, specific cues from a partner, etc.)

POSSIBLE RESPONSES AND RESULTS
Becoming abstinent to avoid pain or embarrassment
Turning to porn or other stimulants as a way of arousing oneself
Negative self-talk
Self-doubt that leaks over into other areas
Shutting down romantic advances from others
Isolating oneself
Dressing modestly to sidestep unwanted attention

Avoiding being naked in front of one's partner

Sabotaging romantic relationships before they evolve to the point where sex becomes an option

Self-medicating when one anticipates a sexual encounter

Initiating sex but putting on the brakes when one is unable to perform

Faking one's enjoyment during sex

Making excuses for why one isn't interested in sex (fatigue, illness, having too much to do, etc.)

Talking negatively about sex so one's partner isn't surprised when one isn't interested

Attempting to prove one's worthiness in other ways

Seeking potential love interests who might also be uninterested in sex or unable to have it

Engaging in solitary sexual experiences

Becoming uncomfortable or evasive when friends talk about sex

Withdrawing from one's partner as a way of avoiding sex (by not giving compliments that will encourage closeness, shunning physical contact, and becoming uncommunicative)

Focusing on meeting a partner's other needs as a way of making up for not meeting sexual ones

Seeking medical or psychological help for one's condition

Being honest with one's partner about the struggle, hoping they'll be supportive and cooperative

Desensitizing oneself to the specific thing one fears in an effort to overcome it

PERSONALITY TRAITS THAT MAY FORM

Attributes: Alert, cautious, diplomatic, discreet, empathetic, independent, kind, loyal, nurturing, patient, perceptive, persistent, private, proactive, protective, quirky, supportive, tolerant, unselfish

Flaws: Apathetic, callous, cynical, dishonest, evasive, hypocritical, inhibited, insecure, macho, oversensitive, pessimistic, resentful, self-destructive, temperamental, timid, uncommunicative, withdrawn

TRIGGERS THAT MIGHT AGGRAVATE THIS WOUND

A partner initiating sex after a long period of abstinence

Being unable to perform at a time when it's very important to do so

A partner expressing dissatisfaction with the sexual relationship

Hearing others joke disparagingly about those with sexual dysfunction

Situational triggers tied to past sexual trauma (certain smells, a song, a location, etc.)

Seeing advertisements for sexual dysfunction products on television or online

OPPORTUNITIES TO FACE OR OVERCOME THIS WOUND

Having a partner who's willing to work on the issue, but knowing one will be risking embarrassment or failure if one agrees

Finding a partner whose unconditional love means they will give up sex (offering one the choice of clinging to feelings of inadequacy or recognizing that one has value beyond sexual abilities)

Realizing that a fear of sex has robbed one of emotional intimacy, and wanting that to change

Feeling the tick of one's biological clock and desiring to start a family

SOCIAL DIFFICULTIES

EXAMPLES
Being extraordinarily shy
Struggling socially as a result of a condition like autism, ADHD (attention deficit/hyperactivity disorder), OCD, social anxiety, or panic disorder
Behavioral disorders or challenges that may set one apart from one's peers
Being a social outcast due to the severity of one's condition

BASIC NEEDS OFTEN COMPROMISED BY THIS WOUND: Love and belonging, esteem and recognition, self-actualization

FALSE BELIEFS THAT COULD BE EMBRACED
I'm a freak.
I don't need friends. I'm happier on my own, anyway.
People will never accept me, so why try to fit in?
If I could just be normal, I'd be happy.
If I pretend to be like everyone else, they'll accept me.
Being different is a curse.

THE CHARACTER MAY FEAR...
Specific phobias or triggers (crowds, being touched, germs, etc.) associated with their condition
Losing control and embarrassing themselves in front of others
Being rejected or ridiculed
Awkwardness in conversation
Losing the people they feel comfortable with
Never finding love or true friendship
Misreading a situation and reacting inappropriately

POSSIBLE RESPONSES AND RESULTS
Having low self-esteem
Avoiding social situations
Avoiding eye contact with others
Adopting abrasiveness or other defensive traits that push people away
Staying on the outskirts of conversations rather than engaging in them
Responding nonverbally (smiling, nodding, shrugging)
Choosing solitary jobs
Participating in activities (like gaming or online chat groups) that provide more time to formulate responses
Preferring to stay home instead of going out
Becoming stressed or worried if one decides to attend an event or go out with friends
Not trying to build new friendships or relationships

Mistrusting the motives of others; expecting them to tease or bully
Hiding the behaviors that make one stand out (compulsions, tics, inappropriate responses, etc.)
Burying one's feelings of hurt or anger and allowing them to build up inside
Withdrawing into oneself and becoming generally uncommunicative with others
Believing the misconceptions of others (that one is rude, self-centered, irresponsible, unkind, etc.)
Clinging to the friends and family one is comfortable with
Mimicking others in an effort to blend in
Engaging in negative self-talk for one's difficulty navigating social situations
Fantasizing about social interactions where one responds appropriately and is accepted by others
Abusing drugs or alcohol as a means of coping
Giving in to peer pressure so one will be accepted
Scorning other marginalized people
Only attending social events when a friend is present
Getting involved in social media where one can connect with less pressure
Pouring oneself into work or hobbies
Reaching out to other marginalized people
Seeking help to overcome social difficulties (through therapy, support groups, medication, etc.)
Focusing on interests where one excels

PERSONALITY TRAITS THAT MAY FORM
Attributes: Cautious, courteous, creative, diplomatic, empathetic, focused, friendly, imaginative, independent, industrious, just, merciful, obedient, pensive, private, quirky, resourceful, studious, talented
Flaws: Antisocial, callous, catty, childish, evasive, frivolous, hostile, inhibited, irrational, jealous, know-it-all, lazy, martyr, needy, nervous, resentful, self-destructive, subservient, uncommunicative

TRIGGERS THAT MIGHT AGGRAVATE THIS WOUND
Being told by a friend that she would rather stay home, then discovering that she went out with others
Experiencing social rejection as an adult like one did as a child
Not being invited to an event (even if it's only an oversight)
Being mocked or teased
Freezing up in a social situation
Feeling rejected when a friend abruptly cancels their plans

OPPORTUNITIES TO FACE OR OVERCOME THIS WOUND
Upon losing a "wing man," one is forced to face a difficult social situation alone
After a lifetime of isolation, a traumatic event makes one realize the need for connection with others
Discovering that one's differences are a benefit rather than a detriment in a particular situation
An awkward interaction with a potential love interest produces a choice: continue to struggle and remain isolated or face one's difficulties and come to grips with them

Failures and Mistakes

ACCIDENTALLY KILLING SOMEONE

EXAMPLES

Driving a car in which a passenger, pedestrian, or cyclist is killed
Unknowingly serving food to someone who's highly allergic to it
A child consuming a fatal dose of medication while in one's care
A child drowning in one's pool or tub
Killing someone while impaired
Instigating a prank or dare that goes wrong
A boating or Jet Ski accident
Peer pressure that ends in an unintentional death (e.g., pushing drinks on a friend who later dies of alcohol poisoning)
The mishandling or misfire of a weapon or firearm
Poor home maintenance (stairs collapsing, someone falling through a rotten floor, etc.)
Hitting someone too hard in a fight
Selling or giving a friend a bad batch of drugs
A sports-related accident
Horseplay between kids that turns deadly
A police officer killing a bystander in the line of duty
Bumping a friend who falls from a high balcony or ledge

BASIC NEEDS OFTEN COMPROMISED BY THIS WOUND: Safety and security, love and belonging, esteem and recognition, self-actualization

FALSE BELIEFS THAT COULD BE EMBRACED

It should have been me.
I am a terrible and worthless person.
I do not deserve to be happy, safe, or loved.
I do not deserve a child of my own when I caused the death of another person's child.
I am only capable of hurting people.
I cannot be trusted with responsibility of any kind.
People will hate me if they know what I did.
I should suffer for the pain I caused.
I can never fix what I did, no matter how hard I try.
It would be better for everyone if I was dead too.

THE CHARACTER MAY FEAR…

Making another mistake that takes someone's life
Responsibility; making decisions that impact others
Losing control (if irresponsible behavior led to the death)
Things not being safe enough (if disrepair or a lack of safety protocol was involved)

POSSIBLE RESPONSES AND RESULTS

Paranoia or obsession regarding circumstances that led to the death (installing safety railings everywhere to avoid someone falling, not allowing one's children near water, etc.)

Over-preparing (e.g., researching dangers tied to a location and packing for a trip accordingly)

Avoiding positions of power and responsibility so one can't screw things up again

PTSD symptoms (flashbacks, anxiety, depression, etc.)

Avoiding friends, family, or the public at large

Not chasing one's dreams because one feels unworthy

Punishing oneself by giving up the things one loves

Taking risks due to the belief that one has no value

Taking risks in hopes death will occur so one may atone for the mistake

Drinking or using drugs to cope

Blaming others for what happened rather than accepting one's role

Avoiding situations and people tied to the event

Being hyperaware of potential danger and safety issues

Choosing to stay close to home most of the time

Becoming a helicopter parent or being overprotective of loved ones

Hiring professionals rather than attempting do-it-yourself repairs

Keeping one's vehicle, home, etc. in top shape

Having well-stocked medical supplies and working fire extinguishers

Taking safety training, CPR, or other life skill courses to be prepared in the case of an accident

PERSONALITY TRAITS THAT MAY FORM

Attributes: Alert, appreciative, cooperative, disciplined, empathetic, focused, generous, gentle, honest, honorable, humble

Flaws: Addictive, apathetic, cowardly, defensive, indecisive, inhibited, irresponsible, martyr, morbid, obsessive, oversensitive, reckless

TRIGGERS THAT MIGHT AGGRAVATE THIS WOUND

Hearing about a similar accidental death on the news or in one's community

Important life milestones for the victim (the anniversary of their death, their birthday, the day they would have graduated from high school, etc.)

Running into a family member of the victim

Experiencing a near-miss similar to the accident (e.g., almost crashing one's car during a rainstorm)

A loved one being involved in an incident that could have turned deadly

Someone being injured on one's property

OPPORTUNITIES TO FACE OR OVERCOME THIS WOUND

Wanting to support a close friend or family member who accidentally hurt or killed someone

A close friend or family member being accidentally killed

The family of the victim filing a wrongful death lawsuit

Being placed in a situation where one has to kill to protect oneself

A situation where one is responsible for another person and must act to keep them alive

BEARING THE RESPONSIBILITY FOR MANY DEATHS

NOTES: Not all people who are responsible for the deaths of others will have this wound—only those who feel remorse.

EXAMPLES
Soldiers and military leaders
People in charge of a country's security (the United States' FBI and CIA, for example)
Pilots who drop bombs on populated areas
Scientists who create weapons for bioterrorism or mass destruction
Fringe military groups and extremists that carry out kidnappings, violence, and genocide
Serial killers and spree murderers
Factory owners who knowingly pollute the environment, causing human and animal deaths
Assassins and violent criminals
Death row technicians
An airline pilot, train engineer, bus driver, etc. involved in a crash that causes many deaths
A drunk driver who causes a large-scale accident
Maintenance workers cutting corners that result in deaths (e.g., faulty carbon monoxide monitors being installed in an apartment building)
Those responsible for mass animal deaths (avid hunters, scientists who experiment on animals, slaughterhouse technicians, veterinarians that euthanize unwanted animals, etc.)
People who work in fur farms or other animal-product industries

BASIC NEEDS OFTEN COMPROMISED BY THIS WOUND: Love and belonging, esteem and recognition, self-actualization

FALSE BELIEFS THAT COULD BE EMBRACED
I can never make up for what I did.
I am a monster.
People will hate me if they find out what I caused.
I don't deserve forgiveness, only punishment.
I should have known what was going to happen and tried to prevent it.
If I had made a better decision, people would still be alive.
I can't trust my own judgment.
No good can balance such evil.

THE CHARACTER MAY FEAR…
Judgment after death
Judgment by others
Their secret getting out
Being in a position of responsibility that will determine life or death for others
Failure and mistakes that put lives at risk
Having their ideas, work, inventions, etc. corrupted and used to bring about more death

POSSIBLE RESPONSES AND RESULTS

PTSD symptoms (insomnia, depression, anxiety, flashbacks, etc.)

Pulling away from family and friends

Living off the grid; separating oneself from society and avoiding people in general

Punishing oneself by denying the things that bring happiness

Thinking of or attempting suicide

Self-medicating through drugs or alcohol

Refusing to care for oneself

Bankrupting oneself through charity donations in an effort to right one's wrong

Researching one's victims as a way to add to the torture and guilt one feels

Avoiding responsibilities or choices that will impact others

Moving to a new city or town to get away from one's past

Quitting one's job—especially if it was part of the event

Avoiding friendships and not allowing people to get close

Lying about one's past

Avoiding making decisions that will impact others

Seeing a therapist

Donating one's time and energy to raise awareness or change laws that factored into the event

Trying to seek justice for the affected families

Advocating for humane treatment, either for animals or people groups

Becoming a vegan

PERSONALITY TRAITS THAT MAY FORM

Attributes: Cautious, independent, industrious, merciful, nature-focused, pensive, persistent, private, proactive, thrifty, wise

Flaws: Addictive, antisocial, cowardly, cynical, defensive, obsessive, paranoid, scatterbrained, self-destructive, temperamental, timid

TRIGGERS THAT MIGHT AGGRAVATE THIS WOUND

Seeing a dead body

Witnessing an accident that causes harm or kills someone

Stories on the news that are similar to the past event

Attending a funeral

Receiving hate mail

OPPORTUNITIES TO FACE OR OVERCOME THIS WOUND

Discovering that those in power are doing nothing to prevent the situation from reoccurring

Being caught in a life or death situation where one must act or others will die

Witnessing someone being duped or groomed to commit an atrocity

Circumstances forcing one back into the position one held when the event occurred (e.g., a bus driver involved in a large-scale accident having to drive people to safety in an emergency)

BEING LEGITIMATELY INCARCERATED FOR A CRIME

NOTES: Serving a jail sentence is a hard thing to go through and can definitely impact a person. But other difficulties arise once the inmate is set free, especially after a lengthy stay in prison. To that end, this entry explores wounds associated with someone who was once incarcerated but has re-entered society.

BASIC NEEDS OFTEN COMPROMISED BY THIS WOUND: Safety and security, love and belonging, esteem and recognition, self-actualization

FALSE BELIEFS THAT COULD BE EMBRACED
I'm not safe; I always have to be looking over my shoulder.
People will only see me as a convict.
I'll always be a screw-up.
No one will ever trust me.
I don't deserve happiness and can never make up for what I did.
I won't be able to realize my dreams.
I've ruined any chance of reconciling with my loved ones.

THE CHARACTER MAY FEAR...
Returning to jail
Losing their few supportive relatives or friends
Not being able to support themselves through legitimate means
Falling back into the unhealthy habits that resulted in the incarceration
Being defined by their crime
That younger loved ones (siblings, children, nieces, nephews, etc.) will follow in their footsteps
Never finding love or acceptance

POSSIBLE RESPONSES AND RESULTS
Struggling with anger and bitterness (toward oneself or others)
Hoarding one's belongings; being overly possessive of material things
Becoming serious about safety (being alert when walking after dark, augmenting home security, etc.)
Fearing the police and other security officials
Obeying blindly out of a desire to stay out of trouble
Rebelling against authority and the law
Habitually (and subconsciously) adhering to one's jail schedule
Continuing to use the prison slang and vernacular one grew accustomed to
Flying under the radar; never drawing attention to oneself
Not thinking for oneself
Withdrawing from others
Falling into addiction as a coping mechanism
Drifting aimlessly without any clear goals

Trying to succeed on one's own and refusing all help

Returning to criminal activity, either because one can't support oneself legitimately or because the activities are habitual or safe

Never speaking about one's jail experiences

Trying to solve problems with one's fists (because of experiences in jail)

Angry outbursts resulting from stress (due to employment roadblocks, being shunned by family, etc.)

Exaggerating one's experiences to make oneself look good to others

Avoiding family due to a fear of letting them down or the belief that they don't want contact

Struggling with friction that occurs when one returns to a family role (having kids who refuse to listen, a spouse who is used to complete independence, etc.)

Sticking close to any family members or friends who reach out after one's release

Avoiding the places, people, and pastimes that were part of one's life before jail

Becoming socially active to effect change

Being grateful for things that others take for granted

Being content with little when it comes to material things

Becoming a hard worker in an effort to prove oneself

Pursuing a career field where one's criminal record isn't a factor

PERSONALITY TRAITS THAT MAY FORM

Attributes: Alert, ambitious, appreciative, bold, cautious, discreet, easygoing, humble, independent, loyal, obedient, patient, pensive, persistent, private, protective, resourceful, simple, thrifty

Flaws: Addictive, antisocial, callous, cocky, confrontational, cynical, defensive, devious, disrespectful, evasive, hostile, martyr, needy, nervous, paranoid, pessimistic, possessive, prejudiced, rebellious, resentful, self-destructive, subservient, timid, uncommunicative, volatile, weak-willed, withdrawn

TRIGGERS THAT MIGHT AGGRAVATE THIS WOUND

Seeing police officers and vehicles on the street

Running into former criminal associates

Being visited by police when there's a crime in the area

Having to check in with one's parole officer

Sirens and flashing lights

Seeing a child or spouse one hasn't seen in a while and regretting the missed time

Small rooms

Being locked or confined in a room

OPPORTUNITIES TO FACE OR OVERCOME THIS WOUND

Wanting to reach out to an estranged love one but being afraid to do so

Being cut out of someone's life and knowing one must repair the damage for reconciliation to occur

Being threatened by police due to one's record and wanting to live a life free of harassment

Seeing one's child acting out as a result of one's absence or a social stigma

CAVING TO PEER PRESSURE

EXAMPLES

Trying drugs or drinking alcohol so one can fit in
Joining others in bullying a classmate
Going along with the group mindset to exclude certain people who are different
Keeping a secret when one knows it's wrong
Covering for friends if they get into trouble (providing an alibi, misrepresenting facts, etc.)
Agreeing to have sex even though it's not what one wants
Pressuring someone into having sex to prove one's prowess to peers
Allowing friends to party at one's house though one's parents (if they knew) wouldn't allow it
Suffering through hazing rituals because it's expected
Quitting an activity because others think it's stupid
Joining a gang, cult, fringe group, club, sorority, team, or religion due to social pressure
Dressing or behaving a certain way because one's social circle demands it
Ending a friendship because one's peers disapprove of that person
Not challenging oneself because friends would see it as being uppity or acting "too good for them"
Compromising one's religious beliefs as a way of blending in
Hiding one's sexual orientation to avoid persecution
Participating in activities that force one to lie to a spouse

BASIC NEEDS OFTEN COMPROMISED BY THIS WOUND: Safety and security, love and belonging, esteem and recognition, self-actualization

FALSE BELIEFS THAT COULD BE EMBRACED

I am a coward for not standing up for what's right.
I don't know who I am.
If people find out who I truly am or what I believe, they will not accept me.
If I hadn't done it, someone else would have.
If I tell the truth no one will believe me.
One person can't change things.
Fitting in is better than standing out.
Blending in is the only way to get ahead.
It's always safer to pretend.

THE CHARACTER MAY FEAR…

Situations that put them in a corner (e.g., fearing parties after giving in to a demand for sex at one)
Authorities and people who have power or influence
A secret being discovered
Being blackmailed
Having to face consequences for what they did under duress

Making a mistake they cannot undo
Becoming a victim
Being cast out by their peers

POSSIBLE RESPONSES AND RESULTS
Hiding one's feelings
Saying and doing what's expected rather than what one wants to do
Retreating into oneself, closing off from family and close friends
One's esteem hitting rock bottom
Feeling trapped by one's circumstances and choices
Fantasizing about escaping one's predicament or going back in time to undo something one did
Sabotaging happiness out of guilt
Punishing oneself (giving away beloved items, pushing away friends, failing on purpose, etc.)
Encouraging others to compromise themselves so one can feel better about one's choices
Self-medicating with alcohol or drugs
Subtly avoiding a group of peers (e.g., feigning illness to avoid a work get-together)
Lashing out at others
Wanting to hurt those who are doing the coercing
Engaging in acts of revenge against those causing the situation
Not thinking about the future
Wanting to talk to someone about it (like a friend or co-worker) but being afraid of being judged
Trying to make up for one's failing to another by showing kindness when peers aren't around
Writing down one's feelings, or leaving a record of what happened
Requesting to work on a different project so one can avoid those applying the pressure
Becoming a voice for justice (e.g., outing offenders either anonymously or openly)

PERSONALITY TRAITS THAT MAY FORM
Attributes: Cooperative, disciplined, friendly, funny, obedient, persuasive, proper, wise
Flaws: Abrasive, apathetic, cowardly, dishonest, disloyal, disrespectful, evasive, gullible, hypocritical, insecure, irresponsible, macho

TRIGGERS THAT MIGHT AGGRAVATE THIS WOUND
Witnessing bullying firsthand
Witnessing exclusion or terrorizing as an adult (among parents, co-workers, etc.)
Being the butt of a prank or joke within one's group of friends or co-workers
Being teased or ridiculed for disagreeing or voicing concerns
Being manipulated by a family member (to come for a visit, help out with a project, etc.)

OPPORTUNITIES TO FACE OR OVERCOME THIS WOUND
One's child hanging out with a bad crowd that is targeting someone or breaking the law
Being asked to cover up a crime (company fraud, a relative's assault, etc.)
Seeing a co-worker being pressured or mistreated while everyone turns a blind eye
A similar situation that provides the chance to make a better choice than last time

CHOOSING TO NOT BE INVOLVED IN A CHILD'S LIFE

EXAMPLES
A biological parent who chose to give up custody rights
A mother or father who gave up a child for adoption
Institutionalizing a child because of a severe physical or mental condition
Moving out of the country after a divorce
A parent who was never around because of work and travel
Immigrating to another country to receive better opportunities but having to leave family behind
Drug or alcohol problems leading to lost custody and visitation rights
Making choices that lead to an incarceration and little access to one's child
Neglecting one's child out of a desire to pursue personal interests or hobbies
Sending a child away to boarding or military school

BASIC NEEDS OFTEN COMPROMISED BY THIS WOUND: Love and belonging, self-actualization

FALSE BELIEFS THAT COULD BE EMBRACED
I can never make up for the past.
The best thing I can do is stay away.
I am to blame for my son or daughter's bad choices because I was never around.
My chance at being a good parent is gone.
People shouldn't rely on me because I'll only let them down.
My child is better off without me.
Now that my child is grown, it's pointless to try and make amends.
I am not worthy of a second chance.
I do more damage than good.

THE CHARACTER MAY FEAR…
Being alone for the rest of their life
Making mistakes that cannot be undone
Letting a loved one down again
Responsibility, especially for others
Having other children, either naturally or through adoption
Being the target of the child's wrath and disappointment
Relationships that mirror a parent-child dynamic (being an uncle, a teacher, a mentor, etc.)

POSSIBLE RESPONSES AND RESULTS
Working long hours so one has less time for thinking
Avoiding places and activities where children are found
Driving past the child's home or school
Watching one's child through social media
Calling one's ex-partner and hanging up

Writing emails or messages but not sending them

Going to kid-friendly venues to feel connected (watching movies that one's child might watch, visiting hangout spots, etc.)

Being hyperaware of children who share similarities with one's child

Pulling out old photos or mementos (if one has them)

Buying gifts for one's child but not sending them

Tracking a child's accomplishments from afar

Mentally rehearsing a conversation that explains why one was absent

Wondering what one's child is doing and imagining their routine

Fantasizing about the relationship one could have with the child if one could be forgiven

Planning trips and excursions one might take with one's child

Volunteering one's time, especially to youth causes

Mentoring young people in one's sphere of influence as a way of making amends

PERSONALITY TRAITS THAT MAY FORM

Attributes: Affectionate, empathetic, generous, idealistic, pensive, persistent, protective, sentimental, tolerant

Flaws: Addictive, impulsive, indecisive, jealous, nagging, needy, nosy, obsessive, perfectionist, uncommunicative, withdrawn, worrywart

TRIGGERS THAT MIGHT AGGRAVATE THIS WOUND

The announcement of a close friend or family member's pregnancy

Seeing bonding examples (a mother and son fishing together, a father and daughter eating ice cream at the park, etc.)

Witnessing a parent's poor parenting style

Having a friend who never makes time for their child

Being invited to a child's birthday party

A co-worker mentioning a parenting problem and asking for advice on what to do about it

Being in places that are special for children (fun centers, theme parks, puppet shows, etc.)

Noticing colored drawings clipped to a friend's refrigerator or clay gifts on a co-worker's desk

Visiting someone's home and seeing a display of family photos

TV commercials and movie trailers that target the child's age group

Friends or co-workers who tell stories about their kids

Being asked if one has kids

OPPORTUNITIES TO FACE OR OVERCOME THIS WOUND

Discovering one will be a mother or father again

Finding out one's child is sick or has been injured

Discovering one's child has gone down a dark path (is in jail, has a drug habit, etc.)

Reaching the step in an addiction recovery program where one must make amends

Falling in love with someone who has children

Caring for someone who had an absentee parent and seeing the damage it continues to cause

Discovering that one's child is suffering abuse or neglect by someone close to them

CRACKING UNDER PRESSURE

EXAMPLES: Someone might crack under pressure…
In an exam room
During a job interview
While giving an important presentation
During a live performance, like a singing, acting, or comedy routine
While being questioned by police
In the middle of a stressful work project
When one must lie convincingly
During an emergency or disaster
When organizing a big event, such as a wedding, conference, or family reunion
While being responsible for someone else (e.g., caring for elderly parents)
While under the scrutiny of a talent scout
In a competition (debates, athletics, a game show, etc.)

BASIC NEEDS OFTEN COMPROMISED BY THIS WOUND: Safety and security, love and belonging, esteem and recognition, self-actualization

FALSE BELIEFS THAT COULD BE EMBRACED
Not trying is better than failing.
I always choke; it's what I do best.
No matter what I do, I'll always disappoint.
Dreams are for talented people.
You only win if you break the rules.
People can't count on me when it matters most.
Settling is the smart choice.
I'm not smart enough or strong enough. I'm defective.
Hope destroys people.

THE CHARACTER MAY FEAR…
Winning something only to lose it
Being placed in a position of power or responsibility
Being incapable of succeeding
Failing and making mistakes
Public humiliation
Being pitied by others

POSSIBLE RESPONSES AND RESULTS
Distancing oneself from those who witnessed the failure
Avoiding locations, people, and activities that remind one of what happened
Choosing what's "safe" over what one really wants
Pretending one is satisfied with the status quo

Pushing oneself harder than necessary, almost as if for punishment
Holding back rather than jumping in
Using a crutch (drinking, smoking, etc.) as an excuse
Thoughts going to the worst-case scenario when one is stressed
Self-defeating behaviors that sabotage one's success (e.g., partying all night and having no time to prepare for an important project)
Lying to get out of commitment or responsibility
Choosing roles where one supports rather than leads
Making excuses if people ask for one's help
Passing the buck to avoid responsibility
Quitting the team or pulling out of an activity
Pretending one has an injury to avoid competing
Secretly following the rise of others in one's area of expertise while feigning disinterest
Second-guessing one's decisions and choices
Quitting when one is getting close to succeeding
Choosing a job that has low-level expectations
Coping through privately drinking
Reaching out to others who have experienced the same pressure
Utilizing self-talk if one must be in the spotlight in some way
Shedding bad habits and replacing them with good ones
Avoiding people who contributed to the pressuring circumstances

PERSONALITY TRAITS THAT MAY FORM
Attributes: Cautious, cooperative, diplomatic, disciplined, discreet, humble, introverted, loyal, mature, obedient, observant, pensive, private
Flaws: Childish, cowardly, cynical, defensive, hostile, humorless, needy, obsessive, resentful, self-destructive, self-indulgent, subservient

TRIGGERS THAT MIGHT AGGRAVATE THIS WOUND
Attending an event similar to the one where one lost control
High-stakes situations where people are being pressured to do well
Being admired for a talent or skill that is tied to the failure
Instances where one's role is vital to success
Being asked to speak in front of a group
Locations or symbols tied to the past event (a sport's trophy, a microphone, a stage, etc.)

OPPORTUNITIES TO FACE OR OVERCOME THIS WOUND
Having a child who is chasing a goal and wanting to support them so they can succeed
A desire to mentor someone else so they can achieve what they want
Being thrust into a situation where lying or deception is critical to survival
Needing money badly enough to consider returning to (or coaching others in) one's chosen profession

DECLARING BANKRUPTCY

NOTES: A bankruptcy may be business-related or personal and often results from three core causes: money mismanagement, a health crisis, and a divorce or breakup. Changes in the economy can also be a factor, especially if the character lacks the education needed to manage risk effectively.

BASIC NEEDS OFTEN COMPROMISED BY THIS WOUND: Physiological needs, safety and security, esteem and recognition, self-actualization

FALSE BELIEFS THAT COULD BE EMBRACED
I'm a loser.
I can't provide for my family properly.
I shouldn't be in charge of others' well-being.
Everyone thinks I'm a total failure.
I have to keep up appearances no matter what the cost.
I need to know where every penny is going to keep this from happening again.
A safety net is more important than happiness.
Having fun now means paying for it later.
Without money and success, I have no value.

THE CHARACTER MAY FEAR…
Going bankrupt again
Trusting the wrong people
Becoming ill or being unable to work
Secrets becoming known
Risk, especially where money is concerned
Losing their home
Having others find out about their past financial difficulties
Being taken advantage of
Losing their family due to broken trust or the change in life circumstances
Being fired or laid off

POSSIBLE RESPONSES AND RESULTS
Making excuses for why one isn't doing better financially
Lying about one's finances to appear more successful to others
Extreme cheapness; getting by on as little as possible
Needing to know where each penny goes each week
Obsessively comparing oneself to others
Drinking to ward off despair or shame
Working constantly; sacrificing one's health and family time
Limiting a child's activities and interests to those that are inexpensive
Growing angry and frustrated when bills come due

Avoiding family and friends, especially those who are successful or well-off

Doing things oneself (home repairs, etc.), even when one isn't qualified

Putting off doctor visits and giving up medications to save money

Having a dour or resentful outlook toward people who fared better than one did

Assuming people are out to take advantage

Making excuses when friends want to go out

Talking about the old days when life was good rather than living in the present

Crossing moral lines to gain back some of what was lost

Hanging onto items from better days even when it's stupid to do so (e.g., refusing to sell a sports car despite being unable to afford the insurance)

Avoiding risks, especially when investing

Re-purposing, re-gifting, and re-using as much as possible

Buying what's on sale rather than what one likes best

Cutting up credit cards (if one still has any)

Shopping secondhand and engaging in bargain hunting

Taking a class or seeking wise counsel on how to manage one's finances

Creating a sensible budget and sticking to it

Teaching financial responsibility to one's children

PERSONALITY TRAITS THAT MAY FORM

Attributes: Analytical, appreciative, cautious, creative, disciplined, discreet, efficient, humble, industrious, meticulous, organized, persistent, private, proactive, protective

Flaws: Abrasive, addictive, childish, confrontational, controlling, cynical, evasive, fanatical, foolish, hypocritical, inflexible, irrational, jealous, judgmental, materialistic

TRIGGERS THAT MIGHT AGGRAVATE THIS WOUND

Getting an unexpected bill and not having enough money saved to cover it

Rumors of layoffs at work

Foreclosure signs on houses or *Going Out Of Business* signs on storefronts

Driving past one's old home or property

Seeing an expensive vehicle one owned in better days

Birthdays and special holidays where gifts are expected that one can't afford to buy

A friend or co-worker talking about an upcoming vacation

Being asked to donate funds for a celebration or event

OPPORTUNITIES TO FACE OR OVERCOME THIS WOUND

An opportunity to start a new business that's a perfect fit

Seeing a friend who also went through financial troubles turn his situation around

A health crisis that forces one to examine what's important: material items or people

A trial separation that will lead to divorce if one can't make the necessary changes

A child who is gifted and requires specialized equipment and training to succeed

Discovering one's family is about to get bigger through an unplanned pregnancy

FAILING AT SCHOOL

EXAMPLES: Struggling throughout one's school career due to…
A learning disorder (dyslexia, dysgraphia, processing disorders, etc.)
A behavioral or mental disorder (anxiety, ADHD, panic attacks, depression, bipolar, etc.)
Medical problems that cause one to miss a lot of school
A sensory processing disorder that makes school an overwhelming experience
Taking medication that interferes with one's ability to focus or learn
Having a low IQ
Getting no support at home
Problems at home (abuse, a family member's addiction, being forced to care for siblings, etc.)
External pressures that make school a low priority (working multiple jobs to provide for one's family, suffering from malnutrition, being homeless, etc.)

BASIC NEEDS OFTEN COMPROMISED BY THIS WOUND: Love and belonging, esteem and recognition, self-actualization

FALSE BELIEFS THAT COULD BE EMBRACED
I'm stupid.
I'm going to fail no matter how hard I try.
I'm no good at school (or math, reading, etc.).
I'm worthless.
My parents won't love me if I don't do well in school.
People won't like me if they find out I'm dumb.
Giving up is better than failing.

THE CHARACTER MAY FEAR…
Others finding out about their difficulties
Having to work with others
Being called on in class
Having a public emotional breakdown from the stress
Overreaching their capabilities
Disappointing their parents or caregivers
That their critics are right about them being worthless

POSSIBLE RESPONSES AND RESULTS
Low self-esteem
Increased anger and resentment toward people who seem naturally gifted
Resentment toward one's family (if stress at home is a factor)
Underachieving; setting low goals to avoid failing at bigger ones
Giving up
Taking frequent trips to the bathroom or nurse during the school day
Skipping school and being "sick" on test days

Not applying oneself so failure can be blamed on a lack of preparation

Becoming the class clown

Cheating on tests and homework

Withdrawing from teachers and other students

Engaging in self-destructive behaviors, like drinking, taking drugs, or promiscuity

Believing one will fail, and doing so (reinforcing the self-fulfilling prophecy)

Lying to family members to hide one's failure

Negative self-talk

Bullying others as a way of going on the offensive

Dropping out of school

Charming one's teachers to get out of trouble

Extorting a teacher in an attempt to get a passing grade

Paying others to write papers and do one's assignments

Redoubling one's efforts in hopes of turning things around

Seeking out tutors or study groups

Asking for more time on assignments or offering to do additional work for extra credit

Asking a trusted adult for help if home circumstances are beyond one's ability to manage

Pursuing interests outside of academics where one excels (sports, the arts, hobbies, etc.)

PERSONALITY TRAITS THAT MAY FORM

Attributes: Charming, creative, disciplined, industrious, patient, persistent, private, proactive, resourceful

Flaws: Apathetic, callous, childish, nervous, perfectionist, pessimistic, rebellious, resentful, rowdy, self-destructive, temperamental, timid

TRIGGERS THAT MIGHT AGGRAVATE THIS WOUND

Another student being lauded for academic success

Being asked to read aloud, present an oral report, or answer a question in class

Seeing one's grade publicly posted

Being told to study more or apply oneself by a critical caregiver

A family member or friend winning accolades for their work

Social media posts that share accomplishments, awards, milestones, and achievements

Receiving a Christmas letter that praises the accomplishments of the sender and their family

OPPORTUNITIES TO FACE OR OVERCOME THIS WOUND

Being shamed by a teacher, classmate, or parent for one's academic weaknesses

A standardized test or other measure that has far-reaching consequences

Being rejected by one's dream college

Being expelled from a program for poor performance

Being caught cheating

Being assigned a work project as an adult that will magnify one's learning difficulty

FAILING TO DO THE RIGHT THING

EXAMPLES: The result of a character failing to do the right thing is often small, such as fleeting guilt or a temporary rift with a friend. But sometimes the natural consequence of a failure can be monumental, resulting in permanent loss, shame, insecurity, and self-loathing. Events like these can be wounding ones that greatly impact our characters over time, such as…

Not standing up for someone who is being bullied, belittled, or victimized

Looking the other way as a crime is committed

Not stepping in when help could have been given (to a vagrant, a child, etc.)

Giving in to peer pressure

Knowing that a relationship is falling apart but not taking steps to fix it

Making choices that cause others to stumble, such as exposing children or siblings to drugs

Taking a bribe

Giving advice that benefits oneself rather than the recipient

Not blowing the whistle on an influential organization or person who is acting unethically

Confirming someone else's lie (that people always ditch when life gets hard, that no one is reliable, that friendship is conditional, etc.)

Not confronting a friend who is endangering herself (with an eating disorder, addictions, unsafe sexual practices, suicidal tendencies, by driving while intoxicated, etc.)

Selfishly neglecting those in one's charge

Telling a secret or private information one promised to keep

Deliberately attempting to hide or twist the truth

Being suspicious of someone but not acting on one's instincts

Exploiting someone who is vulnerable or in need of help

Giving in to destructive temptations, like having an affair or being financially irresponsible

BASIC NEEDS OFTEN COMPROMISED BY THIS WOUND: Love and belonging, esteem and recognition, self-actualization

FALSE BELIEFS THAT COULD BE EMBRACED

I'm a bad person.

I can't be relied upon to do what's right.

I'm untrustworthy.

I'm too cowardly and weak to stand up to others.

It wasn't my fault; something bad would have happened even if I had acted differently.

One person's actions don't matter anyway.

THE CHARACTER MAY FEAR…

Speaking out against friends and losing them

Being responsible for someone being hurt again

Being manipulated or easily led by others

Making the wrong choice or failing again

Putting their own desires above the needs of others

Being punished for their failure

People discovering what they did

Losing their prestige, power, or otherwise being punished if they don't "toe the line"

POSSIBLE RESPONSES AND RESULTS

Relying on others to make important decisions out of a belief that one's instincts are flawed

Refusing to see or acknowledge injustice so one can avoid responsibility

Turning inward; pulling away from family and friends

Doubting oneself and feeling unworthy

Negative self-talk; berating oneself for being a coward

Becoming apathetic or lackadaisical to avoid being put in charge

Overachieving in an effort to prove one's worth to others

Becoming callous to the needs of others so one can avoid making difficult moral decisions

Ignoring problems rather than trying to fix them and failing

Becoming very black-and-white in one's beliefs so it's easy to make decisions

Loosening one's opinions about right and wrong so one can act without experiencing guilt

Playing the blame game to avoid responsibility

Becoming more cautious; carefully considering decisions in order to come to the right conclusions

Getting second opinions before taking action

Working hard to ensure one doesn't make a mistake in the same area again

Having increased empathy for others

Becoming an advocate for others

PERSONALITY TRAITS THAT MAY FORM

Attributes: Alert, ambitious, cautious, discreet, easygoing, honest, honorable, just, merciful, observant, protective

Flaws: Addictive, apathetic, callous, controlling, cowardly, cruel, defensive, devious, evasive, gullible, hypocritical, ignorant, insecure

TRIGGERS THAT MIGHT AGGRAVATE THIS WOUND

Running into the person who was hurt by one's mistake

Always being reminded of the lapse because one was "made an example of"

Being exposed to the courageous acts of others (through media, social networks, friends, etc.)

Watching movies where the hero or heroine sacrifices to save the day

OPPORTUNITIES TO FACE OR OVERCOME THIS WOUND

Seeing someone in need who is being ignored

Being asked to be responsible for others (at work, with one's family, with a friend's child, etc.)

Being asked for an opinion about an important matter and having to find the courage to voice it

Being forgiven by the victim's family members but struggling to forgive oneself

Seeing someone headed down the same road that led to one's own failure

Being the one in need and having to ask someone to make a sacrifice to help

FAILING TO SAVE SOMEONE'S LIFE

EXAMPLES
A failed water rescue
Not stopping a suicide in time
Unsuccessfully preventing someone from choking
Aiding someone after a car accident (e.g., trying to stop the bleeding) but being unable to save them
Intervening during a mugging or physical attack
Failing at reasoning with a criminal during a hostage situation
Failing to protect a child in a school shooting
Being unable to revive a loved one after an overdose
Being unable to prove child abuse to authorities until it's too late
Losing a patient in the ER or at the site of an accident
Failing to rescue a victim from a fire
Being unable to convince an impaired friend not to drive
Being unable to stop a friend from taking stupid risks
Failing to see the signs of a violent situation until it was too late
Being unable to protect a friend from bullying, racism, or another hate-motivated attack

BASIC NEEDS OFTEN COMPROMISED BY THIS WOUND: Love and belonging, safety and security, esteem and recognition, self-actualization

FALSE BELIEFS THAT COULD BE EMBRACED
I can't protect the people I love.
I am weak and ineffective.
It should have been me instead.
It's better to avoid love than to love and lose it.
I am responsible for this death.
I failed the victim, so their responsibilities and burdens must become my own.
You can't rely on the system for justice.

THE CHARACTER MAY FEAR…
Being responsible for others
Making the wrong decision or cracking under pressure
Failing a loved one in need
Dying suddenly
Not knowing critical information when it's needed
Love and connection

POSSIBLE RESPONSES AND RESULTS
Difficulty sleeping
Flashbacks

Obsessing over what happened, trying to figure out one's mistake
Crying frequently or wanting to cry but being unable to
Stomach issues and a lack of appetite due to feelings of guilt or shame
Avoiding responsibility
Believing everyone is talking about one's failure
Making excuses as to why one cannot commit to things
Second-guessing one's decisions
Refusing to act impulsively, or acting extremely impulsively
Avoiding the family members of the victim
Frequently visiting the site of the event
Avoiding the site of the event
Pulling back from family and friends
No longer finding joy in activities and events
Sticking to routines and avoiding spontaneity
Becoming risk-averse
Questioning one's instincts
Downplaying or degrading one's abilities to others
Assessing the dangers and risks for every activity
Being obsessed with death statistics
Digging into the victim's life to understand him or her better
Trying to bubble wrap loved ones to keep them safe, thereby smothering them
Being on constant alert for danger
Becoming safety conscious

PERSONALITY TRAITS THAT MAY FORM

Attributes: Alert, independent, industrious, introverted, meticulous, protective, responsible, sentimental, socially aware

Flaws: Antisocial, controlling, fanatical, humorless, impatient, indecisive, obsessive, perfectionist, withdrawn, worrywart

TRIGGERS THAT MIGHT AGGRAVATE THIS WOUND

A specific place tied to the event (such as water or boats, if a drowning occurred)
Seeing a weapon or item that was used in the event (e.g., a rickety stair railing)
A sound tied to the event, such as glass smashing or tires squealing
Watching a movie or reading a book that has a similar situation to what one experienced
Needing to enter a police station or speak with an officer
Seeing a picture of the person one failed to save
Having to attend a funeral or memorial

OPPORTUNITIES TO FACE OR OVERCOME THIS WOUND

Being in a life or death situation by happenstance
Being put into a position where one is responsible for someone else
Being in the unique situation where one can make a big difference in another person's life
Experiencing a close call and having to react by instinct

MAKING A VERY PUBLIC MISTAKE

EXAMPLES: Public mistakes are nothing new, but in today's technologically advanced world, they are often recorded for posterity—on YouTube, Facebook, and on websites set up with the purpose of never letting others forget. This kind of reminder makes it even more difficult to move on after an embarrassing gaffe like…

Backing a person, cause, or organization that turns out to be fraudulent
Getting caught having an affair
Getting arrested
Being overheard saying something one would like to keep private
Being caught in a public lie
Losing one's temper and making comments one later regrets
Getting drunk and acting inappropriately
Flubbing one's lines during a performance
Literally dropping the ball at a critical moment during a sporting event
Experiencing a wardrobe malfunction
Making public promises that one is unable to keep
Being responsible for a high-profile project or product that fails
Saying something that makes one look stupid or ignorant
Making an accusation that turns out to be unfounded
Accidentally sending a private email to a group of people instead of only the intended recipient
Passing out naked or semi-naked in a public place

BASIC NEEDS OFTEN COMPROMISED BY THIS WOUND: Love and belonging, esteem and recognition, self-actualization

FALSE BELIEFS THAT COULD BE EMBRACED
I'm a public joke. No one will let me forget what I did.
I can't be trusted not to screw up.
I'm terrible under pressure.
My judgment is faulty.
I'm always going to fail.
If I get in front of an audience, I'm going to mess things up.
My career is over (if one has a highly visible career or is a household name).
People are ugly inside, always wanting to tear others apart for making a mistake.

THE CHARACTER MAY FEAR…
Failures and screw-ups
Speaking or performing in public
Letting others down
Further tarnishing their reputation
Saying the wrong thing

Stating their true beliefs and opinions

Going out on a limb for someone only to learn their trust has been misplaced

POSSIBLE RESPONSES AND RESULTS

Shying away from ambitious or challenging opportunities

Becoming very private and withdrawn

Becoming overly cautious or even obsessive-compulsive in an effort to avoid the same kind of mistake (repeatedly checking one's work for errors, over-planning, etc.)

Doubting one's abilities

Trying to forget through alcohol or drugs

Developing an anxiety disorder

Being prone to angry outbursts from suppressing one's emotions

Becoming secretive to keep one's weaknesses from being exploited

Not doing anything without a partner; relying too much on others and not enough on oneself

Avoiding the humiliating scenario (public speaking, online interviews, debates, etc.)

Giving up one's career for something that is lower profile; underachieving

Going into hiding (becoming reclusive, moving to a new place, changing one's name, etc.)

Embracing the false perception caused by one's mistake (becoming promiscuous, flaky, etc.)

Feeling judged by the peripheral people in one's life

Googling one's name to see if others are still obsessed with what happened

Avoiding social networking platforms where one might be reminded of one's mistake

Taking greater care before committing; acquiring information before acting

Becoming highly ambitious or driven in an attempt to overcome one's mistake

PERSONALITY TRAITS THAT MAY FORM

Attributes: Ambitious, cautious, discreet, humble, merciful, private, proactive, responsible, tolerant

Flaws: Defensive, evasive, inhibited, insecure, pessimistic, rebellious, resentful, self-destructive, timid, withdrawn, worrywart

TRIGGERS THAT MIGHT AGGRAVATE THIS WOUND

Watching a video of another person's embarrassing gaffe

Running into old co-workers or teammates who were close to or witnessed the incident

Seeing a TV news van drive by

Randomly being stopped by a reporter and asked to weigh in on a public issue

People who are holding up cell phones to record or take pictures

OPPORTUNITIES TO FACE OR OVERCOME THIS WOUND

Becoming a target of online bullying

Being threatened or extorted by someone willing to drag what happened into the spotlight again

Being faced with a similar situation and almost making the same mistake again

Feeling passion for a cause disdained by narrow-minded people, and needing to decide to support it or give in to the fear of being ridiculed for one's beliefs

POOR JUDGMENT LEADING
TO UNINTENDED CONSEQUENCES

EXAMPLES
A dive off a bridge that results in serious injury
A prank or dare gone wrong
Drinking and driving that results in a car being totaled
Irresponsible drinking on a boat that ends in an accident or drowning
Purposely not telling others where one is going and ending up in trouble, far from help
Street racing that leads to injury or death
Taking drugs without knowing what they are and ending up in the hospital
Ditching a friend who is then attacked or injured
Attempting a stunt (jumping off a roof, car surfing, etc.) and ending up with head trauma
Playing with fire and causing a destructive blaze
Driving underage and accidentally hitting someone
Messing around with a gun and accidentally shooting oneself or another
Shoving or wrestling that causes the other party to fall down stairs or out a window
Filming oneself doing something inappropriate and having it uploaded to social media
Investing money in an unknown venture and losing it all
Gambling more than one can afford to lose

BASIC NEEDS OFTEN COMPROMISED BY THIS WOUND: Safety and security, love and belonging, self-actualization

FALSE BELIEFS THAT COULD BE EMBRACED
I can never make up for this.
One stupid mistake nearly ruined my life—I can never screw up again.
Risk-taking is a fast track to the grave.
Others should make the decisions, not me.
Planning for every contingency is the only way to keep my loved ones safe.
Fun is only safe if it is carefully controlled.
Freedom leads to anarchy.

THE CHARACTER MAY FEAR...
Losing control
Being in charge and, therefore, responsible
Change, risk, and danger
Making another mistake
Letting loved ones down
That they're unreliable and a danger to others
Someone discovering the role they played in the incident

POSSIBLE RESPONSES AND RESULTS

Deep guilt; pulling away from friends and those involved

Difficulty making decisions

Using alcohol or other crutches to cope

Avoiding decision-making (e.g., not responding so someone else will make the choice)

Seeking out opinions because one doesn't trust one's gut

Being obsessive about research and having all the facts

Bubble-wrapping one's children and spouse to protect them

Making choices and decisions for those in one's care so they will not make mistakes

Having a hard time relying on other people; wanting to be in control of things

Allowing others to be in charge and dictate what one should do

Avoiding risky behaviors and being judgmental of those who take risks

An inability to be spontaneous

Overthinking everything

A pessimistic mindset where one expects things to go wrong

Avoiding stepping outside one's comfort zone

Choosing what is safe and known over what is not

Being the wet blanket of the group because one can't let go and have fun

Steering the hobbies and interests of one's children to keep them safe from possible risks

Resisting change

Being highly organized and prepared

Adhering to routines

PERSONALITY TRAITS THAT MAY FORM

Attributes: Analytical, cautious, disciplined, introverted, mature, merciful, meticulous, nurturing, obedient, observant, organized

Flaws: Controlling, indecisive, inflexible, inhibited, insecure, irrational, judgmental, know-it-all, nagging, nervous, obsessive, pessimistic

TRIGGERS THAT MIGHT AGGRAVATE THIS WOUND

The sight of blood, a cast, a scar, etc.

One's child experiencing a near miss, such as a playground fall that results in stitches

News reports or movies that show the same type of foolhardiness one was involved in

Forgetting to pass on a warning and a person being hurt as a result

Being called out for making a mistake or not catching a problem in time

OPPORTUNITIES TO FACE OR OVERCOME THIS WOUND

A son or daughter rebelling as a result of one being too controlling and risk-averse

A loved one wanting to pursue a sport or activity that carries a high risk of injury

Marital problems that occur because one is too structured with no sense of adventure

Failing someone because one was paralyzed by indecision and did not act in time

Bypassing a life-changing opportunity because one couldn't embrace change or take a risk

An attraction to someone who is free-spirited, spontaneous, and enjoys having fun

Injustice and Hardship

AN ABUSE OF POWER

EXAMPLES
Being a victim of police brutality
Being set up for a crime one didn't commit
Being sexually abused by an authority figure (a teacher, member of the clergy, police officer, etc.)
Being deliberately misled or threatened by an employer, causing one to act unethically
One's land or home being ruined, taken, or reassigned at the government's whim
An elderly person being neglected by those being paid to provide care
Being publicly humiliated by a person in authority
Being abused or mistreated by one's parent or guardian
Being victimized by a financial advisor or institution
Donating to a cause and learning that the money was used for someone's personal gain
Being illegitimately fired or laid off
Having one's ideas or work stolen by the person or organization it was entrusted to
A media outlet misrepresenting the facts to achieve its own goals
A ruler or organization that uses money, intimidation, or influence to circumvent the law

BASIC NEEDS OFTEN COMPROMISED BY THIS WOUND: Safety and security, love and belonging, esteem and recognition

FALSE BELIEFS THAT COULD BE EMBRACED
I'm so stupid, I'll fall for anything.
No powerful person or organization is trustworthy.
No one is looking out for me so I have to look out for myself.
I will always be under the thumb of others.
I was targeted because I'm weak.
If others are in charge, I run the risk of being victimized.
I can't trust my own judgment.
Power corrupts. Placing faith in leaders of any kind is foolish.
Justice is blind when it comes to money and influence.

THE CHARACTER MAY FEAR…
Being taken advantage of again
That their instincts about people are unreliable
Trusting the wrong person or organization
Suffering a loss that cannot be recouped, like losing their savings to a dishonest money management company

POSSIBLE RESPONSES AND RESULTS
Distrusting the system (an imperfect judicial process, a failing health system, one's government, etc.)
Choosing to work only with people one personally knows
Avoiding big decisions so one can defer responsibility to others if things go badly

Becoming very traditional; distrusting new ways of doing things

Manically researching facts so one is fully informed and won't be duped again

Suspecting corruption at every level of society

Becoming a conspiracy theorist

Being apathetic; assuming that everyone is corrupt and there's nothing one can do about it

Living off the grid

Disengaging from the kinds of institutions or groups where the abuse occurred (disdaining organization religion, hoarding money rather than keeping it in a bank, etc.)

Requiring full disclosure before one can feel safe working with someone in power again

Seeking to protect one's loved ones from the same kind of abuse

Becoming overly dependent on trustworthy sources to help with decision-making

Aggressively taking control of every area of one's life

Withdrawing from groups or organizations if trustworthiness can't be proven

Circumventing a broken system (delivering justice oneself rather involving police, homeschooling rather than allowing one's child to attend public school, etc.)

Publicly working to bring down the offender or corrupt organization

Being very organized when researching organizations and businesses

Always treating others with honor and respect, especially if one holds a position of power

PERSONALITY TRAITS THAT MAY FORM

Attributes: Analytical, focused, industrious, just, loyal, meticulous, organized, passionate, patient, proactive, protective, resourceful, responsible, studious, traditional

Flaws: Antisocial, apathetic, callous, confrontational, controlling, cynical, disrespectful, fanatical, foolish, haughty, inflexible, irrational, nosy, obsessive, paranoid, uncooperative, withdrawn

TRIGGERS THAT MIGHT AGGRAVATE THIS WOUND

Hearing on the news about a supposedly upright person or group that took advantage of others

Being mistreated again by a different person of power

Facing a situation where one must entrust a child or elderly parent to the very institution that was responsible for the past violation

Suffering ancillary difficulties caused by the initial abuse (an inability to retire due to being scammed out of one's savings, being unable to work due to injuries received from a police beating, etc.)

OPPORTUNITIES TO FACE OR OVERCOME THIS WOUND

A situation where one is in deep trouble and must choose whether to trust an authority figure or not

Seeing the experience affect one's children (becoming cynical, fearing all police, mistrusting their own judgment, etc.) and wanting them to live more fulfilled and happy lives

A person in power turning out to be honorable and trustworthy, challenging one's preconceptions

Abusing power in some way (being an over-controlling parent, perhaps) and then reforming to repair the damage, thus realizing that others are capable of change and may be worthy of trust again

BECOMING HOMELESS FOR REASONS BEYOND ONE'S CONTROL

EXAMPLES

A medical emergency that causes bankruptcy (e.g., due to being unable to obtain insurance)

One's parent suffering from a mental disorder that causes the whole family to be on the street

Being unable to work due to a physical ailment

A weather disaster that destroys one's home

A fire destroying one's uninsured home or apartment

Fleeing an abusive relationship and having nowhere to go

A tragedy that thrusts one into depression, making it difficult to provide for oneself

Minor life events that push a family living on the edge of poverty over the line (a vehicle breakdown, a fender bender, a trip to the hospital, etc.)

BASIC NEEDS OFTEN COMPROMISED BY THIS WOUND: Physiological needs, safety and security, love and belonging, esteem and recognition, self-actualization

FALSE BELIEFS THAT COULD BE EMBRACED

I'm worthless.

I should have seen this coming and planned for this.

Survival is my only priority now; dreams are a thing of the past.

I'll never get back to where I was before.

The system is rigged against people like me.

I am what people think of me (lazy, useless, a drain on society, self-indulgent, etc.).

My children's safety and wellbeing are at stake because of me.

I am a terrible parent (if one's family is also on the street).

THE CHARACTER MAY FEAR...

Family members being split up or children being taken away

Their children being physically or emotionally hurt

Being robbed, attacked, or taken advantage of

Being arrested

What others think (family members or old neighbors, for example)

Never being able to get on their feet again

Giving into depression and developing a problem with alcohol or drugs

Sending their family on a cycle of poverty and homelessness that will last for generations

POSSIBLE RESPONSES AND RESULTS

Trying to find a temporary home with family or friends

Living out of one's car

Falling further into depression

Abusing drugs or alcohol as a way of easing the pain

Becoming disorganized

An inability to focus (due to lack of sleep, poor nutrition, an impairment, or something else)

Suffering deep guilt if others are affected (such as children who are also homeless or a partner who relies on one's support), especially if one feels responsible for the current situation

Finding tricks to save money (showering at truck stops, keeping a cheap storage locker at the bus station, knowing where one can fill up water bottles, etc.)

Becoming protective of one's few material possessions

Turning to unethical means to make money, like being a drug mule or prostituting oneself

Avoiding those in authority who might take away one's child or restrict the freedoms one has

Avoiding responsibility for others (for fear of screwing up again)

Making a plan and sticking to it

Doing what it takes to become financially stable

Avoiding all risks and being very safe with money (after getting back on one's feet)

Making the education of one's children a priority

Working multiple jobs that are below one's capabilities to make ends meet

Prioritizing purchases by necessity and want

Being willing to accept help from friends

PERSONALITY TRAITS THAT MAY FORM

Attributes: Alert, ambitious, cooperative, creative, discreet, empathetic, focused, friendly, hospitable, humble, mature, organized, patient, persistent, private, protective, quirky, resourceful

Flaws: Addictive, apathetic, callous, childish, cynical, devious, evasive, forgetful, ignorant, insecure, jealous, nervous, scatterbrained, self-destructive, stingy, tactless, uncommunicative

TRIGGERS THAT MIGHT AGGRAVATE THIS WOUND

Getting back on one's feet, then receiving an unexpected bill that one can't pay

Walking past panhandlers or people searching dumpsters for bottles to recycle

A car breakdown that leaves one stranded

Receiving an eviction notice when one is personally not at fault (like the building being torn down)

After the crisis has passed, attending family gatherings where others flaunt how well they are doing

OPPORTUNITIES TO FACE OR OVERCOME THIS WOUND

Once off the street, meeting someone who is homeless and wanting to help them achieve stability

Overhearing someone speak negatively about homeless people, and facing a choice: stand up for them by revealing one's past experience or remain silent

Being offered help by another, giving one a chance to overcome a jaded worldview and learn to trust again

Being asked to join a cause benefiting the homeless

BEING BULLIED

EXAMPLES: Bullying can be defined as the ongoing use of power or influence to intimidate someone. Bullies come in many forms, including…
Demanding parents or relatives who did things "for one's own good"
Siblings who had more than the typical share of power due to age, size, or popularity
A jealous friend or resentful classmate
A group of people who joined forces (a subset of classmates or teammates) against others
A teacher or another person in a position of authority
Co-workers who were threatened by one's status or prowess
Social media "friends" who target and ridicule as a way to gain power
Power-hungry employers or well-connected individuals used to getting what they want

BASIC NEEDS OFTEN COMPROMISED BY THIS WOUND: Physiological needs, safety and security, love and belonging, esteem and recognition, self-actualization

FALSE BELIEFS THAT COULD BE EMBRACED
People target me because I'm weak.
My life will never get better; "happily ever after" is for other people.
I am a failure and will never succeed at anything.
If I do what other people want it will go easier for me.
People only get close so they can better manipulate you.
The system (or school, government, company policy, parental fairness, etc.) is a joke.
If people fear me, they won't mess with me.

THE CHARACTER MAY FEAR…
Relationships (due to trust issues)
Isolation
Rejection and abandonment
Violence and pain
Making big mistakes that others will use against them or share online for wide-scale ridicule
People with traits similar to the bullies from their past (manipulative, macho, etc.)
Choosing the wrong person to open up to and having their emotions toyed with
Public speaking, being on display, and situations that make them feel exposed

POSSIBLE RESPONSES AND RESULTS
Being very self-critical and viewing oneself as defective
Being late because one finds it difficult to get up and face the day ahead
Avoiding social events where bullying might occur (office parties, the school cafeteria, etc.)
Finding a safe place to be alone during idle periods (at lunch, between meetings, at home, etc.)
Not making eye contact or engaging others in conversation
Agreeing with one's attacker in an attempt to keep a situation from escalating

Lying to loved ones and pretending everything is fine so others won't worry
Pulling back from relationships to avoid letting people in (and being hurt by them)
Overreacting and sensitivity; feeling deeply wounded even by the smallest offense
Crying easily
Laughing off slights or smaller humiliations in hopes of de-escalating a bad situation
Daydreaming and escapism via books, TV, movies, video games, or writing
Self-medicating to cope (using drugs, alcohol, or food)
Being meticulous with one's appearance to try and fit in
Watching others to see how they behave; emulating them to avoid being targeted
Cutting and other self-destructive behaviors
Suicidal thoughts or attempts
Difficulty eating and sleeping
Not taking care of oneself due to depression
Bullying weaker individuals as a form of release or a means of gaining control
Being hypersensitive to fairness (and unfairness)
Avoiding social media and closing down one's accounts
Downplaying exceptionalities and passions that might make one a target, such as academic success, a love for *Dungeons and Dragons*, or one's passion for and knowledge of trains
Befriending animals or seeking solace in nature
Seeking friendships with "safe people," like those who are outcasts or are much younger
Being deeply moved by small kindnesses or gestures by peers (due to their infrequency)
Engaging in positive self-talk in an effort to find the strength to face everyday situations
Recognizing that the bully is the one who has problems and not oneself
Finding a group to be part of that focuses on friendship and belonging rather than judgment

PERSONALITY TRAITS THAT MAY FORM
Attributes: Cautious, cooperative, independent, mature, nature-focused, nurturing, obedient, private, proactive, protective, resourceful
Flaws: Addictive, antisocial, gullible, hostile, hypocritical, insecure, needy, nervous, self-destructive, subservient, suspicious, uncommunicative

TRIGGERS THAT MIGHT AGGRAVATE THIS WOUND
Running into a bully from the past, or witnessing another person being mistreated
Hearing about a victim of bullying who has committed suicide
Revisiting a location or circumstance that reminds one of past bullying experiences
Being mistreated on a smaller scale (e.g., a friend coercing one to do something one doesn't want to do)

OPPORTUNITIES TO FACE OR OVERCOME THIS WOUND
Being bullied in one's adult workplace or within the community after suffering it as a child
Being in an abusive relationship and realizing that one is allowing the pattern of mistreatment to continue
Seeing signs in one's child that he or she is being bullied and wanting to intervene

BEING FALSELY ACCUSED OF A CRIME

EXAMPLES: It hurts to be accused of something when one is innocent. It's even more devastating when the allegation involves a crime that could result in a humiliating investigation, one's reputation being dragged through the mud, family being impacted, and possible jail time. This can happen with a false accusation of most crimes, including…

Homicide

Sexual harassment of an employee

Discrimination at work

Child or spousal abuse

Sexual abuse (of a student, neighbor, one's child, etc.)

Theft

Corruption (misappropriating funds, bribes, abuse of power, law-breaking, etc.)

Blackmail

Kidnapping

Vandalizing school or neighborhood property

Dealing drugs

Prostitution

BASIC NEEDS OFTEN COMPROMISED BY THIS WOUND: Safety and security, love and belonging, esteem and recognition, self-actualization

FALSE BELIEFS THAT COULD BE EMBRACED

I'll never be able to clear my name.

Even though I was found innocent, people will always wonder about me.

To avoid any hint of wrongdoing, I have to be perfect.

No one will trust me.

This now defines me.

Because of this stain on my reputation, I have to give up my dream (or public office, my career, etc.).

THE CHARACTER MAY FEAR…

New people finding out about the accusation

Family members being mistreated because of what happened

Not being believed

Being falsely accused again of something else

Being rejected due to the accusation

People who hold positions of power and control

Betrayal by someone they trust

POSSIBLE RESPONSES AND RESULTS

Hiding the incident

Instructing loved ones to keep it a secret

Making a change to start anew, like switching careers, moving, or attending a different synagogue

Prejudice toward the kind of person who made the accusation

Limiting interactions by pulling back from friends and social groups or avoiding new people

Becoming defensive at the slightest provocation and feeling one must explain oneself

Needing to immediately address even the smallest of misunderstandings

Avoiding situations where jealousy could result

Getting upset if friends joke and misrepresent the truth about one's involvement in anything

Becoming a people pleaser

Being very loyal to those who stood by one during the accusation

Keeping thorough records in case one is accused of something again

Following the letter of the law out of fear

Having a martyr complex

Adopting a defeatist attitude

Advocating for oneself out of the belief that no one else will

Avoiding scenarios that could lead to a false presumption of guilt (being alone with a student, traveling with a co-worker, etc.)

Being highly attuned to unfairness and injustice

Always believing others—even to a fault—because one doesn't want them to feel the way one did when the accusation was made

Standing up for others who have been falsely accused

Needing proof beyond a shadow of a doubt before accusing someone of wrongdoing

Showing appreciation to those who helped clear one's name

PERSONALITY TRAITS THAT MAY FORM

Attributes: Appreciative, bold, cautious, centered, cooperative, courteous, diplomatic, discreet, easygoing, honest, honorable, independent, just, kind, obedient, private, proper, tolerant, wise

Flaws: Catty, confrontational, cynical, defensive, dishonest, hostile, humorless, insecure, martyr, nervous, oversensitive, perfectionist, pessimistic, temperamental, uncooperative, withdrawn

TRIGGERS THAT MIGHT AGGRAVATE THIS WOUND

Seeing one's accuser prosper without any consequence for what he or she did

Losing a friendship over the false accusation

Being falsely accused of something else, even something small or inconsequential

People who gossip or jump to conclusions about others (in one's social circle, at church, etc.)

OPPORTUNITIES TO FACE OR OVERCOME THIS WOUND

Being punished for the accusation (not getting a promotion, being transferred to a different school, etc.) even though one was acquitted, and needing to choose whether to take it or fight the injustice

After years spent trying to hide from the past, the accusation surfaces again, and one decides to stop running and seek justice and the truth

A friend or loved one suffers mistreatment due to guilt by association, and one must decide to either ignore the unfairness or fight for what is right and just

BEING FIRED OR LAID OFF

EXAMPLES
Being fired for one's poor performance
Being laid off because a department was downsized or a position was outsourced
Being fired for poor performance, an addiction, being unreliable, etc.
Losing a job at a critical time, like when a baby is on the way or a home has just been bought
The company taking an opportunity to legally let one go due to one being a financial drain (e.g., because of medical issues that caused one to need a lot of time off)
A merger that resulted in the majority of employees on one side losing their jobs
Being let go (legitimately or illegitimately) due to friction with one's boss

BASIC NEEDS OFTEN COMPROMISED BY THIS WOUND: Physiological needs, safety and security, love and belonging, esteem and recognition, self-actualization

FALSE BELIEFS THAT COULD BE EMBRACED
To stay employed, I have to work harder than everyone else.
It's safer to be a team player than to disagree with what the company's doing.
I was a fool to try and have a career in this area; I'm not good enough.
I'm worthless if I can't support my family.
Deep down I am defective, and the company knew it.
People will lose respect for me if I can't stay employed.
I have to do whatever it takes to keep a job.

THE CHARACTER MAY FEAR…
Taking risks, especially financial ones
Saying or doing the wrong thing at a new job
Underperforming at work
Abandonment (e.g., a spouse leaving if financial problems impact the marriage)
Changes that could threaten their new job, such as a shifting leadership hierarchy, the company being sold, or technology that could make the position obsolete
Falling into debt while being out of work
Losing the respect of loved ones (a spouse, children, parents, neighbors and friends, etc.)
Being unable to find work

POSSIBLE RESPONSES AND RESULTS
Pretending one still has a job to avoid telling others about the firing
Being disloyal to one's employers out of anger or a sense of betrayal
Absolving oneself of any responsibility for the firing, even if one was to blame
Contacting the people in one's network about job opportunities
Beefing up one's résumé to showcase one's talents and abilities
Anxiety, depression, and self-worth issues
Applying for anything remotely close to one's skillset (if one's finances are in bad shape)

Bending the truth in one's new job if things are looking shaky

Hiding difficulties from employers (an illness, unrealistic deadlines, etc.) rather than risking scrutiny

Worrying about money; carefully watching one's finances

Tying job security and employer satisfaction to one's self-worth

Working late to reinforce one's value and dedication

Being meticulous with one's appearance out of a desire to look good

Turning a blind eye to ethical issues at work

Becoming a "yes man" and always agreeing with the powers-that-be

Needing constant reassurance that one is doing a good job at work

Taking on extra shifts or working holidays to get ahead

Taking a second job to be able to save money, in case something happens

Bringing work home; having a poor work-life balance

Missing out on family time due to work commitments

Sticking with a job that is safe and pays the bills even though one dislikes it

Feeling guilty if one has idle time at work or has to take a legitimate day off

Making sure employers and associates know how much work one is doing

Sucking up to employers and managers

Taking on high-profile projects one may not be suited for out of a desire to prove oneself

Employing oneself rather than being at the mercy of others

Adopting a healthier outlook on work (that it isn't tied to one's value or worthiness)

PERSONALITY TRAITS THAT MAY FORM

Attributes: Alert, cooperative, courteous, efficient, focused, honorable, industrious, loyal, merciful, professional, resourceful, sensible

Flaws: Addictive, insecure, obsessive, perfectionist, resentful, self-destructive, stingy, unethical, weak-willed, workaholic, worrywart

TRIGGERS THAT MIGHT AGGRAVATE THIS WOUND

Hearing rumors about downsizing and possible layoffs

Getting a boss who has other favorites at work

Receiving a poor performance report

A company merger that creates uncertainty

Being put on probation

Seeing one's parent laid off after many years of service and loyalty

OPPORTUNITIES TO FACE OR OVERCOME THIS WOUND

An unexpected financial difficulty (like buying a house, medical bills piling up, or a spouse getting laid off) that makes it especially important to keep one's job

Being fired from another job because of the negative attitude one developed from being let go the last time, and realizing one is creating a self-fulfilling prophesy

One's marriage growing rocky due to subsequent monetary strain, causing one to question the fairness of being held responsible for so much of the family's financial welfare

BEING FORCED TO KEEP A DARK SECRET

EXAMPLES
One's child being a sociopath
A spouse's hit-and-run
The abuse of a family member
A murder cover-up in the family
A horrible deathbed confession that has repercussions for loved ones
One's child being an accomplice in a mass murder
One's spouse belonging to a terrorist organization
An illegal adoption
One's family running a drug smuggling operation
Being related to someone of notoriety, like Hitler, Castro, or bin Laden
A parent embezzling funds from work or stealing money from those who are vulnerable

BASIC NEEDS OFTEN COMPROMISED BY THIS WOUND: Safety and security, love and belonging, esteem and recognition

FALSE BELIEFS THAT COULD BE EMBRACED
How could my own blood do this? I could end up being just like him or her.
I'll be a pariah if people find out.
My silence has made me an accomplice, so I can't tell.
Keeping this secret is best for everyone.
The well-being of my family is more important than the truth.
Telling would make me disloyal.
The secret will come out eventually; I don't have to be the one to disclose it.
You're only guilty if you get caught.
No one could love me if they knew the truth.
People have moved on, so bringing the truth out will only cause more damage.

THE CHARACTER MAY FEAR...
Others finding out
Legal repercussions (being arrested, children being removed from their custody, etc.)
Being rejected by family and friends
Becoming like the guilty person (sharing his or her weakness)
Losing someone's love, a prestigious position, or the respect of their peers if the truth comes out
Being punished or victimized by the one wanting the secret to be kept

POSSIBLE RESPONSES AND RESULTS
Lying and deception becoming second nature
Denial; rewriting the truth in one's mind
Telling conflicting stories (being unable to keep one's lies straight)
Enlisting others who are necessary to keep the secret hidden

Being wary of those who might sniff out the truth

Suffering from nightmares

Depression

Lack of focus and attention to one's duties

Distancing oneself from those associated with the secret (going away to school, moving, etc.)

Avoiding the one who is requiring the secret to be kept

Tiptoeing around the wrongdoer; walking on eggshells

Constantly giving in to the wrongdoer as a way of placating him or her

Physical responses to prolonged stress, like high blood pressure, digestive issues, and headaches

Abusing drugs or alcohol

Keeping the secret but rebelling in other ways to express one's feelings

Becoming temperamental or volatile

Hostility toward the person responsible for the secret

Being nervous around the authorities

Excising things from one's life that one shares with the wrongdoer (hobbies, activities, interests, etc.)

Struggling with opening up to people out of worry one might spill the secret

Subversively helping those negatively impacted by the hidden event

Planning to reveal the secret in a way that maintains one's anonymity

Throwing oneself into other activities as a way of keeping one's mind occupied

Secretly gathering information that can be used against the wrongdoer

PERSONALITY TRAITS THAT MAY FORM

Attributes: Alert, cautious, cooperative, courteous, curious, diplomatic, discreet, easygoing, focused, independent, loyal, mature, meticulous, obedient, observant, patient, private, protective, trusting

Flaws: Addictive, cowardly, dishonest, evasive, forgetful, hostile, impulsive, inhibited, insecure, irrational, irresponsible, nervous, rebellious, resentful, self-destructive, subservient, volatile

TRIGGERS THAT MIGHT AGGRAVATE THIS WOUND

Someone sharing another secret (even a minor one) and requesting it be kept

A clue that makes one wonder if someone else knows about the secret

Running into a victim of the wrongdoer

Being asked outright about the secret and having to lie again to cover it up

OPPORTUNITIES TO FACE OR OVERCOME THIS WOUND

The situation coming to light and one being investigated as an accomplice

When a new relationship develops into something deeper and one has an outlet to tell the secret as a way of releasing the burden and relieving stress

Experiencing friction in one's marriage or another relationship as a result of trying to keep the secret

Suspecting the wrongdoer is continuing with their despicable behavior and needing to choose between what's easy and what's right

BEING FORCED TO LEAVE ONE'S HOMELAND

EXAMPLES: Reluctantly leaving one's country due to…
War
Civil unrest
Extreme poverty
Being trafficked or enslaved and sent somewhere else
A catastrophic natural disaster
The destruction of one's environment in the name of development
A dictatorial government headed down a dangerous path
Persecution because of one's race or ethnicity, religion, political affiliation, etc.
Being accused of a crime one hasn't committed

BASIC NEEDS OFTEN COMPROMISED BY THIS WOUND: Physiological needs, safety and security, esteem and recognition, love and belonging, self-actualization

FALSE BELIEFS THAT COULD BE EMBRACED
I'll never feel at home anywhere else.
No place will be safe for me.
I won't fit in.
By leaving my homeland, I'm sacrificing my identity.
Cowards flee, so I guess that's what I am.

THE CHARACTER MAY FEAR…
Never seeing their family again (if some were left behind)
Facing persecution in the new place (going from one intolerable situation to another)
Being so different culturally that they won't be able to fit in
Losing or forgetting their heritage
Not being able to succeed as an outsider and a transplant
Being sent back to the unfavorable homeland
Never being able to return to their homeland
Their family becoming separated during the crossing
Isolation within the new culture

POSSIBLE RESPONSES AND RESULTS
Difficulty acclimating to the new culture
A deep loneliness that is difficult to dispel
Difficulty meeting one's basic physiological needs, such as shelter, food, or access to clean water
Adhering to the old ways and resisting acclimation
Refusing to learn a new language out of resentment, or giving up because it's too difficult
Flying under the radar due to being in the new country illegally
Fearing anyone in authority

Feeling taken advantage of in the new society, especially if one is there illegally

PTSD symptoms (if one escaped a violent situation)

Becoming possessive of one's items

Hoarding resources and preparing for the worst-case scenario in the new country

Emotional volatility

Becoming violent due to frustration, stress, and personal trauma

Difficulty succeeding at work or school

Depression

Increased anxiety over what may come

Isolating oneself and one's family from people outside of one's culture

Health problems due to lack of hygiene and medical care during the forced move

Feeling caught between two cultures; losing one's sense of identity

Having high expectations for one's children and pushing them to succeed

Finding and building relationships with others from one's country

Making sure one's children maintain a connection to their heritage

Throwing oneself into the culture to learn the language, customs, etc.

Making plans to return to one's homeland one day

A determination to succeed despite the difficulty

Being grateful for new opportunities and the ways life has improved

Appreciating the small things and not taking anything for granted

PERSONALITY TRAITS THAT MAY FORM

Attributes: Adaptable, ambitious, appreciative, courageous, courteous, empathetic, friendly, hospitable, humble, idealistic, independent, industrious, mature, patriotic, persistent, resourceful, responsible

Flaws: Confrontational, devious, hostile, ignorant, insecure, jealous, judgmental, needy, obsessive, possessive, prejudiced, rebellious, resentful, subservient, timid, uncommunicative, violent

TRIGGERS THAT MIGHT AGGRAVATE THIS WOUND

Having to leave one's home again (due to being evicted, fleeing the authorities, etc.)

Experiencing the same persecution in the new place one was subjected to in the homeland

Communication struggles because of language and cultural differences

Being the target of prejudice or discrimination

Finding oneself in a worse situation in the new place than one faced back home

OPPORTUNITIES TO FACE OR OVERCOME THIS WOUND

Losing a loved one (through separation or death) during the forced migration and not wanting that death to be in vain

Learning that a relative back home is in danger, and having to choose between returning or staying

Being threatened with deportation after settling into the new culture

Witnessing one's children turning away from their heritage

After living a long time in the new country, seeing signs that it's headed down the same terrible path of one's homeland

BEING THE VICTIM OF A VICIOUS RUMOR

EXAMPLES: Rumors can be incredibly destructive and hurtful, whether they're started by a friend or family member, a co-worker or employer, an enemy, a complete stranger, a powerful business rival, or an organization that could benefit from tarnishing one's reputation. In today's interconnected world, rumors can have especially far-reaching and long-lasting effects.

BASIC NEEDS OFTEN COMPROMISED BY THIS WOUND: Love and belonging, esteem and recognition, self-actualization

FALSE BELIEFS THAT COULD BE EMBRACED
People will believe this about me anyway, so I might as well embrace it.
I can never achieve my hopes and dreams with this hanging over my head.
Why was I targeted? There must be something wrong with me.
If you try to stand out, someone will always cut you down.
Getting back at them will even the score.
My reputation is ruined. All I can do is quit (my career, passion, business, etc.).
Deep down, people are cruel and hateful. They love seeing someone be ripped apart.

THE CHARACTER MAY FEAR…
Being betrayed by someone (a friend, romantic partner, co-worker, family member, etc.)
Not being believed when it counts most
Revealing personal truths (and possibly having the information used against them)
Being judged and limited by the rumors; not being able to pursue a passion as a result
Being rejected by important people who believe the falsehood
The rumor negatively impacting loved ones

POSSIBLE RESPONSES AND RESULTS
Withdrawing from others
Avoiding places where people have heard the rumor (the workplace, social media, one's school, etc.)
Low self-esteem and diminished self-worth
Analyzing oneself for possible defects to help understand why one was targeted
Staying in rather than going out
Avoiding social events and backing out of commitments
Clinging to a trusted family member or friend
Vacillating between anger, embarrassment, and humiliation
Lashing out at the rumormongers
Investigating to find the source; trying to determine who gains from one's damaged reputation
Seeking vengeance against those who started the rumor
Reluctance to share one's secrets with others

Believing the lie

Embracing the lie and living as if it was true (if the rumor persists)

Cutting off recently formed relationships

Seeking new relationships with people who have no connection to those spreading the rumor

Granting more power to the rumor than it has (believing that every new acquaintance has heard it, that it has spread farther than it really has, etc.)

Becoming paranoid

Physical responses due to prolonged stress (changes in weight and sleeping habits, increased blood pressure and sickness, etc.)

Making it a goal to prove the rumor wrong

Holding back; saying only what people want to hear to avoid further judgment or friction

Changing schools, switching jobs, or moving in an effort to start over

Throwing oneself into other hobbies, interests, or areas of skill as a way of proving oneself

Expressing one's true self through writing, dance, or drawing

Guarding one's words carefully to avoid accidentally starting a rumor that isn't true

Disdaining gossip; refusing to contribute to the vicious nature of spreading rumors

PERSONALITY TRAITS THAT MAY FORM

Attributes: Cautious, diplomatic, discreet, empathetic, hospitable, humble, independent, just, kind, merciful, meticulous, observant, patient, persuasive, private, proper, sensible

Flaws: Confrontational, cynical, defensive, evasive, gossipy, hostile, humorless, inhibited, insecure, martyr, obsessive, paranoid, resentful, timid, uncommunicative, vindictive, volatile, withdrawn

TRIGGERS THAT MIGHT AGGRAVATE THIS WOUND

Overhearing people gossip about someone else

Thinking the rumor has died away only to have someone bring it up again

Being sharply questioned (about work, one's whereabouts, etc.) and having to defend oneself

Someone expressing skepticism over something one has said

Being rejected in a legitimate way (such as losing a condo lease to someone with better credit) but worrying that the rumor is the reason behind it

Seeing the responsible party doing the same thing to someone else

OPPORTUNITIES TO FACE OR OVERCOME THIS WOUND

Being put in a situation where the rumor could become truth (e.g., being offered a bribe after one was accused of taking bribes)

Being punished because of the rumor (a business going under, a marriage ending, etc.) and wanting to fight against the injustice

After becoming jaded by the experience, one realizes there are good people in the world and not everyone can be painted with the same brush

Deciding to quit something because of the rumor only to discover that by staying, one can provide something another person vitally needs

BEING UNFAIRLY BLAMED FOR SOMEONE'S DEATH

EXAMPLES: Someone might be unfairly blamed for a death when they…
Were unable to deter a friend from driving while impaired
Had a disagreement with someone right before he or she committed suicide
Didn't pick up a pedestrian who was then struck by a vehicle while walking home
Weren't able to stop someone's risk-taking behavior
Didn't recognize a friend's distress (like alcohol poisoning) because of their own impairment
Weren't able to protect a sibling from their own bad decisions
Were the eldest child and a tragedy occurred (e.g., playing outside and a younger sister was kidnapped)
Were roughhousing with a friend who suffered a sudden fall or freak accident
Were unable to reach someone in time (a lifeguard and a drowning swimmer, a fireman and the victim of a house fire, a police officer unable to talk down a jumper, etc.)
Needed to save two people but only had the time or resources to save one
Were wearing a helmet during a quad accident but a friend was not
Were driving during a no-fault accident where someone was killed
Took a sick day and the co-worker covering the shift was killed in a robbery
Missed the signs of a loved one's depression and her plan to take her own life
Were a child who was blamed when their mother died during childbirth

BASIC NEEDS OFTEN COMPROMISED BY THIS WOUND: Safety and security, love and belonging, esteem and recognition, self-actualization

FALSE BELIEFS THAT COULD BE EMBRACED
I should have died instead of my sister (or cousin, mother, friend, etc.).
To make amends, I must live life the way the deceased would have if he (or she) had lived.
I will never be able to make it up to the deceased and the person who blames me.
I do not deserve to be happy or have good things happen.
I am a terrible mother (or father, sister, brother, wife, husband, etc.) for not seeing what was unfolding.
I am not capable of being in charge or making important decisions.
To prove I am capable and worthy, I must be responsible for everything and excel at all I do.

THE CHARACTER MAY FEAR…
Relationships and being responsible for others
Vulnerability
Making mistakes, especially if the death was due to poor judgment
Decision-making and choices, especially those that involve other people
Taking a risk and it leading to more loss of life

POSSIBLE RESPONSES AND RESULTS
Extreme guilt and remorse, even though one was not at fault
Walking on eggshells around those who voice blame

Difficulty with trust and relationships
Shifting between confusion and anger at being persecuted
Always wanting to justify or defend oneself
Being unable to move forward in a healthy way (in relationships, by pursing a passion or dream, etc.)
Focusing on the past and what one could have done differently
Withdrawing from friends and family
Being prone to stress and anxiety; needing to go on medication
Drinking heavily or using drugs to escape
Second-guessing oneself
Being defensive about one's responsibility for what happened
Mood swings
Having trouble sleeping; experiencing nightmares about the accident or event
Having low self-worth, and constantly pushing oneself toward perfection to make up for it
Sacrificing oneself for others, even to the point of being taken advantage of
Trying to be all things for everyone by taking on more work and responsibility
Avoiding responsibility, decision-making, and anything that puts one in charge of others
Always taking the easy path
Hesitating to act out of a fear of choosing incorrectly
Becoming overprotective of loved ones
Recognizing one isn't to blame and that one can't buy into the grief of those unable to move on
Working to help the dead party's family (being available, starting a college fund for a child, etc.)
Being slower to blame others until one can be certain of their guilt

PERSONALITY TRAITS THAT MAY FORM

Attributes: Alert, appreciative, honorable, introverted, just, merciful, nurturing, observant, private, protective, responsible, sentimental, socially aware, spiritual, supportive

Flaws: Addictive, compulsive, controlling, defensive, evasive, indecisive, inflexible, inhibited, insecure, morbid, paranoid, pessimistic, resentful, self-destructive, uncommunicative, volatile, withdrawn

TRIGGERS THAT MIGHT AGGRAVATE THIS WOUND

Situations similar to the one that involved the death
Meeting the victim's loved ones unexpectedly during an outing
The annual anniversary of the incident
Encountering things associated with the victim (a stuffed dog, a specific hand lotion scent, a hat she would have loved, etc.)

OPPORTUNITIES TO FACE OR OVERCOME THIS WOUND

Being in charge when something goes wrong (a child gets hurt or one's carpool vehicle breaks down on the roadside) and having to act quickly to save someone
Being rejected by an important person in one's life due to the accident
Feeling unfulfilled in one's job or relationships due to an inability to take risks or be responsible

EXPERIENCING POVERTY

EXAMPLES
Having an addicted or disabled parent who couldn't keep steady employment
Being raised by grandparents on a fixed budget
Living in a refugee camp
Being kicked out of one's home and having to live on the street
Growing up in a dangerous neighborhood
Being forced to flee one's homeland to start over elsewhere
Becoming homeless for reasons out of one's control

BASIC NEEDS OFTEN COMPROMISED BY THIS WOUND: Physiological needs, safety and security, esteem and recognition, self-actualization

FALSE BELIEFS THAT COULD BE EMBRACED
If you don't toughen up, you won't make it.
You do whatever it takes to survive.
Money is everything.
You have to fight to keep people from taking what's yours.
Life is about making sure you always have enough.
The world doesn't care about you when you're poor.
Right and wrong are luxuries I can't afford.
If I make one mistake, it could happen again.

THE CHARACTER MAY FEAR…
Being forced to go without (food, shelter, medicine, etc.)
Being targeted and harmed for what they have
Being victimized (by hate groups, the government, police, criminals, etc.)
Never having anything better in life
That their children will also become caught in a cycle of poverty
That one accident or emergency will push them from poverty into homelessness

POSSIBLE RESPONSES AND RESULTS
Believing the system is rigged; having no aspirations to escape poverty
Doing whatever it takes (good or bad) to get out of poverty: working twice as hard as others, making sacrifices, getting an education, bending ethical rules, etc.
Making grandiose escape plans that one knows one won't ever try
Becoming hardened and tough
Not thinking farther ahead than the next paycheck or rent bill
Spending money foolishly because one wasn't taught to save or be smart with it
Having preconceived ideas about people with money
Believing what one has always been told: *You're stupid, you'll never get out of this neighborhood, you'll never be good at anything.*

Living on high alert, always on the lookout for danger

Living as a multi-generational family unit out of necessity

Making due with less to avoid going soft

Hoarding money, food, medicine, or other supplies to feel safe

Working multiple jobs to make ends meet or to build a nest egg to safeguard the future

Despising those who have discriminated in the past, like police officers, the well-to-do, or one's in-laws

Growing up and continuing the cycle of poverty (getting pregnant at a young age, not finishing school, having minimal skills, etc.)

If one is now affluent, surrounding oneself with symbols of wealth

Pushing one's children to work hard to succeed

Taking good care of one's sentimental or valuable items

Being deeply loyal to those who have been faithful through hard times

Adopting a community mindset so one has support if times get tough again

Avoiding repeating the cycle by making responsible life choices (choosing a stable neighborhood and job, saving for the future, living modestly, etc.)

Promoting education and teaching personal responsibility so one's children are prepared for life

PERSONALITY TRAITS THAT MAY FORM

Attributes: Adaptable, adventurous, ambitious, appreciative, bold, cautious, centered, empathetic, focused, humble, idealistic, industrious, objective, persistent, protective, resourceful, studious, talented

Flaws: Abrasive, addictive, apathetic, callous, confrontational, cruel, cynical, devious, disrespectful, foolish, frivolous, hostile, humorless, ignorant, inhibited, jealous, macho, mischievous

TRIGGERS THAT MIGHT AGGRAVATE THIS WOUND

Experiencing hunger or going without, even for a short time

Bills that come due all at once, leaving one feeling overwhelmed

The threat that if anything goes wrong (a trip to the emergency room, a car dying, a job loss, etc.) it could tip one back into poverty

Seeing a vagrant on the street

Running into a childhood friend who is still stuck in the same situation

OPPORTUNITIES TO FACE OR OVERCOME THIS WOUND

Escaping poverty yet experiencing the same discrimination one did as a child (for race, religion, etc.)

Trying to better one's situation only to be knocked down by random circumstances

Watching a child fall into traps (quitting school, doing hard drugs, etc.) that could lead to poverty

Wanting to follow a passion or dream but being crippled by the negative voices from one's past

LIVING THROUGH CIVIL UNREST

EXAMPLES: Civil unrest is described as disorder caused by a group of people who are often politically or socially motivated. It runs the gamut from small-duration violent protests to larger-scale riots, destruction, and vigilante justice. This kind of atmosphere, when prolonged, can result in societal breakdowns that affect others in the region, the results of which can include…

Shortages of necessary items, such as food, fuel, and water

Threats to public safety

Riots and increased crime

Infringed freedoms (enforced curfews, illegal home searches, confiscation of personal items, etc.)

Destruction of property

The cessation of necessary services like schooling, medical services, postal delivery, garbage collection, cellular service, and public transportation

The discontinuation of commonplace public utilities, such as electricity and gas

BASIC NEEDS OFTEN COMPROMISED BY THIS WOUND: Physiological needs, safety and security

FALSE BELIEFS THAT COULD BE EMBRACED

I should have seen this coming.

The law doesn't apply to me.

Even when life is unjust, it's better to do as I'm told than make waves.

I can only trust and rely on myself.

We will never recover from this.

Safety is only an illusion.

Underneath the surface, everyone is violent.

THE CHARACTER MAY FEAR…

Being killed

A loved one being killed

Being unable to provide for their family

A family member getting injured or falling ill and being unable to obtain medical care

Running out of necessary resources, or having them forcibly taken away

Abandonment by police, the government, or whomever is providing protection during the unrest

Being in the wrong place at the wrong time

Getting involved in other peoples' problems and being punished for doing so

POSSIBLE RESPONSES AND RESULTS

Increased paranoia and suspicion

Reacting impulsively, without thought

Hyperawareness (of changes to one's environment, sounds, emotions, movement, etc.)

Trying to blend in by disguising one's appearance and hiding truths about oneself that are at odds with those causing the trouble

Watching the news incessantly to learn about increased volatility and places to avoid

Beefing up the security at home (building fortifications, keeping track of family, arming oneself, etc.)

Sleeplessness and heightened anxiety

Forming plans (to escape, where to go in an emergency, what to do if the family is separated, etc.)

Only leaving home when it's absolutely necessary

Being careful with one's words due to not knowing who can be trusted

Watching for indicators that one is being surveilled for signs of disloyalty

Avoiding the most dangerous areas, even if it means a big inconvenience

Stockpiling or rationing emergency supplies

Becoming averse to waste of food, fuel, water, clothing, etc.

Worrying over small things; one's mind jumping to the worst-case scenario

Marking possible exits and escape routes

Preparing an emergency evacuation kit in case one must leave immediately

Not helping others in situations where one would have in the past

Researching topics (such as home remedies, basic first aid, or trapping and hunting) so one can be more independent

Reaching out to those in the immediate community to share resources and manpower

Making plans to fight back against those causing the unrest

PERSONALITY TRAITS THAT MAY FORM

Attributes: Adaptable, alert, analytical, bold, cautious, cooperative, decisive, efficient, independent, kind, loyal, mature, observant, organized, proactive, protective, resourceful, responsible, thrifty

Flaws: Antisocial, apathetic, callous, confrontational, controlling, evasive, fanatical, greedy, hostile, humorless, impulsive, inhibited, paranoid, pessimistic, stingy, uncooperative, unethical, violent

TRIGGERS THAT MIGHT AGGRAVATE THIS WOUND

The sound of gunshots, smell of smoke, or other sensory triggers from the time of unrest

Having one's neighbors suddenly move out in the middle of the night

Passing a group of protestors on the commute to work

A union strike at the business where one works that is growing increasingly hostile

Civil unrest being covered in the news

OPPORTUNITIES TO FACE OR OVERCOME THIS WOUND

Experiencing a natural disaster that creates widespread damage and restricts one's access to resources

Unrest in the workplace (a teacher's strike, a union dispute, etc.) that forces one to choose a side

After escaping the unrest by doing unthinkable things, one is faced with an everyday situation that challenges one's moral code

LIVING THROUGH FAMINE OR DROUGHT

NOTES: Droughts (periods of extended dryness) and famine (prolonged scarcity of food) are very different things that often go hand in hand. The duration of famines and droughts can vary; they can last anywhere from weeks to years. But while longer events are more catastrophic, living through even a short period of time without sufficient food or water can be traumatic.

EXAMPLES: There are many causes for drought and famine, including…
The pollution of a community's only water supply
The damming of a distant river or lake that reduces a community's access to water
Deforestation
Meteorological changes
A large number of people moving to a region that an existing water or food supply can't support
An illness or blight that destroys livestock or crops in an area
A war that depletes a country's food supply, leading to restrictions and sanctions
A corrupt government or ruling regime that purposely withholds food from its people

BASIC NEEDS OFTEN COMPROMISED BY THIS WOUND: Physiological needs, safety and security, self-actualization

FALSE BELIEFS THAT COULD BE EMBRACED
The Have-Nots will always be at the mercy of the Haves.
I can't count on anyone but myself.
Survival is all that matters in this world.
I failed my loved ones by not providing adequately for them.

THE CHARACTER MAY FEAR…
Death
Watching a loved one suffer
Surviving when others do not
Being used by others (if the famine or drought was caused by those in power)
Being hungry or thirsty
Living a mediocre life; dying before being able to do anything important
Being insignificant or expendable

POSSIBLE RESPONSES AND RESULTS
Hiding one's meager resources to avoid being targeted and having those resources taken
Being morally flexible if survival is at stake
Becoming dependent on others who represent safety and security
Choosing safety over love (marrying for stability)
Driving one's children to succeed monetarily

Distrusting the wealthy or powerful

Safeguarding against hard times in the future by being miserly, even when one has means

Embracing certain hardships to avoid going soft, in case another emergency hits

Overeating when food is plentiful

Feeling guilty for the little one has when others are going without

Stockpiling food or water against a future famine or drought

Trying to foresee and plan for events that might reduce one's water and food supply

Relocating to a place where famine and drought aren't common

Being resourceful; making the most of what one has

Being sensitive to food or water waste

Studying hard so one can get a job that will ensure security in the future

Educating oneself on the cause of the event so one can take steps to avoid it in the future

Becoming self-sufficient; maintaining a personal food and water source that isn't provided by others

Being generous with what one has because one knows what it's like to go without

Donating money and time to help those without food or water

Working to raise social awareness for people in the same situation

Appreciating what one has

Respecting the earth's resources

Being more environmentally friendly

PERSONALITY TRAITS THAT MAY FORM

Attributes: Adaptable, alert, ambitious, appreciative, courageous, disciplined, empathetic, focused, generous, independent, patient, resourceful, simple, socially aware, studious, thrifty, unselfish

Flaws: Callous, controlling, cynical, devious, greedy, hostile, humorless, impatient, irrational, materialistic, morbid, obsessive, resentful, scatterbrained, selfish, stingy, suspicious, ungrateful, weak-willed

TRIGGERS THAT MIGHT AGGRAVATE THIS WOUND

The water being shut off in one's building (because of a problem, for maintenance, etc.)

A temporary drought in one's area

A power outage that causes food in a fridge or freezer to spoil

Hunger pangs or thirst

Facing a scenario similar to the event that caused the famine or drought in one's past

Seeing people in one's community who don't have enough to eat

Tasting or smelling the one food that was available and had to be eaten constantly during the event

OPPORTUNITIES TO FACE OR OVERCOME THIS WOUND

Having enough (food, water, etc.) but being reluctant to help others for fear of running out

After sacrificing one's morals to survive the crisis, one recognizes a new lack as a result: a loss of self-esteem and identity

Despite cheating death and surviving a devastating drought, one gets a terrible prognosis (an illness, an inoperable tumor, etc.) that will end one's life prematurely

PREJUDICE OR DISCRIMINATION

NOTES: Prejudice is the forming of ideas or opinions without adequate knowledge or facts. People can show prejudice against others based on a person's race or ethnicity, religion, social class, gender, sexual orientation, age, level of education, beliefs, or other criteria. When unfounded judgments are made, discrimination—behaviors or actions taken against individuals due to prejudice—often follows.

BASIC NEEDS OFTEN COMPROMISED BY THIS WOUND: Physiological needs, safety and security, love and belonging, esteem and recognition, self-actualization

FALSE BELIEFS THAT COULD BE EMBRACED
Everyone is prejudiced.
I'll never succeed because my race (or beliefs, religion, etc.) will always work against me.
People will never see the real me, just my (race, gender, disability, etc.).
I will take everything I can because the world owes me.
Friendships and relationships outside of my religion (or race, age, etc.) don't work.
God hates me. I must have done something to be treated this way.
Why accept others when no one accepts me?
The only thing that makes people pay attention is violence.

THE CHARACTER MAY FEAR...
Being attacked or targeted
Their loved ones being attacked and targeted
Their rights being infringed or taken away
Building or achieving something and it being stripped away
Being limited in life because of discrimination
Being ostracized by their own group and losing the security they find there
Becoming what they hate (feeling prejudice and discriminating against others)

POSSIBLE RESPONSES AND RESULTS
Hiding or lying about one's race, orientation, beliefs, etc.
Feelings of inadequacy and self-doubt
Listening to propaganda and feeling ashamed of who one is
Mistrusting the motives of others
Giving up activities or interests that support one's ethnicity, gender, etc.
Being hyperaware of stereotypes and either embracing them fully or avoiding them
Losing one's sense of identity out of a need to be accepted by others
Only hanging out with people one can relate to
Wanting to apply stereotypes to one's opposition but also wanting to rising above that mentality
Believing what others say
Becoming what one is accused of being (fulfilling the prophecy)
Emotional volatility

Reacting to prejudice with violence

Perceiving slights where there are none

Becoming prejudiced against other groups

Suffering in silence; not telling anyone about what's happening

Lowering one's expectations

Hopelessness and depression

Doubting one's abilities

Self-medicating with drugs or alcohol

Having a pessimistic view of the world

Avoiding the people and places who have discriminated against one in the past

Wanting to be politically active but fearing backlash and targeting

Withdrawing into oneself

Refusing to confide in or seek help from people not of one's race, orientation, etc. because of an assumption that they won't understand or care

Trying to be perfect so no one will be able to find fault

Engaging the authorities (or a powerful group) in an effort to stop the prejudice

Fighting the social injustice via protesting, boycotting, or soliciting lawmakers to affect change

Finding a healthy outlet for one's feelings (e.g., joining a group or club of people with similar beliefs)

Rebelling in a healthy way by embracing who one is and dismissing the opinions of others

PERSONALITY TRAITS THAT MAY FORM

Attributes: Ambitious, bold, centered, cooperative, courageous, optimistic, passionate, persistent, socially aware, spunky, tolerant

Flaws: Antisocial, confrontational, disloyal, hostile, hypocritical, ignorant, inhibited, insecure, judgmental, resentful, subservient

TRIGGERS THAT MIGHT AGGRAVATE THIS WOUND

Experiencing prejudice in a place one perceived as being safe (church, a family gathering, etc.)

One's child being the victim of prejudice or discrimination

Seeing a loved one lowering their standards and dreams in the wake of discrimination

Someone with racist tendencies coming into power and threatening one's basic rights

Witnessing a group of people protesting one's race, religion, etc. in one's country

OPPORTUNITIES TO FACE OR OVERCOME THIS WOUND

Having someone not of one's race, religion, age, creed, etc. extend the hand of friendship

While protecting one's rights, the rights of others are infringed, leading to the realization that prejudice can affect anyone, not just those in one's group

Blaming prejudice when one was passed over for a promotion only to discover that the winning candidate was indeed more deserving

Imparting life lessons to a younger person and realizing that society has progressed in the area of discrimination or prejudice, giving one hope

UNREQUITED LOVE

NOTES: In this scenario, the character loves someone who doesn't return that love. Often, the beloved knows about the character's feelings but doesn't feel the same way. In other cases, the beloved is oblivious to how the character feels, and the character is left to pine away in silence.

EXAMPLES: Caring for someone who…
Doesn't care for one in the same way
Is oblivious to one's feelings
Is married or in a committed relationship
Used to be with a best friend or sibling
It's taboo for one to be with (due to race, age differences, religious constraints, family expectations, societal prejudices, etc.)

BASIC NEEDS OFTEN COMPROMISED BY THIS WOUND: Love and belonging, esteem and recognition, self-actualization

FALSE BELIEFS THAT COULD BE EMBRACED
Life isn't worth living without this person's love.
We aren't together because I'm not good enough.
This person is the only one for me.
If I prove my worth, she (or he) will come around.
If I change enough, he (or she) will see what a perfect match we are.

THE CHARACTER MAY FEAR…
Revealing their love
Being rejected by the beloved and losing access to them
Being rejected by other love interests (because if the beloved has turned them down, there must be something wrong with them)
Being ridiculed or laughed at by the beloved or others
Never finding someone who measures up to the beloved
Never finding love at all

POSSIBLE RESPONSES AND RESULTS
Taking every opportunity to be near the person
Stalking him or her (online and off)
Taking an interest in his or her hobbies, passions, and activities
Examining every interaction with the beloved for signs of affection
Missing opportunities for romance with others because of one's focus on the beloved
Sabotaging the person's romantic relationships
Comparing suitors to the beloved and finding them lacking
Doing whatever the person wants out of a desire to win his or her love
Putting the beloved's desires and goals ahead of one's own

Taking pride in knowing the beloved better than anyone else

Fantasizing about being with this person

Becoming depressed and crying frequently

Going through periods of despair where one sees no hope of the dream coming to fruition

Making other relationships secondary (e.g., cancelling a night out with a friend if the beloved asks one to do something)

Always being available (sitting at home instead of going out, waiting for the phone to ring, etc.)

Vowing that if the beloved doesn't return one's feelings, one will never love anyone again

Vacillating between love, resentment, and anger toward the object of one's affection

Using any means possible to gain the beloved's attention

Believing that a personal defect is the reason for the rejection

Self-doubt and decreased confidence; questioning one's intuition

Feeling deeply lonely, even though one might be surrounded by friends and family

Self-medicating through the abuse of drugs, alcohol, or food

Seeking out other partners in an effort to get over one's beloved

Being angry at oneself for being unable to let go

Putting the person out of one's mind as a way of moving on

Focusing on work, school, sports, and other hobbies to get one's mind off the beloved

Seeing one's ability to love wholeheartedly as a gift that can be applied to other relationships

Recognizing that one is just as worthwhile as the beloved and is deserving of happiness

PERSONALITY TRAITS THAT MAY FORM

Attributes: Affectionate, analytical, cautious, diplomatic, discreet, empathetic, flirtatious, friendly, idealistic, loyal, observant, optimistic, passionate, patient, persistent, supportive, trusting, unselfish

Flaws: Catty, cynical, fanatical, foolish, grumpy, gullible, inhibited, insecure, jealous, manipulative, nagging, needy, nosy, obsessive, possessive, pushy, resentful, stubborn, subservient, timid

TRIGGERS THAT MIGHT AGGRAVATE THIS WOUND

Moving on only to misread another romantic situation and how the other party feels

Meeting someone with the same name as the beloved

Watching a co-worker try and cross the "friend zone" with a mutual friend and be successful

The beloved starting a relationship with someone one knows well, such as a friend or sibling

Seeing others fall in love and yearning for the same happiness

OPPORTUNITIES TO FACE OR OVERCOME THIS WOUND

Recognizing a pattern of falling into love with unattainable people and wishing to break the cycle

Noticing that one has changed dramatically in order to gain someone's love (becoming possessive, losing one's will and becoming whatever the beloved wants, etc.) and not liking it

Watching friends meet their soul mates while one is still languishing in this one-sided relationship

Seeing a darker side of the beloved and second-guessing whether he or she is worthy of one's love

WRONGFUL IMPRISONMENT

EXAMPLES
Being mistaken for a criminal with physical similarities
Being set up as a scapegoat for someone else
Being found guilty due to a prejudiced jury or judge
Being found guilty due to the testimony of a mistaken or coerced witness

BASIC NEEDS OFTEN COMPROMISED BY THIS WOUND: Physiological needs, safety and security, love and belonging, esteem and recognition, self-actualization

FALSE BELIEFS THAT COULD BE EMBRACED
God must be punishing me for something I've done.
The system I trusted betrayed me; I'll never be able to trust anyone or anything again.
There's no point in following the rules if I'm going to be punished anyway.
Something was stolen from me and I will never be whole again.
Even if I get out, this will always follow me.
If I let someone else be in control, they're going to take advantage of me.
The only justice I trust comes from my own hand.

THE CHARACTER MAY FEAR...
That they will never get out of jail
Being further victimized through an assault during the incarceration
Rejection; losing loved ones who believe in their guilt
Trusting others
The heartache that hope represents
People or a system that has power over their fate
That those in power will suppress new evidence to cover up the miscarriage of justice
That the truth will never come to light
Losing their identity through the trials of this ordeal

POSSIBLE RESPONSES AND RESULTS
Distrusting those in authority
Flouting the rules since following them didn't do any good
Hating and acting out against the people one believes are to blame
Turning away from one's faith
Becoming suspicious of the institutions and people one formerly trusted
Withdrawing from loved ones (returning letters or not showing up on visiting days) as a way of leaving them before they can do the same
Clinging tightly to loved ones
Being upset by disruptions to one's access to loved ones (letters from home being held by those in charge, visits being cancelled, etc.); seeing these as further injustices
Not trusting what anyone has to say

Doubting oneself

Sucking up to the people who can help or offer protection

Becoming pessimistic or cynical in one's thoughts and words

Lowering one's expectations regarding what one will or can do

Resisting control as much as one can on the inside

Becoming controlling of others

Becoming antisocial; being disillusioned and fighting everyone and everything

Fantasizing about revenge against those who are to blame for one's imprisonment

Engaging in self-destructive behaviors (using drugs, abusing alcohol, picking fights, etc.)

Becoming institutionalized over time; going with the flow of the routine rather than fighting it

Being determined to prove one's innocence as a way of striking back

Educating oneself to self-advocate and try to figure out what happened

Seeking to change the system that's broken

Growing stronger in one's faith

Making the most of one's situation rather than focusing on the things one can't change

PERSONALITY TRAITS THAT MAY FORM

Attributes: Adaptable, ambitious, calm, cautious, focused, industrious, just, observant, organized, pensive, persistent, philosophical, private, proactive, resourceful, socially aware, thrifty, tolerant

Flaws: Abrasive, addictive, antisocial, apathetic, callous, confrontational, controlling, cynical, defensive, hostile, pessimistic, resentful, temperamental, timid, uncooperative, volatile, withdrawn

TRIGGERS THAT MIGHT AGGRAVATE THIS WOUND

Watching TV programming or reading articles about life on the outside

Telling the truth about something else and not being believed again

Being falsely accused of something minor

Being called a murderer, a pervert, a psychopath, etc. (depending on what one is in for)

Talking to other inmates about their lives before jail

Mementos (letters, photos, etc.) that remind one of home

Dates that hold significance, such as one's sentencing date or a child's birthday

OPPORTUNITIES TO FACE OR OVERCOME THIS WOUND

One's appeal being denied

Leaving jail after a sentence ends but facing persecution on the outside

Realizing a dream is out of reach due to one's record and facing a choice: adjust the goal or give up

Experiencing rejection by someone who should be loyal

Evidence coming to light that is being suppressed by those who don't want the case reopened

Misplaced Trust and Betrayals

A SIBLING'S BETRAYAL

EXAMPLES

A sibling starting false rumors or perpetuating existing ones

A sister exposing one's shameful or embarrassing secret, like drug use or deviant behavior

A brother reporting one's crime to the authorities

A sister taking sides with one's rivals out of spite or to gain an advantage

Siblings who stage an intervention for drug addiction, drinking, or hoarding

A sister misrepresenting the truth to one's parents to gain their favor

One's twin openly acting inappropriately around one's husband or wife, then denying it

A brother engaging in an affair with one's partner

A sibling who turns others (family members, friends, a love interest, etc.) against one

A sibling taking advantage of a caregiver role to steal funds from one's elderly parents

BASIC NEEDS OFTEN COMPROMISED BY THIS WOUND: Safety and security,
love and belonging, esteem and recognition, self-actualization

FALSE BELIEFS THAT COULD BE EMBRACED

Whatever I have, someone will always take it.

My sibling only wants to hold me back or ruin my life.

Blood is no thicker than water.

What's the point of trying to excel when I'll only be one-upped by him?

Even my family doesn't respect me.

I am gullible and weak.

I'd be better off as an only child.

When you let people get close, they stab you in the back.

THE CHARACTER MAY FEAR…

Vulnerability

Failure and the resulting ridicule

Achievements being sabotaged

Their secrets and dirty laundry being exposed

Trusting the wrong person

Losing family members due to the sibling's lies (not getting to see nieces or nephews, having parents turn against them, etc.)

Being rejected by a loved one who believes a sibling's lie or skewed account of events

POSSIBLE RESPONSES AND RESULTS

Avoiding family members, especially one's sibling

Refusing to speak to or about the sibling

Talking badly about one's brother or sister to others

Making excuses to get out of social engagements when the sibling will be attending

Having a distanced relationship with nieces and nephews

Cutting the individual out of one's life (online and off)

Not sharing any personal information online

Growing quiet or irritable when one is forced to be around one's sibling

Lying to one's sibling when the truth matters to them

Difficulty sharing personal desires, goals, or feelings with others

Withdrawing into oneself; developing depression or anxiety

Forcing family members and friends to take sides

Being unable to let go; discussing the event often with others

Self-harming to deal with the pain

Turning every situation in which the sibling is involved into a competition

Playing the blame game

Refusing to accept responsibility for the rift or what caused it, even if one shares the blame

Jumping to conclusions; seeing the worst-case scenario when it involves the sibling

Looking for opportunities to take revenge or complicate things for one's sibling

Needing to be the best at everything to prove one's self-worth

Holding onto anger even if an action was justified, such as an intervention meant to save one's life

Being overly sensitive to signs of disloyalty from others

Vetting others carefully before letting them in and opening up to them

Creating healthy boundaries for the toxic people in one's life

Disengaging in a healthy way; refusing to be a player in situations involving power and control

Becoming a safe haven for others who have experienced betrayal and rejection by loved ones

PERSONALITY TRAITS THAT MAY FORM

Attributes: Cautious, disciplined, discreet, empathetic, focused, independent, industrious, introverted, simple, resourceful, tolerant

Flaws: Controlling, cruel, defensive, impulsive, insecure, judgmental, martyr, self-destructive, suspicious, uncommunicative, vindictive, withdrawn

TRIGGERS THAT MIGHT AGGRAVATE THIS WOUND

Perceived disloyalty from someone else

Overhearing unkind gossip or secrets being spilled about someone

Hearing a family member reference the old feud as if one's sibling was innocent

Being falsely accused of being disloyal to a friend, family member, one's child, or co-worker

Family gatherings where one's sibling may be present

OPPORTUNITIES TO FACE OR OVERCOME THIS WOUND

Discovering a dark secret about the sibling and facing a moral conflict as to whether to keep it or not

Learning that a friend has committed a crime and should be turned in, but doing so requires betraying their trust

Seeing one's child pull away due to the untruths being propagated by family members

Working to mend the relationship with the sibling only to be betrayed by him or her again

A TOXIC RELATIONSHIP

NOTES: A toxic relationship is one where the behaviors and attitudes of one person are consistently emotionally (and possibly physically) damaging to the other. While many times this occurs between romantic couples, it can happen between friends, co-workers, an employee and boss, a parent and child, siblings—any relationship where emotions are invested.

EXAMPLES: Relationships where one person…
Controls the other
Is jealous or possessive
Constantly lies
Gets what they want through manipulation and coercion
Physically or verbally abuses the other person, sabotaging their self-esteem
Makes the other person feel small, unimportant, or devalued
Plays the victim, always blaming the other person and denying responsibility for wrongdoing
Is chronically negative (always complaining)
Cheats repeatedly on the other
Is overly perfectionistic, with unrealistic expectations for others
Is extremely competitive and needs to win at everything

BASIC NEEDS OFTEN COMPROMISED BY THIS WOUND: Safety and security, love and belonging, esteem and recognition, self-actualization

FALSE BELIEFS THAT COULD BE EMBRACED
Some people are broken, but I can fix them.
When someone lashes out or hurts me, I shouldn't take it personally.
Leaving people who need you would be selfish and disloyal.
I'm being treated badly by people because I deserve it.
Things will change when we get married (or have a baby, get away from my parents, etc.).
No one else will give me a chance; this is the best I can do.

THE CHARACTER MAY FEAR…
Hurting someone who clearly needs love and acceptance
Not having the strength or will to get out of a bad relationship
Never being good enough for someone else
Being a magnet for negativity and those who are toxic
Being trapped in a situation so long they also become toxic (pessimistic, hateful to others, etc.)

POSSIBLE RESPONSES AND RESULTS
Always giving in to others
Invalidating one's feelings as being selfish, over-reactive, or irrational
Feeling like one can never be oneself; always wearing a mask or adopting a persona to please others
Distancing oneself from everyone except the toxic person

Believing the lies people tell; being gullible

Wanting to "fix" others

Developing a martyr complex

Doubting one's instincts

Internalizing the negative things the toxic person says, or making excuses for that person

Depression

Being drawn to other people who are toxic in some way

Feeling resentful toward those who take but never give, then feeling guilty for the resentment

Adopting a toxic person's bad habits, like gossiping, complaining, lying, or manipulating

Feeling isolated, even in a relationship, because one is used to suppressing one's feelings

Giving more than one receives

Struggling with a problem and having no outlet because one is used to friendships being one-sided

Not wanting to share one's good news with others because one is so used to negative responses

Doing things one doesn't want to do out of fear, guilt, or a sense of obligation

An increasingly negative outlook on life

Avoiding people who are takers

Recognizing the signs of toxicity in other relationships

Being highly empathetic

Being a peacekeeper through fairness and respect

Learning how to stand up for oneself and self-advocate

PERSONALITY TRAITS THAT MAY FORM

Attributes: Adaptable, affectionate, alert, cautious, cooperative, easygoing, empathetic, gentle, humble, loyal, nurturing, obedient, responsible, sentimental, supportive, tolerant, trusting

Flaws: Addictive, dishonest, disloyal, evasive, gossipy, gullible, humorless, hypocritical, ignorant, indecisive, inhibited, insecure, jealous, martyr, needy, subservient, temperamental, timid, weak-willed

TRIGGERS THAT MIGHT AGGRAVATE THIS WOUND

Being around someone who likes to complain and vent

Receiving phone calls, texts, or visits from a toxic friend and feeling emotionally drained

Catching someone in even a small lie, indiscretion, or manipulation

Being asked for one too many favors or sacrifices

Someone making a threat to do something if one doesn't fall in line

Having to steer the conversation out of a danger zone because someone is emotionally volatile

OPPORTUNITIES TO FACE OR OVERCOME THIS WOUND

Recognizing that one is no longer happy and tracing the cause back to the toxic person in one's life

Passing up an opportunity to pursue a dream because of a toxic person and then realizing the mistake

Realizing that one is happier alone than with the toxic person

Meeting someone who is upbeat and optimistic who acts as a reminder of who one used to be before the toxic people set up camp

ABANDONMENT OVER AN UNEXPECTED PREGNANCY

NOTES: Many wounds stem from conditional love: *you didn't try hard enough*; *you embarrassed me*; *you broke my rules.* Having a child, despite the joy that usually accompanies it, is one of the most stressful life events that someone can experience, and if a pregnancy is unexpected or unwanted, the stress compounds. When the person coming to grips with this surprising change is then abandoned by her support system (in the form of parents, a lover, or a spouse), it's devastating. Either parent could be shunned in this situation, but because the mother typically bears the brunt of the rejection, this entry will focus on the wounding event from her perspective.

BASIC NEEDS OFTEN COMPROMISED BY THIS WOUND: Physiological needs, safety and security, love and belonging, esteem and recognition, self-actualization

FALSE BELIEFS THAT COULD BE EMBRACED
Now I'll never achieve my dreams.
What they say about me is true (I'm a whore, I'm stupid, I'm irresponsible, etc.).
The baby is the cause of all my trouble.
Love is temporary.
People always leave when times get tough.
I don't need anyone else.

THE CHARACTER MAY FEAR…
Being abandoned again
The judgment of others
Being spiritually condemned
Always being alone
Being unable to care for herself and her baby
Never achieving a dream because all her time and resources will go toward being a mother

POSSIBLE RESPONSES AND RESULTS
Living in denial; going about life as if one isn't pregnant
Hiding one's pregnancy from others out of the fear that they, too, will respond with rejection
Choosing to have an abortion or give the baby up for adoption
Struggling to meet one's physiological needs
Calling in favors from friends
Turning to people who are likely to help
Trying to reconcile with the offending party
Employing any means to get the offending party back (manipulation, lying, blackmail, etc.)
Becoming a taker; taking the help others give without offering anything in return
Being emotionally unavailable with others
Being so consumed with day-to-day living that other goals (improving oneself, making new friends, furthering one's education, etc.) become impossible

Wallowing in self-pity or blame for what happened
Looking for a replacement partner
Blaming the child for one's abandonment
Running the offending party down at every opportunity
Changing oneself in order to win back the person who left
Maintaining superficial relationships out of a fear of being rejected again
Worrying about one's abilities to cope alone
Doubting one's abilities as a mother
Lowering one's standards for a mate if it means finding someone to help (any port in a storm)
Determining that one (or one's child) will be a better person than those who did the abandoning
Finding a support group
Volunteering to help other women in one's situation
Taking responsibility for one's actions and maturing quickly in order to succeed

PERSONALITY TRAITS THAT MAY FORM

Attributes: Appreciative, ambitious, bold, centered, cooperative, courageous, disciplined, efficient, empathetic, focused, independent, mature, persuasive, resourceful, responsible, simple, supportive

Flaws: Apathetic, callous, childish, cynical, ignorant, inflexible, insecure, irresponsible, judgmental, manipulative, needy, nervous, resentful, self-indulgent, subservient, ungrateful, volatile

TRIGGERS THAT MIGHT AGGRAVATE THIS WOUND

Seeing couples work together to care for a new baby
Running into the baby's father, who clearly wishes the meeting didn't happen
Going to a pre-natal care group filled with couples who are happy about their pregnancies
Experiencing morning sickness or the baby kicking and moving around
Looking in the mirror and seeing the obvious signs of pregnancy
Attending medical appointments and weigh-ins

OPPORTUNITIES TO FACE OR OVERCOME THIS WOUND

Unable to find support, the character realizes that she can't depend on others to help her but must take charge of her own health and the baby's future
The pregnancy taking a turn for the worse that makes it more difficult to get by on one's own
Meeting someone supportive who offers to help, then discovering they're not who they claimed to be
Having an opportunity to help another who has been abandoned by loved ones in a time of need

BEING DISAPPOINTED BY A ROLE MODEL

EXAMPLES
Learning about a pastor's affair
A teacher's arrest or coach's drug peddling being discovered
A parent being charged with propositioning a prostitute
An older sibling being caught selling drugs
A respected boss being caught embezzling from a business or nonprofit organization
A family member scamming seniors out of pension checks
A favorite uncle or aunt being accused of child abuse
One's parent or sibling lying about a severe addiction (to drugs, alcohol, gambling, etc.)
Close friends who preach Christian values but are involved in unethical activities
A parent or close friend's infidelity
A family member or friend who was on the take, like a police officer or judge
An athletic cousin who preached clean living but was caught doping for a competition
A beloved relative's bad choices that led to public humiliation and dragged the family name through the mud

BASIC NEEDS OFTEN COMPROMISED BY THIS WOUND: Physiological needs, safety and security, love and belonging, esteem and recognition

FALSE BELIEFS THAT COULD BE EMBRACED
People are all hypocrites.
I have no one to look up to.
I can't be an example for others; I'll just fail like everyone else.
Why try to be a good person when no one else is?
Why work hard when the world rewards cheaters?
I need to keep my distance from people so they can't abuse my trust.
Following rules is for chumps.
At the end of the day, everyone is just out for themselves.
People pretend to be genuine, but they aren't.
I need to be more of a taker if I want to make it in this world.

THE CHARACTER MAY FEAR...
Trusting the wrong person
Vulnerability or being exposed in some way
Being taken advantage of
Moral failure (giving into temptation or being weak)
Those in authority or positions of power and influence (if this factored into the disillusionment)
Sharing ideas, beliefs, or convictions only to have them stolen or used against them
Responsibility; being viewed as a role model and failing others
Having to place their trust or fate in another's hands

POSSIBLE RESPONSES AND RESULTS

Refusing to share information, especially anything personal

Being distrustful of others; always looking for ulterior motives

Avoiding close friendships or relationships and becoming unsocial

A suspicious nature that makes it difficult to relax around people

Adopting antisocial behaviors and encouraging others to buck the system to expose corruption (if this factored into the original disillusionment)

Watching what one says to avoid giving true feelings away

Antagonism and bias toward people who remind one of the disgraced role model

Avoiding a sport or activity tied to the person who caused the disillusionment

Refusing to make long-term plans or big goals, especially any that rely on others for success

Becoming unteachable; being unwilling to accept instruction from anyone

Cutting the guilty person, organization, or group out of one's life

Being unable to forgive people, even for the smallest transgressions

Avoiding responsibility or decisions that may cause one to fail others

Developing high moral standards and condemning others who do not adhere to one's beliefs

Confronting the role model

Determining to never disappoint those who view one as a role model

Actively seeking out young people to mentor so they'll have a dependable influence in their lives

Fine-tuning one's discernment capabilities so one can judge whether people are trustworthy or not

Finding trustworthy role models for one's children and subtly pushing them toward those people

PERSONALITY TRAITS THAT MAY FORM

Attributes: Alert, analytical, bold, cautious, discreet, empathetic, honorable, hospitable, independent, just, kind, observant, pensive, perceptive, private, proactive, responsible, sensible, wise

Flaws: Abrasive, antisocial, apathetic, confrontational, cynical, defensive, dishonest, evasive, hostile, humorless, uncommunicative, vindictive, volatile, withdrawn

TRIGGERS THAT MIGHT AGGRAVATE THIS WOUND

A news story where a beloved icon (an athlete, singer, or public figure) is caught breaking the law

Learning that the same person who let one down has done it again to someone else

Seeing one's child be devastatingly disappointed by a role model he or she trusted

Friends acting hypocritical (e.g., telling their teens not to drink and drive but doing so themselves)

OPPORTUNITIES TO FACE OR OVERCOME THIS WOUND

Wanting to believe in something bigger than oneself but being afraid the leaders will only disappoint again

Failing in the same way one's mentor failed in the past

Forgiving the role model's indiscretion and becoming victimized by him or her again

Needing a mentor to help with a life decision but recognizing there is no one to turn to due to one's inability to trust

BEING DISOWNED OR SHUNNED

EXAMPLES
Being kicked out of a group or organization one has been loyal to
Being excommunicated from a church
A child running away from home and not returning
A child's abandonment by a parent
A family feud where one is not allowed contact with one's grandchildren
One's child seeking emancipation
An adult being shunned by his parents (after coming out, for converting to a different religion, for marrying outside of the family's race, etc.)
Being disowned for getting pregnant out of wedlock
Being shunned for perceived disloyalty to the family (accusing a sibling of abuse, testifying against an uncle who was guilty of a crime, etc.)

BASIC NEEDS OFTEN COMPROMISED BY THIS WOUND: Physiological needs, safety and security, love and belonging, esteem and recognition

FALSE BELIEFS THAT COULD BE EMBRACED
I can't survive without them.
I need to keep my distance from others so I won't be hurt in this way again.
If I want people to accept me, doing what's right must be secondary to loyalty.
I'm so terrible to be around; people want nothing to do with me.
If they could throw me aside so easily, they didn't love me in the first place.
Love and acceptance are always conditional.
Takers take, and givers are discarded when they have no more to give.

THE CHARACTER MAY FEAR...
Never finding acceptance
Being on their own and failing
Being abandoned again because of a failure or mistake
Never finding someone who will love or accept them unconditionally
That they are as weak (or disloyal, unsuitable, defective, etc.) as others say they are

POSSIBLE RESPONSES AND RESULTS
Bottling up one's emotions
Experiencing a wide range of emotions (sadness, anger, depression, rage, etc.)
Feeling empty inside
Wanting to hurt the people responsible
Rejecting all lessons imparted by the offending party (throwing the baby out with the bathwater)
Obsessing over one's choices that led to the disownment
Critical self-assessments that cause low self-esteem or even self-loathing
Looking for love wherever one can find it

Getting into new relationships that are as toxic as the previous one

Becoming depressed around the holidays and special occasions

Self-medicating

Using social media to stalk those who disowned one as a way of staying connected

Avoiding the places where one might run into former loved ones or group members

Becoming bitter and resentful

Maligning the offending party on social media

Holding grudges

Difficulty trusting people or letting them in

Difficulty committing to long-term relationships

Leaving a loved one before he or she can be the one to leave

Taking subversive measures to contact extended family (nieces or nephews, grandkids, etc.)

Cutting all ties (changing one's phone number, moving, switching schools and work locations, etc.)

Becoming a people pleaser to connect with others and avoid being rejected

Growing anxious when there's conflict and seeking to quickly diffuse it

Highly appreciating being included by others

Being very moved by another's thoughtfulness, such as a birthday card left on one's desk at work

Going through the grieving process

Moving away in an effort to start clean

Finding a support group (at church or in the neighborhood) with a mandate of open acceptance

Examining one's actions to see if or how one may have contributed to the situation

PERSONALITY TRAITS THAT MAY FORM

Attributes: Appreciative, bold, cautious, diplomatic, easygoing, honorable, hospitable, independent, industrious, supportive, tolerant

Flaws: Abrasive, evasive, flaky, gossipy, hostile, insecure, needy, nervous, oversensitive, perfectionist, rebellious, resentful, self-destructive, stubborn

TRIGGERS THAT MIGHT AGGRAVATE THIS WOUND

Rejection, even on a small scale, like being turned down for an after-work drink

Facing an important milestone without the estranged party by one's side

Discovering that the people who disowned one have welcomed new people into the fold (by adoption, embracing a sibling's new boyfriend, opening the doors to new group members, etc.)

Facing a difficult situation where one really needs support but has none

OPPORTUNITIES TO FACE OR OVERCOME THIS WOUND

A healthy relationship turning serious, creating a decision: end it before the other person can do so, or stick it out and risk vulnerability and possible rejection

The offender wanting to reconcile, creating a choice of whether or not one should give them a second chance

A situation where one is tempted to shun one's own child (for drug abuse, theft, violence, etc.)

BEING LET DOWN BY A
TRUSTED ORGANIZATION OR SOCIAL SYSTEM

EXAMPLES
An employee witnessing corruption within his or her company
Discovering that a charity one supports is scamming people out of their money
A prisoner-of-war (POW) being abandoned by his government
A veteran being denied medical or psychological care
Discovering a trusted news network is slanting reports or ignoring stories based on politics or ratings
Being found guilty of a crime one didn't commit
A child being abused or neglected in the foster care system
A student telling teachers and administration about bullying and being dismissed, ignored, or blamed
Dedicating one's life to a company only to be unfairly fired or laid off
Families suffering in a war-torn area while the government does nothing to help
A minority being mistreated by the police
Voters finding out that an election was rigged
Citizens discovering that their government aided terrorists and the country's enemies
Citizens learning that the person in charge of the country is a puppet doing someone else's bidding
Parents learning that a child's education was undermined by curriculum and testing experiments
A citizen discovering that the government approved unhealthy foods or medicines to maintain working relationships with certain lobbyists or companies
Parishioners learning about hypocritical or abusive behavior by the clergy
Citizens falling sick and learning that a local corporation's illegal environmental practices are to blame

BASIC NEEDS OFTEN COMPROMISED BY THIS WOUND: Safety and security, love and belonging, esteem and recognition

FALSE BELIEFS THAT COULD BE EMBRACED
I was too stupid and gullible to see the truth.
Big corporations and organizations are always self-serving and unethical.
Everyone has an agenda.
Educating ourselves is pointless since we're always being misled.
It's better to not engage than to join a group and be betrayed.
Everybody lies.

THE CHARACTER MAY FEAR...
Established organizations and systems, such as government, religion, or public education
Being taken advantage of
Being misled by someone in power
Supporting a person or group who turns out to be unworthy
Speaking out and then being punished for it

POSSIBLE RESPONSES AND RESULTS

Distancing oneself from the guilty organization or business

Mistrusting any large organizations or systems

Finding ways around suspect systems (stashing money at home rather than keeping it in a bank, homeschooling one's child so they don't have to attend school, leaving the country, etc.)

Becoming cynical and negative

Becoming a conspiracy theorist; believing everyone to be suspect

Doubting one's instincts

Allowing one's distrust to seep into all areas of one's life

Always believing the negative, and being susceptible to negative propaganda as a result

Negative self-talk: *I'm so stupid; an idiot would've seen that coming,* etc.

Apathy; accepting the uncomfortable truth with an attitude of despair

Constantly harping about the offending company and what they've done

Passing along mistrust and biases to one's children

Difficulty forgiving transgressions

Refusing to believe people can change

Trying to effect change by bringing the corruption to light

Warning others about the injustice one has seen

Personally vetting organizations before deciding whether or not to support them

Starting a watchdog site to help others find trustworthy charities and businesses

Dedicating oneself to finding the truth rather than taking someone else's word for it

PERSONALITY TRAITS THAT MAY FORM

Attributes: Bold, centered, cooperative, courageous, curious, disciplined, discreet, empathetic, focused, industrious, inspirational, just, organized, passionate, socially aware

Flaws: Apathetic, callous, confrontational, controlling, disrespectful, fanatical, gossipy, ignorant, inhibited, insecure, irrational, melodramatic, nosy, obsessive, paranoid, rebellious, rowdy

TRIGGERS THAT MIGHT AGGRAVATE THIS WOUND

Using social media to shed light on an inconsistency and being shot down by opposition

Speaking out against the company and being dismissed or maligned

Voicing criticism and being punished for it (e.g., criticizing the IRS and suddenly being audited)

Hearing about another corrupt organization taking advantage of innocent people

OPPORTUNITIES TO FACE OR OVERCOME THIS WOUND

Being afraid to speak out against the organization, then learning that others are also being misled

Being asked to join a class-action lawsuit against the organization

Learning that a close friend is falling into the organization's trap

Not wanting to support a group or system but having no choice (like having to send a child to public school)

Being approached by a reporter who offers one an opportunity to blow the whistle

BEING REJECTED BY ONE'S PEERS

EXAMPLES: Being rejected…
Because one lives in the wrong neighborhood or goes to a different school
For being poor or homeless
Because of one's race, religion or sexual orientation
Because one's parent or caregiver is despised (for being in jail, a known philanderer or alcoholic, etc.)
Due to having a notorious sibling or parent and being guilty by association
For embracing beliefs or ideas that go against the popular norm
For a physical disfigurement (being an albino, having severe acne or extreme birthmarks, being morbidly obese, etc.)
For acting in a way that is unsettling (coming across as creepy, dangerous, or unpredictable)
For a publicly humiliating event from one's past, like wetting one's pants or passing out naked
Because one is socially awkward
For having a mental disability, developmental deficiency, or special need
Due to not meeting society's norms in some way (lacking markers of beauty, grace, hygiene, etc.)
Liking things that are considered weird, taboo, or juvenile

BASIC NEEDS OFTEN COMPROMISED BY THIS WOUND: Safety and security, love and belonging, esteem and recognition, self-actualization

FALSE BELIEFS THAT COULD BE EMBRACED
I'll never find love or acceptance.
No one will ever be able to get past my handicap, my situation, etc. to see the real me.
Relationships aren't for people like me.
I am defective.
People like me can only have so much in life. I shouldn't want more.
If I prove my worth in some way, they'll finally accept me.
Because I'm ugly (or stupid, untalented, etc.) I'm worth less than other people.
I don't need anyone else to get by.
Getting back at them will balance the scales.

THE CHARACTER MAY FEAR…
Rejection by others
Prejudice and discrimination for being different
Opening up to or being vulnerable with others only to be abandoned when times get tough
A secret coming to light that could result in further rejection
The kind of person they were rejected by (men, jocks, popular girls, etc.)
That they are unlovable or unworthy of love
Having certain dreams or hopes that society says they cannot obtain

POSSIBLE RESPONSES AND RESULTS
Having low self-esteem and self-worth
Mentally putting oneself down (believing the lie)
Withdrawing from others
Allowing oneself to be mistreated so one can be part of a group
Giving up the habits, hobbies, or beliefs that one is being persecuted for embracing
Hiding the thing that causes one to be mistreated
An inability to trust others
Suspicion of anyone who reaches out
Belittling oneself to make others laugh and gain temporary acceptance
Losing one's identity in an effort to become what is acceptable to others
Giving in to peer pressure
Depression that may lead to self-medicating or self-mutilation
Becoming overly anxious around others, especially in social or performance situations
Pursuing tasks that one believes will result in acceptance by one's peers
Choosing isolating activities that allow one to be alone
Indulging in violent fantasies of comeuppance
Becoming physically aggressive
Becoming emotionally volatile
Seeking vengeance
Distancing oneself from friends who might be contributing to one's social alienation
Throwing oneself into work, school, or other activities where one feels safe or secure
Seeking out other disenfranchised people and groups
Reaching out to an aunt, a counselor, or someone else for advice
Embracing one's uniqueness and choosing not to be victimized by the prejudice of others

PERSONALITY TRAITS THAT MAY FORM
Attributes: Cooperative, courteous, creative, disciplined, discreet, focused, funny, generous, independent, simple, studious, supportive
Flaws: Antisocial, callous, dishonest, frivolous, oversensitive, perfectionist, rebellious, resentful, self-destructive, subservient, volatile, withdrawn

TRIGGERS THAT MIGHT AGGRAVATE THIS WOUND
Negative media coverage, movies, and books that reinforce a hurtful stereotype
Being ignored or treated disrespectfully for no reason whatsoever
Being passed over (for a new position, an award, etc.) and wondering if discrimination was involved
Facing a situation where one needs a friend or supporter but having no one

OPPORTUNITIES TO FACE OR OVERCOME THIS WOUND
Finding oneself rejecting someone else for little reason and realizing one may also have biases
Trying to get involved with another group but being rejected by that one, too
An opportunity where one can confront the guilty party for being shamed, bullied, or traumatized
A son exhibiting behaviors that led to one's rejection and worrying that he'll suffer the same way

CHILDHOOD SEXUAL ABUSE BY A KNOWN PERSON

NOTES: This kind of abuse encompasses sexual behaviors, touching, or penetration. While it can be inflicted by a stranger, this entry will focus on what happens when the abuser is a trusted individual with access to the child, such as a relative, family friend, teacher, classmate, parent of a close friend, or babysitter.

BASIC NEEDS OFTEN COMPROMISED BY THIS WOUND: Physiological needs, safety and security, love and belonging, esteem and recognition, self-actualization

FALSE BELIEFS THAT COULD BE EMBRACED
This is my fault; I invited it because of something I said or did.
I deserved it because I'm worthless (or a bad daughter, student, athlete, friend, etc.).
No one is safe; even those closest to me try to hurt me.
People take advantage because I let them.
When I'm friendly or helpful, people hurt me.
I must have wanted it because I didn't fight back (or say no, struggle hard enough, resist, etc.).
I'm powerless to change my life for the better.
I'm broken now, beyond repair.
Bad people only deserve bad things.
When you trust people, they hurt you.
No one could ever love someone as terrible as me.
Standing out (by excelling, being talented, wearing nice clothing, etc.) is an invitation to be hurt.
It's better to be alone than to be betrayed.
Love is a weapon used to hurt people.

THE CHARACTER MAY FEAR...
Intimacy and sexual feelings
Love, and having it taken away or perverted in some way
Being touched or exposed
Telling someone and not being believed
Being alone with their attacker (or someone like them)
Doing or saying something that is misconstrued as a sexual invitation
Trusting the wrong person and having that trust betrayed
That the same thing will happen to someone they love
Being abandoned and blamed by family members and friends when the truth is discovered

POSSIBLE RESPONSES AND RESULTS
Becoming reclusive; avoiding family or friends
Mood swings, like being quick to anger
Certain triggers producing confusing or inexplicable feelings
Changing one's manner of dress to cover oneself more completely or be less noticeable

Giving up passions, interests, or activities that one associates with the abuser

Close relationships becoming strained if family members pressure one not to talk about it

Resenting family members who want to act like nothing happened

Worrying about the worst-case scenario and adopting pessimistic thinking

Developing an eating disorder or engaging in self-harm (cutting, scratching, etc.)

Becoming addicted to a substance as a means of coping

Being achievement-driven at work, in relationships, or as a parent to make up for being "unworthy"

Being unable to accept compliments (by minimizing one's role or responding with self-deprecation)

Difficulty asking for help

Trouble accepting gifts and compliments, and feeling discomfort when others bestow a kindness

Trust issues; having a difficult time taking someone at their word

Difficulty reading people and situations

Having a spotty memory of the event(s) or certain details associated with it

PTSD symptoms (panic attacks, depression, believing one will die early, etc.)

Sexual dysfunctions like hypersexual activity, risky sex, premature interest in sex, being unable to enjoy sex, or sexual preferences that may not be considered mainstream

Difficulty being open in a relationship; experiencing anxiety at becoming vulnerable

Being uncomfortable with one's body and it being seen by others

Flinching when touched (especially if it's unexpected) and avoiding situations where it might happen

Becoming overprotective or irrational about the safety of one's children or loved ones

Repressing one's pain out of a desire to not make others feel uncomfortable

Resolving to be more present, alert, protective, and available for one's own children

Becoming a mentor for a child or teen who has experienced sexual abuse

Actively seeking to protect the rights of children

PERSONALITY TRAITS THAT MAY FORM
Attributes: Alert, analytical, bold, courageous, decisive, empathetic, honorable, independent, introverted, loyal, observant, organized, perceptive, persistent, proactive, resourceful, sensible, socially aware, talented, wise

Flaws: Abrasive, addictive, controlling, cruel, cynical, evasive, foolish, hostile, inflexible, inhibited, insecure, irrational, irresponsible, needy, nervous, rebellious, self-destructive, suspicious, uncommunicative, volatile

TRIGGERS THAT MIGHT AGGRAVATE THIS WOUND
Seeing the perpetrator with a small child

Reading about a public case where a victim reported abuse and was vilified or not believed

Sensory triggers that remind one of the abuse (smells, sounds, locations, etc.)

Engaging in sex or sexual touching

OPPORTUNITIES TO FACE OR OVERCOME THIS WOUND
Being unable to forgive the perpetrator when he or she seeks to make amends

Being asked to speak publicly about one's abuse

Seeing signs that could mean one's child has been abused

Realizing one's negative coping behaviors are limiting one's happiness, and wanting to change that

DISCOVERING A PARTNER'S SEXUAL ORIENTATION SECRET

NOTES: No one is honest all the time, and the occasional white lie can be harmless. But the more intimate the relationship, the more serious it is when one person deceives the other. When the lie itself revolves around who a person is on their most basic level, it escalates from a lie to a betrayal. The other person is left wondering what else the partner hasn't been honest about, how she could have missed something so obvious about the most important person in her life, and how the relationship will inevitably change because of this revelation. It's no wonder that a lie of this caliber can cause a lasting wound.

BASIC NEEDS OFTEN COMPROMISED BY THIS WOUND: Love and belonging, esteem and recognition, self-actualization

FALSE BELIEFS THAT COULD BE EMBRACED
I can't trust anyone.
I'm destined to be alone.
My instincts suck.
This happened because something is wrong with me.
I'm gullible enough to believe anything.
No one will ever want to be with me now.
People are never honest about the things that count.

THE CHARACTER MAY FEAR...
That their judgment and instincts are impaired
Missing the obvious warning signs again
Being the last to know
Being betrayed by someone close
Trusting the wrong person and being deceived again
Being pitied and becoming the object of gossip

POSSIBLE RESPONSES AND RESULTS
Experiencing anger or rage toward one's ex
Worrying about the possibility of contracting a disease (if the partner was also unfaithful)
Confusion over what to tell one's children
Confusion over what to do (loving the partner but knowing any love they return is limited)
Trying to salvage the relationship through therapy or other means
Ending the relationship at once
Wanting to vent to friends but worrying about being viewed as homophobic, intolerant, or uncaring
Becoming homophobic
Distrusting those of the same gender or orientation as one's partner
Not trusting anyone's word at face value
Mistrusting even one's closest friends

Looking for deceit; believing that every person has a hidden agenda
Believing that others are guilty until proven innocent
Avoiding seeing old friends out of embarrassment
Avoiding family functions where awkward questions will be asked
Dropping out of social circles one used to frequent with one's partner
Lashing out at the person on social media
Outing the person as a means of avenging oneself
Laughing it off or making jokes about it to avoid showing one's hurt
Hounding friends to find out if they knew or suspected the truth about one's partner
Avoiding new romantic relationships
Not telling others the truth about why the relationship ended
Choosing partners who embody a clear sexual preference (being highly macho, overtly feminine, etc.)
Choosing partners with biases (homophobes, those with an extreme standpoint on sexual identity, etc.)
Struggling with bouts of depression
Being healthily cautious when starting new relationships in the future so one's eyes are wide open
Being more appreciative of the trustworthy people in one's life
Adopting honesty as a core character trait
Seeking partners for whom honesty is a core trait
Training oneself to become more observant, perceptive, or analytical to avoid being fooled again

PERSONALITY TRAITS THAT MAY FORM
Attributes: Analytical, bold, cautious, discreet, empathetic, honest, honorable, loyal, merciful, meticulous, observant, perceptive, philosophical, private, socially aware, traditional
Flaws: Abrasive, antisocial, callous, cruel, fanatical, haughty, inflexible, judgmental, macho, nosy, paranoid, prejudiced, promiscuous, resentful, self-destructive, vindictive, withdrawn

TRIGGERS THAT MIGHT AGGRAVATE THIS WOUND
Recalling clues to the truth that one didn't recognize at the time
Friends or family members saying that they suspected the truth from the beginning
Overhearing hurtful gossip
Catching another loved one in a big lie
Being the last to know something, even when it is an oversight or completely harmless

OPPORTUNITIES TO FACE OR OVERCOME THIS WOUND
Suspecting a friend's partner of living a lie and having to choose whether or not to speak up
A love interest being honest and transparent about their past but disclosing something worrisome, like infidelity with a previous partner
Seeing the ex move on while one is alone, miserable, and mired in insecurity and distrustfulness
Entering a new relationship and discovering that one's partner has lied about something important, such as their name, marital status, or criminal record

DISCOVERING A SIBLING'S ABUSE

EXAMPLES
Witnessing the abuse firsthand (seeing or hearing it occur)
Discovering the abuse after the fact when one's sibling opened up about it
Realizing a sibling has allowed herself or himself to be victimized in order to shield one from harm
Learning about the abuse in a sibling's suicide note
Being told about it by a friend or family member the sibling had confided in

BASIC NEEDS OFTEN COMPROMISED BY THIS WOUND: Safety and security, love and belonging, esteem and recognition, self-actualization

FALSE BELIEFS THAT COULD BE EMBRACED
I failed because I didn't protect him (or her) from this.
How did I not know? I'm too stupid to see what's in front of me.
I should have taken the abuse myself.
I am unworthy of love, respect, or trust.
I can't help others; I will only fail or let them down.
Because I failed my sister when she needed me most, I deserve only pain and unhappiness.
This failure is a permanent stain; I deserve the guilt it brings.
I can't protect the people I love.
I don't deserve to feel safe and secure—not when my sibling had that taken away.

THE CHARACTER MAY FEAR…
Trusting people, especially ones who are like the abuser
Being responsible for others and screwing it up
Misreading people and missing a threat
Being unable to protect loved ones
Failing to protect someone again
Being rejected for being a bad sister or brother
Being exploited when they are at their weakest

POSSIBLE RESPONSES AND RESULTS
Denial (initially); not wanting to believe that one was wrong about something so important
Subservience to one's sibling to alleviate guilt and make up for the perceived past failing
Trying to help "fix" the sibling
Anger and outbursts, even violence
Blaming adults close to the situation for not preventing the abuse, even if they didn't know it was happening
A desire for revenge
Not taking anyone at face value; believing that trust must always be earned
Seeing signs of abuse where there are none

Second-guessing one's decisions, especially in situations where one is responsible for others
Growing overprotective of loved ones
Viewing any secret as toxic; developing a compulsion to speak the truth
Cutting all ties with the abuser
Digging into suspected secrets to uncover the truth
Wanting to know where loved ones are at all times
Fine-tooth-combing one's memories to find clues one might have missed
Being confused about conflicting emotions (relief over not being abused oneself, guilt for being relieved, hatred toward family members for not catching the abuse, etc.)
Placing oneself in risky situations that increase the likelihood one will be hurt out of a deep sense of guilt and believing one deserves pain
Backing away from responsibility for fear of messing up again
Deep feelings of shame that keep one from being near the abused sibling
Self-harm, medicating with alcohol or drugs, or other self-destructive behaviors
Becoming very alert and observant out of fear of missing the signs again
Offering unconditional love and support to the sibling
Encouraging the sibling to seek counseling and offering to go with them to show support

PERSONALITY TRAITS THAT MAY FORM
Attributes: Affectionate, alert, appreciative, courageous, empathetic, generous, honest, honorable, humble, introverted, kind, loyal, merciful, nurturing, obedient, observant, patient, perceptive, persistent, private, protective, resourceful, responsible, spiritual, supportive, unselfish
Flaws: Confrontational, cowardly, humorless, inhibited, insecure, nervous, paranoid, promiscuous, reckless, self-destructive, subservient, suspicious, timid, uncommunicative, violent, volatile, withdrawn, workaholic

TRIGGERS THAT MIGHT AGGRAVATE THIS WOUND
Seeing signs (even false ones) that a loved one is being abused, such as personality shifts or acting out
Seeing the abuser and one's sibling together at church, a birthday party, or other event
A memory surfacing that was a clue to the abuse but one didn't recognize it at the time
Being touched unexpectedly (not seeing the interaction coming)
Situations where one's sibling is being criticized or judged by others

OPPORTUNITIES TO FACE OR OVERCOME THIS WOUND
Being blamed by the sibling for not recognizing or stopping the abuse
Family members not believing the sibling and siding with the alleged abuser
Resentment toward one's parents for not intervening (even if they also had no idea the abuse was occurring) which causes a rift, and wanting to move past those feeling to repair the relationship
Wanting to be close to one's sibling again after the discovery but having to forgive oneself to do so
Having children who fight constantly and wanting them to realize they should value a sibling's love

DOMESTIC ABUSE

NOTES: Domestic abuse is any ongoing pattern of behavior by an intimate partner intended to exert power and control over the other. Males or females can be targeted, and the mistreatment can be physical, sexual, psychological, and verbal in nature.

EXAMPLES

Constant accusations of things the victim isn't guilty of, such as cheating, lying, or disrespect
Verbally shaming the victim (at home, in public, or around family members)
Distancing or isolating the victim from family and friends
Controlling the victim's money and finances and making important decisions for them
Dictating the victim's physical appearance (hairstyle, clothing choices, makeup, etc.)
Physical violence and threatening the victim through words, facial expressions, and posture
Pressuring the victim or forcing her into sexual activity she isn't comfortable with
Stalking (online and off)
Destroying the victim's property or threatening their loved ones and pets
The perpetrator blaming the victim for the abusive behavior
Gaslighting (manipulation using denial, misdirection, and contradiction to disorient a victim, causing them to question their own sanity, abilities, actions, and beliefs)

BASIC NEEDS OFTEN COMPROMISED BY THIS WOUND: Physiological needs, safety and security, love and belonging, esteem and recognition, self-actualization

FALSE BELIEFS THAT COULD BE EMBRACED

If I were more intelligent (or a better husband, etc.), she wouldn't treat me this way.
If you love someone deep enough, they'll change.
This is what love is.
I'm defective and don't deserve any better.
Other people will always have power over me if I let them get close.
I'm weak and I always will be.

THE CHARACTER MAY FEAR...

Uncertainty and the unknown (from living in constant fear of what will happen next)
Retribution from the abuser, should they try to leave
For the safety of their children
Not being able to care for themselves financially or raise the kids alone
The removal of their children if the authorities should find out
Being perceived as weak if the abuse becomes known
That the abuser is right; believing the lie that they are stupid, unlovable, or worthless

POSSIBLE RESPONSES AND RESULTS

Conforming one's will to the abuser's and losing all sense of self
Catering to the abuser's needs and following a routine based on their demands

Internalizing what the abuser says (believing that one is lazy, slutty, stupid, ugly, etc.)

Provoking or taking abuse to shield others in the household, like one's children

Depression, dissociation, and gaps in one's memory

Fearing for one's life or the life of one's children as abuse escalates

Secretly honing an ability (self-defense, a career skill, etc.) to help one escape

Aligning with people who could help one escape, like a police officer, a social worker, or someone with a room to rent

Leaving with nothing (not wanting to provoke more rage by taking things)

Seeking sanctuary (with a friend, at a shelter, at a home for families at risk)

Being hyperalert even after one is freed from the situation

Having flashbacks and nightmares

Experiencing anxiety or panic attacks when one feels threatened

Fear-driven behavior and actions; expecting the worst to happen

Feeling nervous when out; routinely scanning for an exit or escape and looking over one's shoulder

Keeping one's guard up; having difficulty trusting anyone new

Feeling followed and watched; struggling to find a normal routine

Worrying one is too weak to cope, too broken to succeed (believing the lie)

Falling apart when the kids aren't around (through crying, depression, or self-medicating)

Avoiding new relationships

Struggling with intimacy and trust

Seeking out free or subsidized counseling

Talking out one's fears with others who have been through the process

Cutting or dyeing one's hair and changing a wardrobe both to feel safe and to embrace a new start

PERSONALITY TRAITS THAT MAY FORM

Attributes: Adaptable, affectionate, appreciative, cooperative, courteous, discreet, gentle, humble, merciful, nurturing, obedient, traditional

Flaws: Cynical, defensive, dishonest, flaky, forgetful, fussy, martyr, needy, nervous, subservient, timid, uncommunicative, weak-willed

TRIGGERS THAT MIGHT AGGRAVATE THIS WOUND

Seeing one's child expressing violence that is clearly a response to abuse they witnessed

Flashing back to a particularly abusive experience

Being contacted by one's abuser after leaving

Seeing a child with suspicious bruising or a friend with frequent wounds

OPPORTUNITIES TO FACE OR OVERCOME THIS WOUND

Being too afraid to pursue a relationship with someone who seems great, then questioning one's choice

Realizing that one is repeating the cycle of abuse with one's children or a new partner

Losing a job, friend, or lover due to a substance abuse problem that's being used to mask one's pain

Meeting a survivor who embodies strength, and wanting to find one's own

FINANCIAL RUIN DUE TO A SPOUSE'S IRRESPONSIBILITY

EXAMPLES: Experiencing financial devastation due to a spouse…
Secretly overextending their credit and being unable to hide the lie any longer
Investing in questionable companies and initiatives that go bad
Draining joint accounts to pay for a habit (drinking, drugs, prostitutes, gambling, etc.)
Being fired or laid off and depleting the savings account to avoid admitting it
Falling prey to scams and not wising up in time
Loaning a friend or relative money that is never paid back
Who is a hoarder, collector, or compulsive shopper
Running up credit card debt or a personal line of credit to support a failing business
Borrowing money from questionable people who then call in the debt

BASIC NEEDS OFTEN COMPROMISED BY THIS WOUND: Physiological needs, safety and security, love and belonging, esteem and recognition, self-actualization

FALSE BELIEFS THAT COULD BE EMBRACED
I can't trust anyone to handle money but myself.
My instincts and judgment are flawed, especially when it comes to relationships.
Trusting other people is foolish.
I need to use my head, not my heart.
The only way my future is safe is if I am in control.

THE CHARACTER MAY FEAR…
Trusting the wrong person
Living in poverty or becoming homeless
Going into debt
Making a bad decision that leads to more instability
An illness or disaster that further stresses their financial situation
Taking risks
What the future will hold

POSSIBLE RESPONSES AND RESULTS
Leaving one's spouse
Difficulty trusting others; always wondering if they're being honest or hiding things
Obsessively watching one's bank account
Insisting on maintaining separate finances in future relationships
Demanding to know how money is being spent within the family (wanting to see receipts, etc.)
Restricting access to one's accounts and investments
Refusing to use credit cards
Clipping coupons
Only engaging in free or cheap activities

Becoming stingy (e.g., resenting having to kick in money for a co-worker's birthday cake)

Feeling guilty when spending money on oneself

Buying used items instead of new ones

Minimizing the importance of holidays to avoid having to buy gifts

Not going out with friends to avoid spending money

Reusing and repurposing items

Going without

Becoming risk averse

Taking advantage of any money-making opportunity

Taking on extra jobs and sacrificing downtime to do so

Becoming protective of what one has left

Taking charge of one's finances in a realistic and expectable fashion, rather than leaving them for someone else in the family

Consulting a financial advisor or family member with wisdom in this arena to figure out what to do

Creating a plan to climb out of debt, and sticking to it

Becoming less concerned with material things

PERSONALITY TRAITS THAT MAY FORM

Attributes: Analytical, cautious, centered, decisive, disciplined, efficient, focused, industrious, just, mature, meticulous, organized, persistent, proactive, protective, resourceful, sensible, simple, thrifty, wise

Flaws: Apathetic, catty, compulsive, controlling, disloyal, fussy, greedy, humorless, impatient, inflexible, insecure, irrational, judgmental, nagging, nosy, obsessive, possessive, resentful, stingy, workaholic, worrywart

TRIGGERS THAT MIGHT AGGRAVATE THIS WOUND

A glitch in one's banking records that temporarily shows a great loss

A loved one asking for money

Learning that a family member is ignoring the budget and being extravagant with household funds

Seeing unfamiliar purchases on one's credit card statement

Witnessing the good fortune of others, like a friend's vacation or a co-worker's new car

OPPORTUNITIES TO FACE OR OVERCOME THIS WOUND

Being scammed by someone else

An event that threatens one's financial stability (a loophole in one's home insurance that doesn't cover a fire, an illness that leaves one unable to work for an extended period, etc.)

A situation that forces one to choose between a job and family (a sick spouse, a child needing more attention or support, etc.), which puts one's financial security in jeopardy

Stinginess and control issues damaging a new relationship

FINDING OUT ONE WAS ADOPTED

EXAMPLES

Being told about the adoption by one's parents

Learning about the adoption by accident (overhearing a conversation, finding a birth certificate, etc.)

A jealous or spiteful relative hinting at the information, making one curious

Finding out when a serious illness requires knowledge of one's medical history

Confronting one's parents because of personal suspicions (because one does not look like them, due to cryptic comments by a distant relative, etc.)

Finding out after the death of one's parents

Being approached by strangers claiming to be one's birth parents or siblings

BASIC NEEDS OFTEN COMPROMISED BY THIS WOUND: Love and belonging, esteem and recognition, self-actualization

FALSE BELIEFS THAT COULD BE EMBRACED

If my real parents gave me away, there must be something wrong with me.

I don't belong anywhere; no one wants me.

I probably should never have been born.

I don't know who I am.

If my parents can lie to me, then I can't trust anyone.

If my parents could abandon me, anyone can and probably will.

If I put walls up, people can't manipulate my feelings.

Love makes everything hurt more.

THE CHARACTER MAY FEAR…

Abandonment and rejection

Trusting the wrong person

Vulnerability and intimacy

Meeting their birth family and being rejected a second time

Being loved less than their siblings (especially if the siblings weren't adopted)

Being taken away from their adopted family by the birth parent

Being lied to about other things

POSSIBLE RESPONSES AND RESULTS

Mood swings (anger, betrayal, gratitude, mistrust, guilt, confusion)

Examining family interactions, searching for signs that one is being treated differently or loved less

Living in denial; refusing to seek out one's roots or past

Growing obsessive about the past (asking constant questions, needing to know one's roots, etc.)

Difficulty trusting people

Struggling with one's identity

Over-focusing on the differences between oneself and one's adoptive family

Having a hard time saying goodbye or letting people go

Always striving to prove one's worthiness to friends

Questioning what people say without cause; looking for or expecting deceit

Pulling back from adopted family members

Medicating with alcohol or drugs

Engaging in risky behavior as a way of acting out

Becoming subservient out of a desire to please one's adoptive family (out of fear of abandonment)

Experiencing anxiety or situational depression

Double-checking facts rather than taking someone at his or her word

Developing insecurities about one's performance at work or school

Experiencing relief, since one has always felt different, then feeling guilty about it

Rejecting adoptive family mementos or heirlooms; feeling unworthy of them

Cynicism; developing a negative outlook

Daydreaming about reconciling with one's birth parents

Seeking to find one's birth family

Rejecting one's birth family and embracing one's adoptive family

Having newfound respect for honesty and openness

Seeing oneself as being chosen by one's adoptive family rather than rejected by one's birth family

PERSONALITY TRAITS THAT MAY FORM

Attributes: Adaptable, analytical, appreciative, centered, curious, diplomatic, easygoing, empathetic, happy, private, sentimental, supportive, wise

Flaws: Abrasive, addictive, confrontational, cynical, disrespectful, gullible, hostile, needy, uncommunicative, ungrateful, withdrawn, workaholic

TRIGGERS THAT MIGHT AGGRAVATE THIS WOUND

Situations where a sibling comes out on top, even if parental favoritism isn't a factor

A scenario where one must decide whether or not to lie to one's children, like them asking how babies are born or if Santa Claus is real

Filling out insurance forms that ask for family medical history

One's birthday and adoption dates

OPPORTUNITIES TO FACE OR OVERCOME THIS WOUND

Unexpectedly conceiving a child and having to face the adoption choice oneself

A difficult medical situation where knowing one's history is important because of possible genetic factors

Discovering that one's birth was a result of rape or incest

Tracking down one's birth family only to discover they have passed on or don't want contact

Deciding not to look for one's birth parents only to later learn of an inheritance that they left behind

Adopting a child and being forced to decide when (or if) to tell them about it

FINDING OUT ONE'S CHILD WAS ABUSED

NOTES: Parents have many roles, but one of the most instinctive is that of the protector. Keeping one's child safe is not just a moral duty; it kicks into gear on the most basic of levels the moment that child comes into a person's care. So when someone discovers that their child has been abused, it shakes them to the core, challenging their beliefs about their capabilities and worth as a parent. The lies and associated guilt and self-blame associated with this wound are more deeply entrenched if the child said nothing because she felt she couldn't go to her parent or if the child tried to reveal what was happening—e.g., she acted out and the behavior was written off as attention-seeking—or she tried to say something but wasn't immediately believed.

EXAMPLES: Learning, after the fact, that…
One's partner or a close relative had abused one's child
The abuse occurred at a trusted family friend's house
One's child was hit or touched by a teacher or person in authority
The abuse took place while one's child was in the care of a neighbor or babysitter
The child suffered abuse while one was asleep or in another area of the home
The abuse occurred while one's child was on a supervised trip (for school, church, sports, or a club)
The abuse happened during a custody visit (either by the ex or someone associated with them)

BASIC NEEDS OFTEN COMPROMISED BY THIS WOUND: Safety and security, love and belonging, esteem and recognition, self-actualization

FALSE BELIEFS THAT COULD BE EMBRACED
I am a terrible parent. I couldn't even protect my child.
I should have seen what was happening and stopped it, so this is my fault.
I placed my child in danger. He or she is safer with someone else.
If I don't do a better job of protecting them, this will happen again.
My child isn't safe with anyone but me.

THE CHARACTER MAY FEAR…
Letting go of their child, even for short periods of time
Missing obvious signs again
Trusting others
Their own judgment about people and safety
Continued failure as a parent
Devastating repercussions from the abuse (their child turning to drugs or alcohol, the child blaming and rejecting them, the development of a debilitating mental disorder, etc.)

POSSIBLE RESPONSES AND RESULTS
Deep anger and hatred toward the offending party
A desire for revenge
Needing to know where one's child is at all times

Checking on one's children frequently (with or without their knowledge)
Being suspicious of anyone—even a trusted friend or family member—who shows an interest in one's child
Trying to protect one's child to the point where it disrupts routines and causes fear to bloom
One's mind always going to the worst-case scenario
Being unable to leave children in someone else's care (choosing to homeschool them, switching jobs so one is always home after school, etc.)
Difficulty sleeping
High anxiety
Being overly generous and agreeable with one's child—even spoiling them—out of guilt
Needing to know and be familiar with the child's friends
Seeking to bring the abuser to justice
Not seeking justice due to fear that the process will further traumatize one's child
Only allowing sleepovers in one's own home
Difficulty leaving one's child alone even for short periods of time, regardless of their age
Second-guessing one's decisions; losing confidence in one's abilities and personal radar
Becoming more engaged in the life of one's child
Seeking advice on the best way to help one's child
Making healthy sacrifices on behalf of one's child (proactively putting him in therapy, cutting hours at work so one can spend more time at home, etc.)

PERSONALITY TRAITS THAT MAY FORM
Attributes: Alert, analytical, bold, cautious, decisive, discreet, empathetic, gentle, loyal, nurturing, observant, pensive, perceptive
Flaws: Addictive, confrontational, controlling, cynical, defensive, fanatical, fussy, hostile, humorless, impatient, inflexible, irrational, obsessive, paranoid, pessimistic, stubborn, uncommunicative, vindictive, worrywart

TRIGGERS THAT MIGHT AGGRAVATE THIS WOUND
A situation where the child leaves one's protection, like attending a sleepover at Grandma's house
One's child exhibiting behavior issues
Seeing one's child cry or hearing their sobs
Interacting with parents who are lax about monitoring their children
Visiting or passing by the place where the abuse occurred
Observing adults interacting with children where the child appears resistant or upset

OPPORTUNITIES TO FACE OR OVERCOME THIS WOUND
The abuser being released on a technicality and going free
The child being removed from one's custody
The abuse unearthing buried memories of one's own abuse as a child
Seeing behaviors in other kids that match those of one's child prior to the abuse being discovered
Learning that this wasn't the abuser's first crime against a minor, and recognizing that if one doesn't take action, it will occur again

GETTING DUMPED

NOTES: When it comes to common wounds, getting dumped is at the top of the list—so much so that it's almost a rite of passage, a part of growing up. Being rejected by a beloved person is painful enough, but sometimes the method can be particularly traumatizing, such as being broken up with via text message, getting dumped in favor of someone else, being left at the altar, or learning that the relationship is over when the lover posts about it on social media. Despite the universality of being dumped, it's always a painful experience that can be a deeply wounding one.

BASIC NEEDS OFTEN COMPROMISED BY THIS WOUND: Love and belonging, esteem and recognition

FALSE BELIEFS THAT COULD BE EMBRACED
My judgment is flawed for not seeing this coming.
It's better to be alone than to risk this kind of pain again.
He or she was my one true love. I'll never have a relationship like that again.
I'll always be alone.
I am too stupid (or untalented, ugly, unworthy, etc.) to love.

THE CHARACTER MAY FEAR…
Rejection by others
Being embarrassed or humiliated
Finding love only to lose it again
Trusting the wrong partner; opening up only to be hurt again
Never finding true love
Living life alone
That there's something defective about them that contributed to the rejection

POSSIBLE RESPONSES AND RESULTS
Periods of depression, negative self-talk, and wallowing
Comparing oneself to others and finding oneself lacking
Analyzing the relationship in detail in one's mind, trying to spot where it went wrong
Periods of hopelessness
Sticking like glue to one's friends
Difficulty adjusting to being single
Making repeated attempts to repair the relationship
Entering into a rebound relationship
Jealousy and anger if one's ex-partner moves on before one does
Drinking too much
Avoiding dating altogether
Working longer hours to have less time for being alone
Bad-mouthing one's ex or others like him or her
Pessimism about life in general

A deep aversion to making oneself vulnerable again

Seeking transactional kinds of relationships (e.g., those that are purely for sex)

Shying away from potential love interests as a fear of vulnerability kicks in

Sabotaging new relationships before the other person gets a chance to reject one as a partner

Overcompensating for a perceived weakness (acting macho, accentuating one's beauty, etc.)

Growing more jaded if one experiences a dating drought or has a string of disappointing encounters

Being judgmental or close-minded about committed relationships

Experiencing jealousy of others who are in healthy relationships

Wanting to always be active (going out, having plans, etc.) to distract one from feeling lonely

Engaging in unhealthy behavior as a means of numbing the pain, such as promiscuity or prostitution

Choosing partners who are timid or needy, and encouraging their dependency

Seeking out one's single peers to fill the void (via gaming marathons, workouts, bar-hopping, etc.)

Going through the stages of grief

Soul-searching to recognize problems in the past relationship or the part one might have played in it not working out

Identifying areas where one could become a stronger partner

Identifying areas for self-improvement that will lead to personal fulfillment

Doing something new as a way of turning over a new leaf (taking a dance class, getting a dog, volunteering at the hospital, learning Italian, etc.)

PERSONALITY TRAITS THAT MAY FORM

Attributes: Adaptable, analytical, bold, cautious, diplomatic, discreet, empathetic, flirtatious, idealistic, independent, mature, optimistic, patient, pensive, philosophical, private, sentimental

Flaws: Callous, childish, disloyal, humorless, insecure, macho, melodramatic, nagging, needy, obsessive, promiscuous, resentful, self-destructive, temperamental, vindictive, whiny, withdrawn

TRIGGERS THAT MIGHT AGGRAVATE THIS WOUND

Seeing the ex with a new flame

Being surrounded by couples within one's group of friends

Being stood up by a friend for a dinner date

Passing by a spot one used to visit with one's partner

The anniversary of the previous relationship

Getting into an argument with a new partner

Starting a new relationship and seeing warning signs (real or perceived) that things aren't going well

Being invited to an important event (a family reunion, wedding, or awards ceremony) and having to go solo

OPPORTUNITIES TO FACE OR OVERCOME THIS WOUND

Going through another break-up for the same reasons cited by one's ex

Recognizing that by refusing to accept what happened, one is allowing the wounding to continue

Being in a long-term relationship that isn't working and realizing that it needs to end

Being loved by someone else and recognizing that one is desirable and worth loving

HAVING ONE'S IDEAS OR WORK STOLEN

EXAMPLES
Telling an idea to someone at work who then presents it to higher-ups as his own
Collaborating on a successful song with a partner and receiving no credit for it
Sharing one's writing with a critique partner who steals the essence of the story and publishes it herself
Pitching a new invention to an investor who files the patent for it under his own name
Doing most of the work on a project and a co-worker taking credit and being promoted for it
Struggling to sell one's new product only to have a large, successful organization create the same thing and mass market it
Making an important discovery (scientific, medical, etc.) and having an employer lay claim to it
Netting a big client, then having one's boss take the credit
Discovering that one's software or app has been pirated and distributed, cheating one of revenue
Seeing knockoffs of one's work being sold by others

BASIC NEEDS OFTEN COMPROMISED BY THIS WOUND: Esteem and recognition, self-actualization

FALSE BELIEFS THAT COULD BE EMBRACED
No one can be trusted.
I'll never come up with an idea as good as that one.
I'm better off working alone.
If you start to get ahead, someone will always pull you down.
Why respect the rules of good conduct when no one else does?
To get by in this world, you've got to look out for number one.
You're only guilty if you get caught.

THE CHARACTER MAY FEAR...
Being taken advantage of again
Never being acknowledged for anything
Trying to gain recognition in a specific area that is highly competitive
Having to work with others
Sharing their ideas or work with others

POSSIBLE RESPONSES AND RESULTS
Being reluctant to share fully with others
Difficulty working collaboratively
Trust issues that seep into all areas of one's life
Losing favor with co-workers due to one's inability to collaborate
Giving up on succeeding in the arena where one's work was taken
Seeking to discredit the thief
Suing the offending party

Sabotaging the thief

Refusing to work with that person again

Playing the martyr

Becoming a resentful and bitter person

Suffering from stress-related health issues (frequent illness, aches and pains, stomach problems, etc.)

Assuming that all people are unethical and only want to benefit themselves

Stooping to new lows in order to succeed; adopting the if-you-can't-beat-'em-join-'em attitude

Never being fully open with anyone, even loved ones

Looking for signs of disloyalty in others

Clinging to those who have proven themselves completely trustworthy and loyal

Not wanting to meet new people; keeping one's distance professionally and socially

Baiting people in conversation in hopes they will reveal their true motives

Taking action to bring the thief to justice

Deciding to take the idea farther and do it better than the thief could ever do

Viewing the theft as a sign that one is headed in the right direction

Accepting that if one came up with this good idea, others will follow

Enjoying the process of learning and doing rather than focusing only on the endgame

Taking steps in the future to protect one's work before sharing it with others

Recognizing that the time spent developing the idea was valuable and meaningful rather than a waste

PERSONALITY TRAITS THAT MAY FORM

Attributes: Cautious, confident, diplomatic, discreet, enthusiastic, focused, independent, just, optimistic, passionate, patient, persistent, persuasive, private, quirky, resourceful, wise

Flaws: Catty, confrontational, controlling, cynical, devious, fussy, inflexible, irrational, obsessive, paranoid, perfectionist, possessive, resentful, stingy, stubborn, suspicious, uncooperative

TRIGGERS THAT MIGHT AGGRAVATE THIS WOUND

Being forced to work with others

People who show excitement or enthusiasm for what one does or is working on

Seeing the thief gain great success and accolades from one's idea

A request to see a file, article, or schematic that one has created

OPPORTUNITIES TO FACE OR OVERCOME THIS WOUND

A health scare that makes one see that bitterness about the past event is only causing harm

Realizing that one's continued negative focus on the past is stifling creativity and making it impossible to excel

Coming up with a new idea that forces one to make a choice: continue to live an unfulfilled life or pursue a dream and risk being taken advantage of again

Inventing something that could benefit a great many people but being afraid to act on it out of fear it will be exploited

Wanting to pursue a new idea but needing the collaboration and expertise of a partner for it to succeed

INCEST

NOTES: Incest is defined as sexual relations between closely related family members, such as between siblings or a parent and child. It occurs most frequently between a sexually predatory older relative and someone younger, but it also occurs in communities where marrying outside of one's race or culture is considered taboo.

BASIC NEEDS OFTEN COMPROMISED BY THIS WOUND: Safety and security, love and belonging, esteem and recognition, self-actualization

FALSE BELIEFS THAT COULD BE EMBRACED
He (or she) says that because we love each other, it's ok.
We have a special bond.
I'm disgusting. No one will ever want to be around me if they find out.
Telling will just make things worse.
I deserve this because I am a terrible person.
This is my fault; my behavior somehow led to this.
If someone has power over you, they will hurt you.
People use love to get what they want.

THE CHARACTER MAY FEAR...
The abuser
People like their abuser (men, women, authority figures, adults, etc.)
Sex and intimacy
The incest being discovered, bringing shame and humiliation with it
Getting pregnant by their abuser
Loved ones discovering the relationship and rejecting them because of it
Being asked to keep an important secret from someone else

POSSIBLE RESPONSES AND RESULTS
Alcoholism and drug addiction
Self-harming
Eating and sleeping disorders
Thoughts of suicide and attempted suicide
Rebelling against those in authority
Volatile emotions; acting out with violence
PTSD, anxiety disorders, and phobias
Being protective of younger siblings who could also be victimized
An inability to trust others
Difficulty being intimate with others
Low self-worth
Conflicted feelings about what happened (especially if it was consensual)
Not trusting one's instincts; second-guessing one's decisions

Anger toward one's parents (whether they knew or not) for not protecting one as a parent should

Not being able to remember chunks of one's childhood

A tendency to disassociate when highly stressed

A generalized feeling of powerlessness

Confusing sex with love

Entering into abusive relationships as an adult

Sexual promiscuity

Having little or no interest in sex; avoiding sexual encounters

Shutting down one's emotions during sex

Living in denial about what really happened

Having a distanced relationship with one's parents, especially if they encouraged one to not tell anyone about the abuse after discovering it was happening

Being stuck emotionally at the stage of life when the incest occurred

Worrying that one's children will suffer the same fate at someone else's hands

Deciding against having children

Seeking therapy in an effort to heal

Viewing oneself as a survivor rather than a victim

Vowing to take control of one's life in a healthy way; not allowing oneself to be victimized again

Empathizing with others who are in a chronically unjust situation (suffering from a mental disorder, being disowned, telling the truth but not being believed, etc.)

PERSONALITY TRAITS THAT MAY FORM

Attributes: Affectionate, cooperative, courteous, discreet, easygoing, empathetic, imaginative, nurturing, pensive, protective, sensual, socially aware, studious, supportive

Flaws: Addictive, childish, compulsive, controlling, dishonest, evasive, hostile, ignorant, impulsive, inhibited, insecure, nervous, perfectionist, pessimistic, promiscuous, rebellious, self-destructive

TRIGGERS THAT MIGHT AGGRAVATE THIS WOUND

Missing a period

Seeing the family member after an extended absence

Seeing an adult touch a child the way one was touched (frequent arm squeezing, back rubs, touches that linger, etc.) prior to the act

OPPORTUNITIES TO FACE OR OVERCOME THIS WOUND

Finding oneself in another toxic relationship and realizing the incest is at the root of one's problems

Facing a situation where one's abuser will go free or possibly abuse someone else if one doesn't speak out against him or her

After being unable to enjoy or even want sex, one realizes that facing the past is the only way to heal

An emergency situation where one must build trust quickly with a victim, and revealing one's past victimization is the most effective way to do it

INFIDELITY

EXAMPLES

A spouse engaging in a one-night stand or giving in to desire after drug or alcohol use

One's husband or wife having an affair with someone at work

Discovering one's spouse is cheating through online chat rooms or voyeur sites

A partner being caught with a prostitute

A partner who visits an ex and old feelings rekindle, leading to intimacy

Discovering that a spouse has multiple relationships or even a second family

One's spouse turning to a friend for companionship and advice

One's spouse struggling with sexual identity and choosing to explore it with others

A partner who accepts someone's sexual advances out of a strong need for approval

A partner who finds satisfaction elsewhere because of a lack of intimacy at home

A partner cheating emotionally (sharing intimate feelings with someone outside of the marriage), making one feel betrayed

Discovering one's partner has cheated with a family member (a sibling, cousin, parent, etc.)

Trying to rebuild a marriage after infidelity only to learn that one's spouse is cheating again

BASIC NEEDS OFTEN COMPROMISED BY THIS WOUND: Physiological needs, safety and security, love and belonging, esteem and recognition

FALSE BELIEFS THAT COULD BE EMBRACED

I am unworthy of love.

I am an unsatisfactory lover.

No one could ever be attracted to me.

This is my fault for not being good enough.

There is no such thing as a committed relationship.

All men (or women) cheat and I am better off alone.

If I let people in, they'll only hurt me.

If I want a relationship to last, I have to comply with my partner's whims.

THE CHARACTER MAY FEAR...

Intimacy and sex

Love (because it leads to vulnerability)

Being betrayed by someone they trust

Trusting the wrong person

Being alone forever

Being perceived as weak or gullible

That their instincts are unreliable and they will continue to make life-impacting mistakes

POSSIBLE RESPONSES AND RESULTS

Leaving one's partner

Avoiding dating and close relationships

Second-guessing one's actions and choices, especially those involving trust and relationships

Becoming evasive; keeping one's emotions close to the vest

Looking for signs of deceit in potential romantic partners

Following up with someone or questioning them to determine if they are telling the truth

Paranoia; expecting one's partner to account for his or her time away

Control issues; difficulty giving a partner privacy

Wearing clothing that hides one's body

Obsessive dieting or worrying about one's weight and appearance

Going through a period of turning inward, not wanting to get involved with anyone else

Jumping into a rebound relationship

Engaging in risky sexual behavior as a way of getting back at one's partner

Avenging oneself on the spouse's lover

Sabotaging a partner's relationships with those of the opposite sex

Withholding forgiveness from a partner even if he or she is contrite and wants to reconcile

Decreased interest in sex

Lying about the infidelity due to embarrassment or to save one's children from shame

Ignoring the infidelity; living in denial

Learning to be independent

Discovering that one is stronger than one thought

Leaning on those who are supportive and trustworthy

Giving one's lover a second chance while maintaining reasonable requirements and expectations

PERSONALITY TRAITS THAT MAY FORM

Attributes: Adaptable, alert, honorable, independent, loyal, merciful, nurturing, perceptive, private, proactive, protective, sensible, supportive

Flaws: Catty, insecure, irrational, jealous, needy, obsessive, possessive, resentful, self-indulgent, suspicious, vindictive, withdrawn

TRIGGERS THAT MIGHT AGGRAVATE THIS WOUND

Having sex for the first time since the affair

Seeing the person with whom one's partner cheated

Receiving divorce papers

Having to get checked for a sexually transmitted disease or other condition following the cheating

Seeing one's ex (during custody swaps, at the grocery store, around the neighborhood, etc.)

OPPORTUNITIES TO FACE OR OVERCOME THIS WOUND

A new relationship progressing to the point where vulnerability and openness are expected

Falling for someone in a new relationship and finding out they cheated on a previous partner

Wanting to reconcile with one's partner but being unable to make oneself vulnerable again

Learning that a friend was able to forgive a cheating partner and wondering if one has the strength or willingness to do the same

LEARNING THAT ONE'S PARENT HAD A SECOND FAMILY

NOTES: To many, the scenario seems ridiculous, the stuff of fiction: a parent who has a second family, complete with children. How could that be perpetuated over the long term? How would the families not know? Yet it happens often enough to have become familiar. And with the seemingly impossible logistics of such a scenario, it's no surprise that the parent does usually end up getting caught, leaving a trail of betrayal, lies, destroyed families, and wounded loved ones in their wake. Whether one makes this awful discovery as a child, teenager, or grownup, the results can be long lasting.

BASIC NEEDS OFTEN COMPROMISED BY THIS WOUND: Love and belonging, esteem and recognition

FALSE BELIEFS THAT COULD BE EMBRACED
Given the choice, people will always choose someone else over me.
If I had been better behaved (or smarter, prettier, etc.), he would have been happy with us.
I'm defective in some way.
I'm stupid; a smart person would have seen what was happening.
Everybody lies.
If I wasn't enough for my mother (or father), I won't be enough for anyone else.

THE CHARACTER MAY FEAR...
The parent choosing the other family over theirs
Being rejected by others
Never finding someone who can love and accept them unconditionally
Their family falling into poverty if the parent leaves
Being lied to
Betrayal by a person deemed trustworthy
Ending up like the betraying parent

POSSIBLE RESPONSES AND RESULTS
Denial and disbelief
Dulling the pain through self-medication (or acting out, for younger victims)
Feelings of anger and rage toward the offending parent
Doubting oneself
Wondering if the parent's feelings were genuine at all or just an act
Examining oneself for weaknesses and reasons why the parent might have done such a thing
Perfecting perceived weaknesses to gain the parent's love (doing well at school, making oneself more physically attractive, excelling at a sport, etc.)
Becoming obsessed with the other family
Distancing oneself from the guilty parent
Determining to never be gullible or ignorant again
Obsessing over past family details, looking for the clues one missed

Trying to uncover other lies one has been told, believing there must be more

Difficulty trusting others

Becoming controlling as an adult

Being confused by conflicting emotions (love, anger, shame, fear, etc.) about one's parent

Viewing other close family members with distrust, wondering if they're being honest

Withdrawing into oneself; not sharing with others

Becoming very protective of the other parent, who was also duped

Taking a hard stance on lying; disassociating from those who cross the line

As an adult, worrying that one's partner is lying and living a secret life

Spying on one's partner to make sure he or she is telling the truth

Disdaining marriage

Becoming independent so one won't have to rely on others

Accepting dishonesty and unfaithfulness from partners because it's what one is used to

Being drawn to men or women similar to the betraying parent

Stifling one's emotions; not expressing them

Glomming onto anyone who shows one affection

Choosing partners who are needy and dependent

Talking to someone trustworthy about what happened

Determining to always be honest with one's children and to keep one's word

Working hard to never become like the offending parent

PERSONALITY TRAITS THAT MAY FORM

Attributes: Alert, bold, cautious, cooperative, curious, diplomatic, honest, honorable, idealistic, just, loyal, mature, merciful, obedient, observant, proper, responsible, talented

Flaws: Abrasive, controlling, dishonest, disloyal, humorless, insecure, irrational, jealous, manipulative, needy, nervous, nosy, obsessive, paranoid, perfectionist, possessive, rebellious

TRIGGERS THAT MIGHT AGGRAVATE THIS WOUND

Wanting to talk about what happened but being shut down by other family members

Coming in second (in a contest or game, or being picked last for a team)

Being rejected in favor of someone who is better in some way (being turned down for a promotion, a potential lover choosing to be with someone else, etc.)

Discovering the person one is dating is also dating someone else

OPPORTUNITIES TO FACE OR OVERCOME THIS WOUND

After reliving this betrayal with a partner, one resolves to date more carefully, since one deserves better

Experiencing unconditional love with a partner and realizing that the betraying parent's choice to seek a family elsewhere speaks to their shortcomings, not one's own

Despite achieving a difficult life-long dream, one is unable to grasp contentment and realizes that only through accepting oneself (weaknesses and all) can true happiness be found

LEARNING THAT ONE'S PARENT WAS A MONSTER

EXAMPLES: Learning that one's mother or father…
Was a pedophile
Has committed murder
Was a serial killer
Abused children (physically, emotionally, or both)
Liked to cause animals pain or kill them for fun
Poisoned people to make them sick
Kidnapped people and enslaved them in a hidden basement or at another property
Was a human trafficker
Exploited vulnerable people for personal gain
Practiced sacrifices and taboo blood rituals
Was a cannibal
Liked to torture others

BASIC NEEDS OFTEN COMPROMISED BY THIS WOUND: Safety and security, love and belonging, esteem and recognition, self-actualization

FALSE BELIEFS THAT COULD BE EMBRACED
How did I not see the signs? My judgment can't be trusted.
Everything I know is a lie.
My mom (or dad) isn't human, so maybe I'm not either.
People will judge me no matter what I do because of this, so why try to fit in?
My parent never loved me—how could they, and do what they did?
I need to stay away from people for their own protection.
I can never accomplish anything worthy or great with this hanging over me.
People will only see me as the child of a pedophile (or serial killer, madman, etc.) so I have to keep this a secret from everyone.
People will target me now, so I can never let down my guard.

THE CHARACTER MAY FEAR…
Themselves and what they might be capable of because they have the same genes
People discovering who their parent is
Being universally hated
Reporters, the media, and other information-gathering sources
Being thrust into the public eye
Trusting the wrong person with the truth
Becoming a mother or father and passing along defective genes

POSSIBLE RESPONSES AND RESULTS
Changing one's identity (adopting a new name, creating a false history, etc.)
Struggling with one's identity and having low self-worth

Having mixed emotions regarding the parent

Moving when one feels threatened (even if it is just in one's own mind)

Keeping secrets

Avoiding relationships (friendships and romantic ones)

Keeping to oneself; not engaging with neighbors or one's community

Avoiding family members and friends from one's past

Avoiding social media

Frequently searching one's name on social media to see if anything comes up

Avoiding places and situations that serve as a reminder of what one's parent did

Beating oneself up for normal urges and thoughts, believing they're indications of something sinister

Refusing to read books or watch movies with situations that hit close to home

Obsessively reading books or watching movies close to one's situation to gain insight and answers

Deciding not to have children

Striving for independence so one never has to rely on anyone again

Choosing a job that has little opportunity for human interaction

Going off the grid in an effort to keep one's parentage a secret

Constantly re-examining old clues to see if one should have known what was going on

Blaming oneself for the victim's pain because one didn't see what was happening

Surreptitiously keeping track of the victims or their families to see how they're doing

Throwing oneself into social awareness associated with the parent's crime

Anonymously doing something for a victim's family as a way of making restitution (paying off medical bills, asking a therapist friend to reach out, arranging for a paid vacation, etc.)

Refusing to let the parent's crime keep one from succeeding in life

PERSONALITY TRAITS THAT MAY FORM

Attributes: Appreciative, calm, centered, courageous, disciplined, focused, generous, gentle, honorable, pensive, protective, socially aware, wise

Flaws: Addictive, antisocial, self-destructive, temperamental, timid, uncommunicative, uncooperative, withdrawn, worrywart

TRIGGERS THAT MIGHT AGGRAVATE THIS WOUND

Being approached by a police officer (if this is how one learned the truth about one's parent)

Media coverage of a similar crime, such as captives being discovered in an underground dungeon

Sensory stimuli associated with the parent (their accent, having one's hair ruffled, etc.)

Seeing people who match the victim's type (redheads, new mothers, prostitutes, etc.)

Being questioned in a related case because of one's association with the guilty parent

OPPORTUNITIES TO FACE OR OVERCOME THIS WOUND

Being asked to testify but knowing that doing so will make one's parentage public

Being confronted by one of the victims

Having one's new identity cracked by an investigative journalist or private detective

A victim offering forgiveness despite one being unable to forgive oneself

LOSING A LOVED ONE DUE TO A PROFESSIONAL'S NEGLIGENCE

EXAMPLES: Experiencing the death of a loved one…
At the hands of an inexperienced or impaired medical practitioner
From being given the wrong medication
In a mass transit crash (bus, taxi, plane, train, etc.) where the operator was under the influence
From illegal chemicals or toxins used in the construction of their home
From food poisoning contracted at a restaurant or through improperly managed grocery items
When a negligent chef serves food the loved one is deathly allergic to
At the public pool while the lifeguard wasn't paying attention
In the care of an inattentive babysitter
From a misdiagnosis
When poorly constructed scaffolding collapses on a busy sidewalk
In a hostage standoff being overseen by an incompetent negotiator
Due to excessive or unnecessary police force
In a freak skydiving or bungee jumping accident with an inept instructor or defective equipment
In a car accident due to an automotive defect caused by either the manufacturer or a mechanic
On a poorly maintained amusement park ride
When a therapist doesn't notice or act upon signs of suicide

BASIC NEEDS OFTEN COMPROMISED BY THIS WOUND: Safety and security, love and belonging

FALSE BELIEFS THAT COULD BE EMBRACED
My instincts don't work; I was a fool for trusting the doctor (or the system, the police, etc.).
It's my fault for putting my trust in the wrong person (or company, institution, etc.).
I can't keep my loved ones safe.
I wasn't thorough enough in my research.
I am powerless. Something like this could happen again and I can't do a thing about it.

THE CHARACTER MAY FEAR…
Places associated with the loved one's death, such as a hospital, ski hill, or jail cell
Sensory triggers (the smell of diesel, the sound of helicopter rotors, the taste of soy sauce, etc.)
Losing another loved one unexpectedly
The practitioner going unpunished and someone else dying as a result

POSSIBLE RESPONSES AND RESULTS
Being unable to forgive the guilty party
Taking personal vengeance on the one to blame
Adopting an attitude of apathy and despair
Becoming overly protective of remaining loved ones
Becoming safety conscious to the degree that it impacts relationships and impairs happiness

Looking for the dangers, faults, and flaws in everything
Struggling with enjoying life and relaxing in the moment
Feeling helpless and disillusioned about how the world works
Blaming God for the random senselessness of it all
Losing one's faith or growing stronger in it
Needing someone to blame for every little thing that happens
Lacking closure; always wondering why it happened and how one could have avoided it
Avoiding places similar to the location where the death happened
Pulling away from loved ones out of the fear of getting too close and losing them too
Isolating oneself
Self-medicating
Difficulty choosing new practitioners (and making choices in general) that could have repercussions
Focusing so much on the lost loved one that others are neglected
Suing the responsible person or company
Striking out at the guilty party through social media attacks, poor reviews, and billboard notices
Going on a quest to find answers for closure
Working to ensure nothing like this happens to anyone else
Vetting new companies; not accepting their trustworthiness without proof
Forgiving oneself for, and letting go of, perceived guilt
Starting a charity to honor the loved one's memory
Cherishing every moment with remaining loved ones; not taking anything for granted

PERSONALITY TRAITS THAT MAY FORM

Attributes: Affectionate, appreciative, bold, disciplined, empathetic, focused, idealistic, just, passionate, pensive, persistent, persuasive, protective, sentimental, spiritual

Flaws: Abrasive, addictive, apathetic, callous, confrontational, controlling, humorless, inattentive, morbid, nagging, obsessive, pessimistic, possessive, resentful, self-destructive, suspicious, ungrateful

TRIGGERS THAT MIGHT AGGRAVATE THIS WOUND

Having to visit the same kind of establishment and trust those employed there
Needing to find a new doctor or professional and being paralyzed with fear and indecision
Hearing about a professional's negligence that results in someone's death
Seeing TV lawsuit ads for no-fault injuries and malpractice suits
Discovering that the practitioner is back at work

OPPORTUNITIES TO FACE OR OVERCOME THIS WOUND

An emergency situation where one must make a decision regarding the welfare of a loved one
Upon learning that the professional has opened his doors in another town, one must fight to permanently put him out of business, reliving the wounding event in the process
A situation where one realizes that one can't be responsible everything—including taking the blame for the death that occurred

MISPLACED LOYALTY

EXAMPLES

Learning that one was a pawn for someone else
Being used by a love interest to get to one's best friend
Discovering that a friend used the relationship to gain access to a popular group, club, or organization
Defending a friend and discovering that he or she was guilty of the accusation
Being thrown under the bus by a family member
Trusting a mentor with a secret only to have him or her tell someone else
Overhearing a close friend's hurtful gossip
Being excluded from one's group based on unfair criteria like race, sexual orientation, immaturity, personal values, etc.
Having a family member choose someone else over oneself
Standing by someone who doesn't return the favor when the chips are down
Being physically intimate with someone and learning the person wasn't interested in a relationship
Doing a favor for a friend, then learning that the activity was illegal (e.g., delivering a package that ended up containing drugs, evidence in a court case, or laundered money)
Being let down by a trusted organization or social system
Telling the police the truth but not being believed
Having one's ideas or work stolen by a relative

BASIC NEEDS OFTEN COMPROMISED BY THIS WOUND: Love and belonging, esteem and recognition

FALSE BELIEFS THAT COULD BE EMBRACED

I can't trust my own instincts.
I'm so gullible; I believe anything anyone says to me.
No one can be trusted.
People are only looking out for number one.
People aren't worthy of loyalty. If you believe that, you're a fool.
I need to look out for myself.

THE CHARACTER MAY FEAR...

Intimacy with others
Making themselves vulnerable to others
Sharing personal information with anyone
Professions of loyalty from others and being obliged to take responsibility for them
Being betrayed by a loved one
New people seeking friendship
Misreading other people's motives and being duped

POSSIBLE RESPONSES AND RESULTS

Blaming oneself for being gullible

Negative self-talk

Withdrawing from others

Not opening up to others

Clinging to the friends and family members one knows are trustworthy

Obsessively going over the betrayal in one's mind, trying to figure out what one did wrong

Laughing it off; acting as if the betrayal was no big deal

Claiming that one knew what was happening all along

A reluctance to rely on anyone else

Difficulty asking others for help

Becoming cynical; refusing to give anyone the benefit of the doubt

Convincing oneself that one doesn't need more friends

Pushing existing friends away so they can't cause the same hurt

Keeping busy so one doesn't feel lonely

Avoiding places where one might run into the betraying person

Assuming that everyone has an agenda

Becoming disloyal

Making promises carefully and thoughtfully so one can never be accused of betrayal

Truly appreciating the trustworthy people in one's life

Never breaking another person's trust

Recognizing the signs of misplaced loyalty in others and warning them ahead of time

Studying people so one can learn to read them better and avoid being misled in the future

PERSONALITY TRAITS THAT MAY FORM

Attributes: Analytical, appreciative, bold, cautious, centered, decisive, diplomatic, discreet, honorable, pensive, private, proactive, proper, responsible

Flaws: Apathetic, antisocial, callous, catty, know-it-all, needy, obsessive, oversensitive, subservient, suspicious, timid

TRIGGERS THAT MIGHT AGGRAVATE THIS WOUND

Suspecting that one is being used again by someone else

Not knowing if a friend can be trusted or not

Seeing a loved one be taken advantage of in a similar way

Catching a friend in a lie

Making time for someone only to be blown off or dismissed again

OPPORTUNITIES TO FACE OR OVERCOME THIS WOUND

Finding that one is guilty of betraying the trust of someone else

Being given the chance to join a group instead of living on the fringes of community and having to decide whether or not to do it

Accusing a friend of disloyalty, then realizing the person was devoted after all

Seeing a friend in need, which gives one the choice between continuing to live in isolation or making oneself vulnerable again by offering them support

TELLING THE TRUTH BUT NOT BEING BELIEVED

EXAMPLES

Telling someone that one is being abused (by a parent, coach, uncle, etc.) and not being believed

Reporting a crime and the police responding with skepticism

Being accused of stealing or lying and all proclamations of innocence fall on deaf ears

Being sentenced and punished for a crime one did not commit

Having a parent believe someone else over one's account of what happened

Repeatedly being called a liar by one's parents, caregivers, or those in authority

Confiding in a teacher or principal about an inappropriate situation and being labeled a troublemaker

Giving an eyewitness account of something and it being dismissed as not credible

Giving an account of something that challenges society's belief systems and being belittled for it (seeing a ghost, talking to God, spotting a UFO, experiencing the supernatural, etc.)

BASIC NEEDS OFTEN COMPROMISED BY THIS WOUND: Physiological needs, safety and security, love and belonging, esteem and recognition, self-actualization

FALSE BELIEFS THAT COULD BE EMBRACED

If I tell, I'll only get into trouble.

People say honesty is the best policy, but it isn't.

People only believe what they want to hear.

I can't count on anyone to stand beside me when it matters most.

It's better to tell people what they want to hear.

The people who should protect you will betray you in the end.

The only one who can look out for me is me.

THE CHARACTER MAY FEAR…

Not being believed when it matters most

Persecution

Being wrong about what they believe to be true

Rejection by others as a result of being too honest

Being taken advantage of, hurt, or otherwise victimized, and having no recourse

Trusting the wrong person and being betrayed

Those with power or authority twisting the truth to serve their own needs

POSSIBLE RESPONSES AND RESULTS

Not valuing honesty or integrity because no one else does

Manipulating others so they'll believe what one wants them to (rather than relying on honesty)

Telling people what they want to hear as a way of avoiding problems

Not opening up or sharing one's past experiences because one expects to not be believed

Lying compulsively to mask feelings and avoid being hurt by others

Not being able to take a joke about lying; dealing poorly with being teased

Needing assurances that one is believed in even the most benign situation

Explaining oneself and one's motivations when it isn't necessary

Indignation when one's word is questioned

Suffering a complete meltdown when one is challenged about the truth

Proving one's loyalty at every opportunity

Keeping to oneself so one's word will never be questioned

Being unable to keep a secret if it requires one to lie to others

Compulsively needing to reveal the truth to others if they are being misled by someone else

Giving overly detailed answers to prove one is being truthful

Relying on humor, generosity, or charm to win people over

Resenting those one knows is lying when others take them at their word

Taking steps to prove one's honesty (keeping notes, recording conversations, etc.)

Angry reactions if one's words are twisted or taken out of context

Being compulsively honest; refusing to tell even the smallest lie

Embracing the truth completely and having a highly tuned sense of fairness

Never making assumptions; always searching for facts

Giving others the benefit of the doubt so they won't experience the same sense of unfairness

Learning to read people so one will know if they're telling the truth and won't have to guess

Becoming extremely articulate to minimize chances for misunderstandings

PERSONALITY TRAITS THAT MAY FORM

Attributes: Cautious, courageous, disciplined, discreet, empathetic, funny, honest, honorable, independent, just, loyal, meticulous, nurturing, persistent, persuasive, protective, responsible, socially aware, wise

Flaws: Antisocial, compulsive, cynical, defensive, dishonest, disloyal, evasive, fanatical, hostile, inhibited, insecure, judgmental, know-it-all, needy, nervous, obsessive, oversensitive, paranoid, perfectionist, pessimistic, prejudiced, rebellious, resentful, timid, uncommunicative, weak-willed, withdrawn

TRIGGERS THAT MIGHT AGGRAVATE THIS WOUND

Being forced to call someone out who is lying

Being lied to by one's child or spouse

One's word being doubted while someone with a conflicting story is believed

Being treated so poorly in a situation that one suspects prejudice is to blame

OPPORTUNITIES TO FACE OR OVERCOME THIS WOUND

Having to discern the truth when two people are telling opposing stories

Facing a situation where lying is the greater kindness because the truth will cause unnecessary hurt

Being accused of wrongdoing and having to choose between accepting the blame to make things easier or proving one's innocence

Discovering a friend is being hurt and encouraging them to speak up so the wrongdoer is held accountable

Specific Childhood Wounds

A NOMADIC CHILDHOOD

EXAMPLES
Growing up in a military family where one had to move often
Having parents who struggled to find work and were always traveling to where the jobs were
Having a parent who was transferred often at work due to a specialization
Being abducted by one's parent (perhaps without knowing) and constantly moving as a result
Parents who were addicts and moved frequently because of financial difficulties or evictions
One's parent being a diplomat who traveled a lot
Parents whose jobs required them to move on assignment (historians, missionaries, scientists studying an aspect of nature or geography, etc.)
Being part of the foster care system
Having parents who were homeless
Living in a war-torn country where one had to move around for safety

BASIC NEEDS OFTEN COMPROMISED BY THIS WOUND: Safety and security, love and belonging

FALSE BELIEFS THAT COULD BE EMBRACED
Staying in one place means trouble.
Nothing is permanent.
Relationships are only temporary.
I don't belong anywhere.
Getting attached means getting hurt.
Sticking around means settling.
I'm happier on the road.

THE CHARACTER MAY FEAR...
Getting attached to someone or something
Commitment
Being abandoned by others
Being found by the wrong people
Responsibility that would tie them down
Never fitting in

POSSIBLE RESPONSES AND RESULTS
Fighting the "new kid" stigma; worrying about school or being bullied, and acting out as a result
Constantly hoping (and convincing oneself) that this move or change will be different
Daydreaming of one's perfect home
Wanting a close friend (or pet) but being afraid to get attached
Clinging to a treasured item (a battered backpack, a pebble from one's old yard, etc.)
Not bothering to unpack everything after a move
Craving a routine to feel normal

Feeling anxious when a routine is established

Difficulty forming long-term relationships

Not asking questions that might cause one to care or become invested

Having few possessions

Being accepting of change, even if one wishes things to be the same

Being highly inflexible about certain things

Having few ties to favorite places (restaurants, parks, neighborhoods, etc.)

Trying to convince oneself that one is happier on the road

Resentment toward traditional families

Craving normalcy (a home-cooked meal, belonging to a club or group, etc.)

Worrying that one will be abandoned by one's parents (as a child or an adult)

Moodiness and irritability when one has stayed too long in one place

Growing bored at seeing the same view for too long (if one has acclimated to this lifestyle)

Relocating as a way of escaping emotion (after a breakup, after the death of a pet, etc.)

Struggling with control issues

Wanting to stay and put down roots as an adult but feeling a compulsion to move

Feeling disconnected from one's birth country or cultural identity (if one has moved beyond it)

Always staying in the same place as an adult, even when it's unwise or unsafe to do so

Viewing one's circumstances (good or bad) as temporary

Being highly practical

Being more accepting of differences in cultures, languages, socioeconomic diversity, etc.

PERSONALITY TRAITS THAT MAY FORM

Attributes: Adaptable, adventurous, cautious, extroverted, imaginative, independent, introverted, loyal, spontaneous, thrifty

Flaws: Antisocial, apathetic, cynical, hostile, impulsive, inflexible, irresponsible, manipulative, pessimistic, promiscuous, rebellious

TRIGGERS THAT MIGHT AGGRAVATE THIS WOUND

Having to travel for work

Unbearably long car rides and commutes

Seeing exhausted child travelers hefting small backpacks as they wait to board a bus

Packing or unpacking for a necessary move

Having to let go of something cherished because it's old or ruined

A parent or pet passing away

OPPORTUNITIES TO FACE OR OVERCOME THIS WOUND

Being in a dying marriage but not wanting to disrupt the lives of one's children

Having to move for financial or medical reasons

A spouse's career changing to one that requires a lot of travel

The threat of deportation after one has settled into a community

A war or other event that causes unrest, forcing one to flee

A PARENT'S ABANDONMENT OR REJECTION

EXAMPLES
Being abandoned as an infant (on a doorstep, in a dumpster, on the side of the road, etc.)
A parent giving up his or her rights and turning the child over to the state
Being left with relatives for long periods of time with little communication from one's parent
Being left alone as a young child to fend for oneself
Having a parent who frequently left for long periods of time without warning or apology
Being subjected to a life of foster care when one's parent left or was imprisoned
Being rejected due to stigma, superstition, or prejudice (because of albinism, a deformity, etc.)
A parent who used rejection and abandonment as a form of emotional abuse

BASIC NEEDS OFTEN COMPROMISED BY THIS WOUND: Physiological needs, safety and security, love and belonging, esteem and recognition

FALSE BELIEFS THAT COULD BE EMBRACED
No one wants to be with someone who is defective.
If I achieve enough, I will be worthy of love.
I need to push others away before they have a chance to leave me.
Choosing to be alone is better than chancing rejection.
If you let someone in, they will only hurt you.
Someone better will always come along to take my place.
People always leave when times get tough.

THE CHARACTER MAY FEAR…
Being abandoned by those who should be trustworthy
"Normal" relationships (due to abandonment being the norm)
Inadvertently driving others away due to some flaw or failing
That they're defective in some way, making it impossible to be loved
Never being truly loved and accepted
Letting someone in and being hurt again

POSSIBLE RESPONSES AND RESULTS
Searching inwardly to determine what one may have done to contribute to the rejection
Distrusting authority or parental figures
Maintaining shallow relationships
Abandoning others before they have a chance to leave
Sabotaging budding relationships because of a knee-jerk response to fear
Closing down emotionally before people can get too close
Engaging in unhealthy relationships out of a need for love
Struggling to set healthy boundaries
Becoming clingy and needy

Becoming possessive of others
Being apathetic about one's relationships
Worrying that conflict will lead to the other person leaving
Shutting down and creating distance when things get tough instead of working through it
Becoming obsessed or paranoid; demanding frequent proof of someone's love
Worrying about infidelity in relationships
Frequently transitioning out of situations (jobs, schools, churches, neighborhoods, etc.) where relationships are being formed
Not putting down roots in any one place
Becoming a loner
Not committing to anything
Being obsessed with loving family relationships (wanting what one cannot have)
Trying to strengthen the relationship with one's parents despite repeated rejections
Not following through on responsibilities
Becoming fiercely independent
Becoming a people pleaser out of a need to be accepted and loved
Pursuing people who aren't likely to return one's affections
Not taking risks to avoid any possible rejection
Putting the needs of others first so they will always feel valued
Becoming incredibly loyal to those who love consistently
Never taking on a responsibility one can't fulfill
Being grateful for the people in one's life who are dependable and caring

PERSONALITY TRAITS THAT MAY FORM
Attributes: Adaptable, appreciative, cautious, cooperative, courteous, empathetic, kind, loyal, protective
Flaws: Apathetic, callous, inhibited, insecure, manipulative, needy, oversensitive, rebellious, resentful, subservient, withdrawn

TRIGGERS THAT MIGHT AGGRAVATE THIS WOUND
Being evicted from an apartment or one's lease not being renewed
Being let go or fired from one's job through no fault of one's own
Being criticized for a mistake, choice, or decision
A close friend getting married and moving away
Being rejected even in a small way (being snubbed by a neighbor, one's idea being dismissed, etc.)

OPPORTUNITIES TO FACE OR OVERCOME THIS WOUND
Being abandoned again by a fiancé, spouse, parent, or long-time friend
Being asked to make a long-term commitment to a person, job, organization, etc.
Deciding never to get close to anyone again, then experiencing a deepening of feelings for someone
A parental figure passing away
Being loved by another and realizing that blame for the past abandonment lies with one's parent rather than with oneself

BECOMING A CAREGIVER AT AN EARLY AGE

EXAMPLES
Caring for one's siblings because parents were addicts, neglectful, absentee, or mentally ill
As a new adult, taking full responsibility of siblings upon the death of one's parents
Having to care for an ill or incapacitated parent or relative
Bearing extra responsibilities because one's single parent had to work all the time to provide for the family

BASIC NEEDS OFTEN COMPROMISED BY THIS WOUND: Physiological needs, safety and security, love and belonging, esteem and recognition, self-actualization

FALSE BELIEFS THAT COULD BE EMBRACED
I am the only person who can keep us afloat.
Adults can't be trusted or counted on.
I'm as capable as any adult (if one is still underage).
Family is about obligation, not love.
Wanting things for myself is selfish and counter-productive.
I have value because others need me.
Asking for help is a sign of weakness.
Being upset about my circumstances is a sign of ingratitude.
Other peoples' needs are more important than my own.
I'll never achieve my dreams so there's no point in having them.
Emotions are pointless and only get in the way.

THE CHARACTER MAY FEAR...
The authorities finding out (if the caregiver is a minor)
Losing someone in their charge
Important details slipping through the cracks
Someone discovering a shameful secret, such as the parent being an alcoholic or hoarder
Following in a parent's footsteps (choosing the wrong partner, being unfulfilled, etc.)
Poverty and becoming homeless
Becoming like the adult one is caring for or replacing (an addict, a terrible parent, etc.)
Developing the same illness or debilitating condition and having to rely on others
Feeling or expressing certain emotions (if it is unsafe to do so)
A loss of identity; never being able to escape the trap of caring for others

POSSIBLE RESPONSES AND RESULTS
Putting oneself last (taking on extra jobs, going without sleep or food, etc.)
Anticipating the needs of others
Becoming hypercautious about factors that allow one to care for others (safety, hygiene, etc.)
Overprotecting the people in one's charge
Pushing one's siblings hard so tough love will make them resilient

Resenting peers who have fewer responsibilities

Distrusting people in authority

Perfectionism

Becoming evasive, withdrawn, or deceptive (if one has a secret to keep)

Repressing one's emotions

Making do with less

Having no patience for frivolity or "silly" endeavors (while secretly craving such things)

Losing touch with one's peer group

Gravitating toward more mature peers

Giving up hobbies, interests, and friends due to having no time for them

Feeling guilty for wanting freedom

Straining under home pressures, especially if neglect or abuse are present

Growing rebellious and acting out

Doing whatever it takes to escape the situation

Rationalizing guilt for leaving one's siblings: *Once I get a place of my own, they can move in with me.*

Being careful with one's relationships, especially if parental abandonment was a factor

Taking on and succeeding at jobs one didn't know one could do

Being highly practical

Noticing what others miss

Enjoying the small things

Becoming thrifty and innovative

PERSONALITY TRAITS THAT MAY FORM

Attributes: Bold, mature, meticulous, persistent, protective, resourceful, responsible, sensible, thrifty, unselfish

Flaws: Controlling, cynical, evasive, fussy, humorless, impatient, inflexible, obsessive, resentful, uncooperative, withdrawn, worrywart

TRIGGERS THAT MIGHT AGGRAVATE THIS WOUND

A friend being showered with gifts at Christmas while one's family has to go without

A bare cupboard or pile of overdue bills

A sick sibling who needs medicine that one must somehow acquire

Being invited out by friends and being unable or unwilling to go

Having to buy secondhand or depend on handouts

Briefly being part of an intact and ideal family, then having to return to one's situation

OPPORTUNITIES TO FACE OR OVERCOME THIS WOUND

A chance to do something one wants that would interfere with responsibilities at home

An event that makes it difficult for one to be the caretaker (i.e., being evicted)

Being threatened with the removal of one's charges

Struggling in school and knowing that failing would sabotage the chance for a better future

Having difficulty coping as a caregiver but being unable to seek help due to guilt, shame, or distrust

BEING RAISED BY A NARCISSIST

EXAMPLES: Being raised by a parent who…
Withheld love and affection via the silent treatment
Demanded excellence and then took credit for one's successes
Rarely displayed physical affection
Critiqued every mistake and misstep
Showed anger instead of compassion when an injury or life event caused inconvenience
Pitted siblings against one another, encouraging competition
Displayed cruelty, possibly employing emotional and physical abuse
Refused to help when needed
Frequently undermined one's progress and then blamed one for being stupid
Caused everyone to walk on eggshells due to their high expectations, mood swings, etc.
Made threats and manipulated to get their way
Expected others to cater to them because they were special or important in some way
Purposely took statements out of context to use them against others
Gave conflicting advice to create a no-win situation
Lived out personal dreams through their children

BASIC NEEDS OFTEN COMPROMISED BY THIS WOUND: Safety and security, love and belonging, esteem and recognition, self-actualization

FALSE BELIEFS THAT COULD BE EMBRACED
Love is how people manipulate you.
Love is conditional.
I am a failure and a burden to those around me.
Wanting something for myself is selfish. I need to put others first.
I am too flawed to ever be loved by anyone.
To matter, you need to be the best.
To avoid being hurt, hit first.

THE CHARACTER MAY FEAR…
Rejection and abandonment
Experiencing certain emotions and having them used as weapons
Deep relationships that require vulnerability to succeed
Failures that will prove the parent correct about their deficiencies
Being punished for their mistakes and failures
Trusting the wrong person and being taken advantage of
Repeating the cycle with one's children

POSSIBLE RESPONSES AND RESULTS
Struggling to identify one's feelings because one is used to putting the parent's feelings first
Difficulty choosing a direction because one can't identify what one wants

Saying that things are fine when they're not

Deferring to others, especially when one is under pressure

Being unsure what healthy boundaries look like

Struggling with vulnerability, intimacy, trust, and sharing one's feelings

Being a people pleaser and needing praise to feel valued

Trying to be perfect in all things

Becoming clingy or needy; having dependency issues

Being driven to achieve accolades but feeling uncomfortable receiving them

Low self-worth; feeling stupid or deficient regardless of one's achievements

Choosing a career because it was what a parent wanted

Being taken advantage of because one is unable to self-advocate

Changing one's role to become what others need

Making excuses or forgiving a parent's behavior out of a desire to gain their love

Believing one is to blame when something goes wrong, even when it's irrational

Beating oneself up for personal failures

Always putting one's needs first (repeating the narcissism cycle)

Becoming a bully as a way to cope; striking first to avoid being crushed

As an adult, cutting ties with the offending parent

Choosing to practice self-love in hopes of healing and achieving greater self-worth

Building a relationship with someone who fills a healthy parental or mentoring role

Being deeply moved by acts of kindness and displays of affection

Being hypersensitive to the needs and feelings of others

Using a journal to process emotion and express one's thoughts

PERSONALITY TRAITS THAT MAY FORM

Attributes: Adaptable, alert, analytical, appreciative, mature, meticulous, obedient, observant, organized, perceptive, persistent

Flaws: Addictive, defensive, dishonest, gullible, indecisive, inhibited, insecure, jealous, judgmental, manipulative, materialistic, perfectionist

TRIGGERS THAT MIGHT AGGRAVATE THIS WOUND

Criticism, no matter how constructive or respectfully it's phrased

Falling short, failing, or making a mistake

Spending time with a friend's family and participating in a normal parent-child activity

Phone calls and visits with one's parent

Coming in second (or third, last, etc.)

OPPORTUNITIES TO FACE OR OVERCOME THIS WOUND

Trying to reconnect with a sibling who shared the parent-enforced dysfunction

Realizing one's marriage will fail if one can't learn to resolve the self-esteem issues

Needing help and having to ask for it regardless of how vulnerable it makes one feel

Experiencing joy at someone's gift of encouragement and unconditional support and realizing this emotion was missing from one's toxic upbringing

BEING RAISED BY AN ADDICT

NOTES: Many factors will determine how deep this wound will be, such as whether the addict was one's sole parent, if abuse was involved, and the quality of life the character experienced in this environment.

BASIC NEEDS OFTEN COMPROMISED BY THIS WOUND: Safety and security, love and belonging, esteem and recognition, self-actualization

FALSE BELIEFS THAT COULD BE EMBRACED
People drink because they can't stand to be around me.
No one would notice if I ceased to exist.
I can't protect my loved ones (if there were siblings one failed to protect from abuse).
If I let people in, they'll only be disappointed.
No one will be there for me if I really need it.
I'm weak; I'm going to become just like my parent.
There's no safe place for me in this world.

THE CHARACTER MAY FEAR...
Violence, sexual abuse, or both
Conflict
Being abandoned
Life spinning out of control
Becoming just like their parent
Having to rely on others
Functional relationships (since dysfunctional ones have become normal)
Affirmations of love or acceptance (since these have always proven to be false)

POSSIBLE RESPONSES AND RESULTS
Difficulty relaxing; being in a perpetual state of guardedness
Carefully reading a situation before responding to it
Anxiety and depression
Having a hard time telling if someone is joking; being uncomfortable with humor, teasing, or pranks
Keeping one's deepest thoughts and desires private
Not rocking the boat
Drinking or doing drugs to feel connected to one's parent
Difficulty expressing what one wants and needs
Shying away from conflict and even healthy debates
Rebelling, or wanting to rebel, from being so emotionally stymied
Keeping secrets
Choosing what's safe over what one really wants
Double-checking things to make sure all is as it should be

Feeling close and grateful to people who keep their word

Continuing the cycle (becoming a drug user, drinking too much, engaging in illegal activities, etc.)

Being pessimistic

Denial, especially as to how bad a situation is and how one is coping

Being a people pleaser

Putting the needs of others first

Being hard on oneself

Fleeing from situations that make one feel vulnerable

Wanting clear rules and boundaries; craving predictable routines

Becoming a caretaker of others out of habit

Taking on more responsibility than is healthy

Finding it difficult, if not impossible, to speak up or complain

Letting emotions build up until there's an explosion

Needing to be given clear directions and understand the exact expectations

Having less fear of the specific dangers one was exposed to as a child

Shutting down when a confrontation flares up

Lying or distorting the truth to protect others

Feeling shame and embarrassment keenly

Always waiting for the other shoe to drop

Having strong peacekeeping skills; being able to persuade others, calm tempers, etc.

Finding an outlet for safe expression (playing an instrument, writing poetry, gardening, etc.)

Only making a promise when one knows with certainty that one can deliver on it

PERSONALITY TRAITS THAT MAY FORM

Attributes: Adaptable, alert, analytical, cautious, cooperative, loyal, mature, nurturing, organized, perceptive, persuasive, proactive, responsible, tolerant

Flaws: Addictive, antisocial, controlling, cynical, dishonest, evasive, hostile, humorless, uncommunicative, volatile, withdrawn, worrywart

TRIGGERS THAT MIGHT AGGRAVATE THIS WOUND

The smell of alcohol or pot

Raised voices and heated arguments

Driving with someone who is drunk

Having to care for a friend who's had too much to drink or has passed out

Loud music, parties, and celebrations where people let loose

The sound of clinking glass bottles or a beer can being crumpled

OPPORTUNITIES TO FACE OR OVERCOME THIS WOUND

Marrying someone with a drinking or drug problem

Watching the parent's health decline and wanting to mend old fences before it's too late

Wanting to be a good parent and recognizing that one must let go of one's dysfunctional past

Becoming an addict as an adult and realizing how the habit is affecting one's child

BEING RAISED BY NEGLECTFUL PARENTS

EXAMPLES: Neglect can best be described as a caregiver's ongoing failure to provide for a child's basic needs. It can be physical, emotional, mental, or medical in nature. Child or teen victims of neglect could be said to have been raised by parents who…

Refused to take the child to routine medical check-ups

Suffered from a mental disorder or another disability that rendered them unable to adequately care for others

Often failed to feed their child

Didn't make their child go to school

Withheld love and affection

Knew about and didn't stop their child from engaging in dangerous behavior, such as abusing drugs or alcohol

Were neglectful due to their addictions

Were so absorbed in their own lives they neglected the basic care of their children

Were unintentionally neglectful due to having to work multiple jobs or travel often for work

BASIC NEEDS OFTEN COMPROMISED BY THIS WOUND: Physiological needs, safety and security, love and belonging, esteem and recognition, self-actualization

FALSE BELIEFS THAT COULD BE EMBRACED

I am unlovable.

I'm not worth taking care of. I am a burden to others.

My needs are not important.

I've done something to deserve this treatment.

I'm invisible. My life will always be this way.

I can't depend on others for my survival; I have to fend for myself.

Adults can't be trusted.

My parents' love must be earned.

This is what love looks like.

THE CHARACTER MAY FEAR…

Never being loved or accepted by anyone

Being hungry or not having enough to eat

Embarrassment (over their clothing, home, appearance, etc.)

Other people discovering how they were raised

Being mistreated by others

Having to rely on someone else

Never being able to rise above their circumstances

Repeating the parents' mistakes with their own children

POSSIBLE RESPONSES AND RESULTS

Hoarding materials such as food, clothing, or toys

Clinging to anyone who shows love and affection

Being highly protective of one's siblings

Pulling away from peers so no one discovers one's situation at home

Being evasive and keeping secrets

Confusion over why one's family and home life is different than others

Trying to be obedient, helpful, perfect, etc. in order to receive attention and love

Developmental delays, especially social ones, from certain life lessons not being passed on

Developing mental disorders such as depression or eating disorders

Having to learn through trial and error what others have already mastered or know

Difficulties focusing or succeeding in school

Sacrificing secondary needs to meet imperative ones (e.g., giving up self-actualization to gain love)

Turning to a life of crime to secure primary needs

Self-destructive behaviors, like self-harming, engaging in risky sexual activity, etc.

Resisting being responsible for others as an adult

Difficulty forming attachments, even with one's spouse or children

Trying to provide for the needs of others so they can avoid the same experience

Struggling to parent effectively

Becoming determined to rise above one's circumstances

Being moved by small acts of kindness more so than other people

Applying oneself to an activity, hobby, or interest as a means of escape

Becoming self-reliant out of necessity

Practicing empathy and kindness to combat one's feelings of inferiority

PERSONALITY TRAITS THAT MAY FORM

Attributes: Adaptable, ambitious, focused, independent, industrious, mature, nurturing, private, resourceful, responsible, simple, thrifty

Flaws: Addictive, antisocial, apathetic, callous, compulsive, controlling, cruel, cynical, devious, dishonest, disrespectful, evasive, hostile, humorless

TRIGGERS THAT MIGHT AGGRAVATE THIS WOUND

Perceived neglect (being stood up, messages not being returned, etc.) by the people one trusts

Being let down by the system (e.g., being refused aid or medical coverage)

Hearing friends talk about their happy childhood memories and close family dynamics

Medical difficulties caused by poor nutrition or lack of proper medical care

Being forgotten on important days, such as a birthday or graduation

OPPORTUNITIES TO FACE OR OVERCOME THIS WOUND

Suspecting that a child in one's circle is being neglected in some way

An unexpected change, such as having to take on multiple jobs to make ends meet, that threatens one's children with the kind of neglect one faced

Developing an illness and worrying that one will be unable to provide for those in one's care

Striving to advocate for one's children but going too far and creating unhealthy dependency

BEING RAISED BY OVERPROTECTIVE PARENTS

EXAMPLES: Being raised by parents or caregivers who…
Worried constantly about one's safety
Enforced confining rules (early curfews, not allowing dating, etc.) meant to keep one safe
Discouraged experimentation and taking risks
Made all of one's decisions
Constantly hovered
Intervened before mistakes could be made, removing the chance for one to learn from them
Chose one's friends, rather than trusting one to make those choices
Were overly suspicious of organizations, the government, religions, etc.
Taught fear (i.e., of being victimized) to ensure one would heed their advice

BASIC NEEDS OFTEN COMPROMISED BY THIS WOUND: Love and belonging, esteem and recognition, self-actualization

FALSE BELIEFS THAT COULD BE EMBRACED
I'm incapable of making my own decisions.
People will take advantage of me if I'm not careful.
The world is a dangerous place where bad things are likely to happen.
Being safe is the most important thing.
Mistakes and failure must be avoided at all costs.
I need someone looking out for me.
It's better to let others lead because they are more suited than I am.
People in power only want to control the rest of us.

THE CHARACTER MAY FEAR…
Failure or making dangerous mistakes
Taking risks
Making the wrong decision
Change; stepping outside of their comfort zone
That they're incapable or inept
The outside world or specific portions of it that were the focus of a parent's worry
Being responsible and letting others down

POSSIBLE RESPONSES AND RESULTS
Difficulty making decisions
Second-guessing one's choices; fretting after the fact
Relying on others to make important choices
Blindly trusting leaders
Avoiding risks; always taking the safest path
Not wanting to be put on the spot
Becoming a follower rather than a leader

Susceptibility to manipulation

Overreacting when one is forced into making snap decisions

Frantically studying all of one's options and getting advice before moving forward

Questioning the motives of others

Thinking about what will go wrong when one is making plans

Overthinking things and worrying about what could happen

Doubting or underestimating one's skills and capabilities

Avoiding responsibility

Having low ambitions; lacking the desire to put oneself out there where one could be easily hurt

Developing panic attacks, phobias, or anxiety

Being overprotective of one's own children (continuing the cycle)

Feeling smothered by rules and rebelling against people in authority

Taking foolish risks because one wasn't able to do so as a child

Acting as though one is invincible

Becoming sneaky or devious as a way of getting around the rules

Not learning from mistakes as an adult, since one couldn't make and learn from them as a child

Using fear tactics and manipulation to sway others to one's line of thinking

Overcompensating with one's children by being too permissive

Recognizing that making mistakes is part of the learning process and shouldn't be feared

Taking control of one's life and making decisions for oneself

Seeing the positive side of one's upbringing, such as being shielded from unnecessary exposure to dangerous elements

Aligning with wise and trustworthy people who can help one with decision-making

PERSONALITY TRAITS THAT MAY FORM

Attributes: Adaptable, cautious, easygoing, innocent, introverted, loyal, obedient, pensive, protective, traditional

Flaws: Childish, controlling, devious, evasive, gullible, ignorant, indecisive, inhibited, insecure, irresponsible, lazy, ungrateful, weak-willed

TRIGGERS THAT MIGHT AGGRAVATE THIS WOUND

Being given a project or duty that affects many people and fearing the responsibility

Facing an important decision that has far-reaching ramifications

Being micro-managed by one's spouse

Making a mistake that opens one up to danger or risk

A real or perceived threat from the organization or entity feared by one's parents

OPPORTUNITIES TO FACE OR OVERCOME THIS WOUND

Being faced with an exciting change that would require one to leave the comfort zone

Realizing one's children are growing anxious about things due to one's anxiety

Realizing one's parents' fears were irrational and wanting to see the world in a more balanced light

Making an important decision and succeeding, learning that one is more capable than one believed

Learning something important because of a mistake and being able to apply it to help others

BEING RAISED BY PARENTS WHO LOVED CONDITIONALLY

EXAMPLES: Parents who showed love…
If one got good grades
As long as one's actions met approval
When one behaved as expected
When one gained accolades and awards for performances
As long as one kept everything organized and clean
If one fit the mold provided
When choices and decisions aligned with parental wishes
When one's physical appearance and bearing met a parent's high standards
Provided one didn't cause embarrassment
When one had control over one's emotions
When one showed the correct level of respect and appreciation

BASIC NEEDS OFTEN COMPROMISED BY THIS WOUND: Love and belonging, esteem and recognition, self-actualization

FALSE BELIEFS THAT COULD BE EMBRACED
I am only worthy when I achieve great things.
I can earn love by being obedient.
I must have absolute control of my emotions and impulses.
Trying doesn't matter; winning does.
I will be whatever I am expected to be.
Others know what is best for me.
Pushing someone to be the best is how you show love.
Pretending is better than disappointing people with the truth.
Love is a tool used to get what you want.

THE CHARACTER MAY FEAR…
Disappointing people, especially loved ones, by failing
Being anything less than exceptional
Rejection
Competition (especially for love)
Isolation
Changes that are impossible to predict or prepare for

POSSIBLE RESPONSES AND RESULTS
Anxiety; being filled with self-doubt
A need for approval and praise
Feeling one must always be a giver rather than a taker
Doing as requested without hesitation
Anticipating the needs of others

A need to tell others about accomplishments to prove one's value

Faking emotions around others rather than expressing one's true feelings

Checking in to get feedback: *Is this okay? Did I do what you wanted?*

Sharing one's joys but not one's disappointments or fears

Respecting people who are proactive, successful, and powerful

A lack of closeness with siblings (if competitiveness was an issue growing up)

Needing to be in charge so one can influence the outcome

Functioning best when working within strict guidelines and instructions

Struggling in situations that require creativity or faith

Always being prepared

Being one's own worst critic

A compulsion to be the best in all things

Micro-managing others to ensure optimal results

Being materialistic; having an attachment to brands that are well-known and respected

Turning even fun things into a competition

Avoiding activities where one is not gifted or there's a good chance of failure

Choosing partners that are at times emotionally distant

Requiring tangible evidence of love (i.e., needing to be told *I love you* frequently)

Being hard on one's children and pushing them to do their best

Having no patience for people who complain or whine

Being very affectionate with one's partner

Being thoughtful

Tying one's worth to achievement and success

PERSONALITY TRAITS THAT MAY FORM

Attributes: Adaptable, affectionate, bold, decisive, disciplined, efficient, extroverted, honorable, industrious, kind, loyal, meticulous

Flaws: Cocky, judgmental, know-it-all, materialistic, nagging, needy, obsessive, perfectionist, possessive, pushy, subservient, stingy

TRIGGERS THAT MIGHT AGGRAVATE THIS WOUND

Competition within the family

When past failures are brought up in jest at gatherings

One's parent openly praising someone else to make the character try harder to succeed

Losing or failing (at work, a game, a competition, etc.)

Driven and successful co-workers (who are, therefore, a threat)

OPPORTUNITIES TO FACE OR OVERCOME THIS WOUND

Meeting someone who loves unconditionally and doesn't require one to "prove" love

Wanting to mend fences with a parent whose health is failing

Having a passion for something that relies on luck or chance rather than skill

An injury, illness, or accident that impairs one's ability to excel in a specific area

BEING SENT AWAY AS A CHILD

EXAMPLES
Being placed in a boarding school
Being sent to live with a relative because of a parent's inability to provide the right sort of care
Being sent to live with one parent because the other parent is unable to deal with behavioral issues
Being placed in a special needs school or care facility
Mandatory placement in a juvenile detention center
Being enrolled in a school to deal with an embarrassing incident
Being sent to live with a foreign host family against one's wishes
Being placed in a reprogramming facility to eradicate perceived deviant behaviors (like sexual orientation) that go against the family's beliefs
Being sent to foster care or placed in an orphanage

BASIC NEEDS OFTEN COMPROMISED BY THIS WOUND: Safety and security, love and belonging, esteem and recognition

FALSE BELIEFS THAT COULD BE EMBRACED
When you need them most, people abandon you.
My value is in what I can contribute, not in who I am.
Parents only love kids who are easy.
People reject me because I'm flawed, so why try to be anything else?
If I keep people at a distance, they can't reject me.
I don't need anyone. I'm stronger on my own.
I don't deserve love and companionship.
If you let people in, they weaken you.
The best way to solve problems is by ditching the people causing them.

THE CHARACTER MAY FEAR…
Experiencing abandonment as an adult (e.g., one's child choosing to live with the ex)
That no one will love them due to their deep flaws
Rejection (being chosen last, excluded, or forgotten)
Connecting with others and opening themselves up to hurt
Doing the wrong thing and driving people away
Never belonging or being accepted

POSSIBLE RESPONSES AND RESULTS
Seeking out relationships that are conditional (transaction-based, one-night stands, etc.)
Engaging in superficial personal relationships
Viewing sexual interest as love
Not getting attached to people

Needing to be in control

Convincing oneself that certain things don't matter (challenging dreams, love, etc.)

Refusing to get a pet because it will one day die and leave one alone

Trying to be the best at everything to prove one has value

Doing things in hopes of earning approval

Negative thoughts that sabotage one's self-worth

Being a people pleaser

Needing to be complimented, catered to, and reassured of one's value

Poor relationships with one's siblings, especially if they were treated differently growing up

Choosing a life where one is alone and doesn't need other people for anything

Trust issues; having a difficult time asking for help

Abandoning others before they can leave

Encouraging others to be dependent so they won't leave

Using sarcasm, unfriendliness, or undesirable behaviors to keep people at a distance

Choosing an unfulfilling career that one's parents will approve of

Living off the grid

Being highly protective or possessive of others

Not keeping in touch with family, especially one's parents

Not tolerating rivals; either taking them out or disengaging so one doesn't have to compete

Choosing easy goals to avoid disappointment

Antagonism toward authority figures

Struggling with self-identity, especially if brainwashing was part of one's past

Difficulty opening up to others and forming close bonds

Becoming an advocate for others

PERSONALITY TRAITS THAT MAY FORM

Attributes: Cautious, disciplined, discreet, introverted, nature-focused, obedient, persistent, private, protective, resourceful

Flaws: Abrasive, antisocial, controlling, disloyal, grumpy, hypocritical, inhibited, insecure, jealous, judgmental, needy, obsessive

TRIGGERS THAT MIGHT AGGRAVATE THIS WOUND

Family reunions or get-togethers

Being exposed to loving and accepting family units

Real or perceived failures, such as being turned down for a date or job

Places similar to those one had to attend as a child, such as a reformatory or church

A disapproving tone of voice

OPPORTUNITIES TO FACE OR OVERCOME THIS WOUND

Having to travel often for work, thereby leaving loved ones at home

Going through a divorce

Meeting someone who is open, accepting, and offers unconditional love no matter what

Being valued and loved by a parental figure (e.g., a neighbor who takes one fishing)

BEING THE PRODUCT OF RAPE

NOTES: This discovery, at any age, will be difficult and can lead to many self-worth and identity concerns. But the fallout can have greater impact if the child learns of his or her lineage at a formative age or during an already difficult time. Other factors to consider are the responses of those around the child who know about the situation, if the child was abused or mistreated as a result, and if he or she was raised by a biological parent or adoptive ones.

BASIC NEEDS OFTEN COMPROMISED BY THIS WOUND: Safety and security, love and belonging, esteem and recognition

FALSE BELIEFS THAT COULD BE EMBRACED
I am a monster because the same blood flows through my veins.
I am unworthy of being loved.
This curse will follow me forever. I am tainted.
If people discover what I am, they will despise me.
Life would be easier if I was dead.
My parents would never have adopted me if they'd known.
My mother would have aborted me if she could have.
I'm defective, a ticking time bomb.
My life is a constant reminder of the evil in this world.

THE CHARACTER MAY FEAR...
That deviancy is genetic
Sexual contact
Their own children growing violent or become offenders
People finding out and passing judgment, which will lead to rejection and abandonment
Being targeted for the parent's crime
Never finding someone who can overlook their past
Becoming a victim of violence as a sort of karmic justice

POSSIBLE RESPONSES AND RESULTS
Lacking confidence and self-esteem
Feeling guilty for being alive; having suicidal thoughts
Believing one's identity will always be The Child Of A Rapist
Pulling away from friends, hobbies, and activities
Finding it hard to concentrate on other things
Feeling empty, emotionally numb, and depressed
Struggling to find joy in life
Going through periods of self-disgust and self-loathing
Sabotaging promising relationships because one believes one deserves to be punished
Trying too hard (to be beautiful, talented, good, etc.) out of a desire to be loved
Feeling shame and humiliation, as if people will immediately know that one is the product of rape

Studying the faces of strangers and wondering who the rapist was

Wanting to know more about the rapist because he is one's parent, and feeling guilty about it

Looking for signs that those who know are disengaging or have secret negative feelings

Clinging to people out of a fear of rejection

Keeping one's past a secret and being terrified others will find out

Questioning one's maternal or paternal abilities

Always putting the needs of others first; sacrificing one's happiness, needs, desires, etc.

Developing an eating disorder

Believing one is the cause of a loved one's unhappiness

Self-medicating with drugs or alcohol

Believing one has to prove oneself in order to have value

Becoming a workaholic in order to become the best in one's field

Becoming aware of the unfairness of certain labels in society

Questioning how people judge; believing that a person's present actions, as opposed to those from the past, are what matters

Trying to focus on one's good qualities rather than things outside one's control

Seeking therapy to process one's complicated feelings

PERSONALITY TRAITS THAT MAY FORM

Attributes: Affectionate, appreciative, courageous, curious, empathetic, nurturing, protective, unselfish

Flaws: Addictive, impulsive, inhibited, insecure, irrational, martyr, needy, obsessive, paranoid, scatterbrained, self-destructive, subservient, suspicious, timid, withdrawn, workaholic, worrywart

TRIGGERS THAT MIGHT AGGRAVATE THIS WOUND

One's birthday

When a friend announces she's pregnant

Receiving a friend or family member's birth announcement

TV shows or movies that feature rape as part of the story line

Media coverage of rapists or violence against women

Seeing items that one knows were part of the rape (a knife, a gun, duct tape, etc.)

Going through old files and finding one's adoption paperwork

Being contacted by one's birth mother

Walking by an abortion clinic

Seeing a pro-life or pro-choice protest

OPPORTUNITIES TO FACE OR OVERCOME THIS WOUND

The parole of one's rapist parent

Discovering a support group for others in the same situation and having to decide whether to share one's feelings or try to cope alone

Locating one's biological parents and wanting to contact them

Discovering that one's biological parent is dying

A desire to have children

EXPERIENCING THE DEATH OF A PARENT
AS A CHILD OR YOUTH

NOTES: A parent dying—from an illness, accident, or another cause—is especially difficult when one is a child or young adult. In this case, a parental death leaves a huge void. The potency of this wound may be especially difficult if violence was involved, if the death was unexpected, or the relationship was strained. The dynamic between the child and the remaining parent (if there was one) and the quality of care given would also effect the depth of the scar caused by this event.

BASIC NEEDS OFTEN COMPROMISED BY THIS WOUND: Safety and security, love and belonging

FALSE BELIEFS THAT COULD BE EMBRACED
People die when you need them most.
It's better to hold back than love someone completely.
Nothing is certain, so why worry about the future?
I will never have a relationship as good as the one I lost.
I won't be a good mother (or father) because I had no role model to show me how.
If I'm too busy to think, I won't have to feel.
I am a burden to the people around me.
People don't want to hear about my pain so it's best to just shut up about it.

THE CHARACTER MAY FEAR…
Losing a loved one
Dying and what comes afterward
Being abandoned or rejected
Places, events, or situations similar to the ones that led to the parent's death
The vulnerability that comes with fully loving someone
Getting sick (if symptoms were part of the parent's death)
Being responsible for others and failing them

POSSIBLE RESPONSES AND RESULTS
Viewing life differently due to a loss of innocence
Regressing to an earlier age (if one is still a child)
Insomnia or restless sleeping habits
Physical aches, pains, and stomach issues
Anxiety and depression
Panic attacks and separation anxiety disorder, especially if the parent was taken violently
Difficulty feeling truly secure
Becoming overly-sentimental and wanting to live in the past
Guilt, shame, or anger as one's memory of the parent grows foggy over time
Feeling resentment or envy of people who have both parents

A lack of ambition

Having a difficult time imagining the future

Self-medicating with drugs or alcohol

Becoming overly attached to people and things, which could escalate to hoarding

Using work as a shield to avoid people and relationships

Becoming fiercely self-reliant so one never has to depend on others

Acting out through deviant behavior (committing crimes, abusing alcohol or drugs, etc.)

Struggling with situations that lack structure or boundaries

Choosing emotional numbness over feeling deeply

Struggling with building healthy, balanced relationships

Becoming a hypochondriac

Worrying about others and what will happen in the future

Growing superstitious when it comes to death or keeping loved ones safe

A memory block that affects one's recall of the dead parent (if one was young when it happened)

Deeply wanting and needing nurturing but being unable to ask for it

A feeling of incompleteness that persists throughout life

Associating love and acceptance with sexual activity

Not wanting to celebrate personal life events because it's too painful without one's parent

Thinking often about who one would be and what life would be like if one's parent was still alive

Appreciating small things that most people overlook

Noticing the absence of things more than other people do

PERSONALITY TRAITS THAT MAY FORM

Attributes: Affectionate, appreciative, nurturing, observant, patient, philosophical, protective, responsible, sentimental, spiritual, unselfish

Flaws: Addictive, antisocial, compulsive, dishonest, disorganized, disrespectful, evasive, forgetful, withdrawn, workaholic, worrywart

TRIGGERS THAT MIGHT AGGRAVATE THIS WOUND

The date of the parent's death

Special life events (graduation, getting married, having a baby, buying a home, etc.)

A difficult decision or personal struggle where parental advice would be welcome

Big holidays that reinforce the specialness of family (Thanksgiving, Hanukkah, etc.)

Attending funerals

Coming across old mementos

OPPORTUNITIES TO FACE OR OVERCOME THIS WOUND

Losing a second parent or grandparent

A living parent growing ill

Becoming a parent oneself

Meeting someone who suffered a similar loss and being able to process it together

GROWING UP IN A CULT

NOTES: A cult is characterized as a fringe organization (often, but not always, defined by a religious belief system) that espouses ideologies and practices believed by others to be dangerous or extreme. This entry will focus on people who were once ensconced in a cult but at some point escaped or turned their backs on it.

BASIC NEEDS OFTEN COMPROMISED BY THIS WOUND: Safety and security, self-actualization

FALSE BELIEFS THAT COULD BE EMBRACED
I am weak-minded, an easy target.
My judgment can't be trusted.
I'll never be free from the ideas that were put into my mind.
All religions are out to brainwash and control people.
You can never really trust an organization's stated motivation.
I'm a disloyal or selfish person (for leaving the cult and one's family and friends).
I can't trust anyone.

THE CHARACTER MAY FEAR...
Their children being pulled into a cult
Someone finding out they were associated with the cult
Organized religion in general
Being manipulated or controlled by anyone
Being on their own
Having to make decisions
Not being able to trust their own mind (due to the cult's brainwashing)
Trusting someone and being taken advantage of
Being assaulted, especially if physical, sexual, or emotional abuse was common in the cult

POSSIBLE RESPONSES AND RESULTS
Avoiding or despising religious groups and organizations
Becoming controlling (in an effort to avoid being controlled again)
Avoiding organized groups, even those that aren't religious in nature
Keeping one's guard up with others
Being extremely private
Suffering from low self-esteem and feelings of low self-worth
Reacting with anger if someone crosses a privacy line
Difficulty making decisions for oneself
Feeling conflicted about one's time in the cult
Keeping secrets
Difficulty recognizing truth from fiction (due to brainwashing by cult members)
Questioning one's decisions; worrying that one's choices are poor ones

Withdrawing from others out of a fear of not being able to trust their motives

Worrying about being taken advantage of by others

Being paranoid that one is being pursued by members of the cult

Suspecting others of dishonesty and deceit

Worrying over the fate of loved ones still in the cult

Being overly cautious; avoiding risk

Distrusting certain aspects of the outside world that one was taught were bad

Feeling isolated by one's experience

Difficulty assimilating into society

Struggling with guilt over leaving one's family and friends behind

Fearing what will happen to one's eternal soul due to leaving the cult

Defending the cult and its practices

Depression and panic attacks

Confusion regarding healthy relationships (what they look like, appropriate boundaries, etc.)

Adhering to and acting on deeply ingrained superstitions related to the cult (engaging in ceremonial cleansings, prayers, etc.)

Being overly protective of one's children

Becoming studious so one can make informed decisions and not be easily led by others

Keeping a journal and writing about what one experienced as a way of working through it

Developing discernment; more easily recognizing manipulation and propaganda

Teaching one's children how to tell truth from deception

Pursuing independence

Joining a support group for ex-cult members

PERSONALITY TRAITS THAT MAY FORM

Attributes: Analytical, appreciative, cautious, independent, industrious, persistent, persuasive, protective

Flaws: Antisocial, callous, controlling, cynical, defensive, evasive, inflexible, inhibited, insecure, judgmental, nervous, paranoid, possessive

TRIGGERS THAT MIGHT AGGRAVATE THIS WOUND

Bumping into someone from the cult

A friend's growing enthusiasm for an organization or religion

A member of a group or organization aggressively pursuing one to join

Seeing a news story about a cult on TV or online

Overhearing others talking disparagingly about one's former cult

OPPORTUNITIES TO FACE OR OVERCOME THIS WOUND

A family member being drawn into a belief system that one fears might be extreme

Suspecting that one is being stalked or watched by members of the cult

Being blamed and shamed by family members who are still part of the organization

Being contacted by a loved one stuck in the cult who wants help getting out

A journalist or police officer asking for details about one's childhood

GROWING UP IN FOSTER CARE

EXAMPLES: Being placed in foster care due to…
One's surviving parent passing away and not having any relatives to take responsibility
One's parents dying and relatives being unwilling to take one in
Being taken away from drug-addicted or otherwise neglectful parents
Being given up for adoption but never finding a home
Being abandoned by one's parent
A parent's abuse causing one to be removed from the home
Being given up because of one's extreme behavioral, medical, or cognitive challenges
One's only parent being incarcerated, hospitalized, or placed in a mental facility

BASIC NEEDS OFTEN COMPROMISED BY THIS WOUND: Physiological needs, safety and security, love and belonging, esteem and recognition, self-actualization

FALSE BELIEFS THAT COULD BE EMBRACED
I am defective.
I am unworthy of love.
This world only cares about people who are whole (if one has a disability or specific challenge).
I don't know who I am.
I will never find a place to belong or call home.
No one wants someone who's broken.
People are inherently cruel.
The powerful always take advantage of the weak.

THE CHARACTER MAY FEAR…
Loving or becoming connected to someone only to lose them
Rejection and abandonment
Poverty
Being bullied, abused, and hurt
Trusting someone and being betrayed
That life will never get better
Becoming attached to any person or place
People in positions of strength, power, and authority

POSSIBLE RESPONSES AND RESULTS
Behavioral volatility; growing angry quickly
Keeping secrets and being uncommunicative
Lying or making up untruths, even when they aren't important
Telling people what they want to hear
Being highly private
Being very protective of one's possessions and close relationships

Avoiding locations, activities, and groups that have a strong family focus

Keeping a bug-out bag or secret stash of items in case one has to leave quickly

Steering conversations away from personal topics

Pushing people away as a defense mechanism

Difficulty sharing certain things

Craving routine, yet being unable to adapt to it easily

Wanting stability and permanence but questioning whether one deserves these things

Looking for exits; being watchful for danger or threats

PTSD symptoms (being in constant fight-or-flight mode, startling easily, etc.)

Trust issues; difficulty taking people at their word

Daydreaming of a future time when one is independent and not under the thumb of others

Being disdainful of promises due to a desire to avoid more disappointment

Difficulty asking for help, relying on people, or admitting that one needs others

Being surprised when people follow through or do what they say

A tendency to hoard certain things (money, food or items symbolizing what one was denied, etc.)

Being emotionally unattached in relationships; choosing partners for convenience or shared goals

Viewing sex as being different than intimacy

Living sparsely; not forming attachments to places or things, yet craving something permanent

Being highly empathetic; wanting to save others who are at risk and going to great lengths to do so

Becoming fiercely loyal to the few people one allows to get close

PERSONALITY TRAITS THAT MAY FORM

Attributes: Adaptable, alert, analytical, perceptive, persuasive, private, proactive, protective, resourceful, sentimental, thrifty, wise

Flaws: Abrasive, addictive, antisocial, apathetic, confrontational, cruel, cynical, devious, dishonest, violent, withdrawn

TRIGGERS THAT MIGHT AGGRAVATE THIS WOUND

Someone failing to show up when they said they would

A break-up that causes one to be alone again

Seeing parents who are mistreating or ignoring their children

Sensory or situational reminders of one's negative foster care experiences

Finding oneself back in the foster home's neighborhood

Being innocently asked about one's childhood or hometown

Locations where families typically gather (picnic sites, campgrounds, amusement parks, etc.)

OPPORTUNITIES TO FACE OR OVERCOME THIS WOUND

Being in an accident that could have left one's child parentless, and realizing one needs other people

Trying to help a distressed foster child but being unable to draw him or her out

Wanting to become an advocate for children (perhaps by becoming a foster parent or social worker)

Desiring a relationship with someone who also struggles with trust and connection

GROWING UP IN THE PUBLIC EYE

EXAMPLES
Coming from a family with extreme wealth
Having a parent who is important and well connected (e.g., the head of a government organization)
Having a parent who is a famous movie star, entertainer, athlete, etc.
Being part of a royal family
Being part of a very old and powerful family—of aristocrats, for example
Having an infamous parent, such as a serial killer or terrorist bomber
Being famous oneself (a singing prodigy, an actor, a beauty queen, etc.)
Being famous for an unusual talent, like being able to talk to the dead or heal people
Coming from a political family (of senators, governors, diplomats, etc.)

BASIC NEEDS OFTEN COMPROMISED BY THIS WOUND: Safety and security, love and belonging, esteem and recognition, self-actualization

FALSE BELIEFS THAT COULD BE EMBRACED
I don't know who I am, just what I'm supposed to be.
I can't afford to make mistakes.
People expect me to be just like my famous mother (or father, grandparent, etc.).
Everyone wants me to fail because I'm famous.
People only want to use me for my fame.
The cards are stacked against me. (if one's fame is negative)
Without my fame, I am nothing.
I have the same genes; what if I'm a monster too? (if the fame came from a parent's notoriety)

THE CHARACTER MAY FEAR...
Trusting the wrong person
Public embarrassment
Making a decision that will haunt them forever
Never measuring up
Letting people down
Taking risks
Being vulnerable and being taken advantage of or betrayed
A secret being discovered that could ruin their reputation

POSSIBLE RESPONSES AND RESULTS
Being obsessive about one's appearance (clothing, hair, behavior, etc.)
Holding back rather than taking risks out of a fear of publicly screwing up
Being more mature than one's peers; having to grow up fast in the limelight
Being unable to relate to "regular" peers
Keeping secrets or avoiding voicing one's opinion

Obsessing over one's imperfections

Being very hard on oneself

False bravado; pretending to be overly confident

Having few genuine close friendships

Becoming a "mean girl" or something similar to shield oneself from haters

Doing what one is told and not thinking for oneself

Working hard and not making time for oneself; trying to keep up with expectations

Engaging in anonymous activities to feel like a regular person (wearing disguises, visiting chat boards with a fake name, etc.)

Using alcohol to loosen up and not feel so self-conscious

Using drugs to cope with high expectations or to escape

Purposely acting in ways that defy the expectations of others

Becoming entitled; believing one is above the law

Trying to buy one's way into situations or out of trouble

Needing things to be bigger, better, and riskier to enjoy them

Not knowing who one is because one is always playing a part for the media

Messy burnouts and meltdowns from the pressure

Seeking therapy (and help for addictions, if one has them)

Striving to distinguish oneself in healthy ways

PERSONALITY TRAITS THAT MAY FORM

Attributes: Adaptable, cautious, cooperative, courteous, disciplined, discreet, extroverted, generous, hospitable, independent, introverted, kind, loyal

Flaws: Addictive, callous, cocky, compulsive, confrontational, cynical, defensive, evasive, extravagant, foolish, frivolous, volatile, whiny, workaholic

TRIGGERS THAT MIGHT AGGRAVATE THIS WOUND

Discovering that a trusted friend is only interested in one's fame and lifestyle

A friend revealing one's well-kept secret

Being ripped apart in the media for spurning reporters

Being misrepresented in the tabloids

Being swarmed by paparazzi or fans when one was hoping to get away and de-stress

Having one's privacy invaded by the media

An entitled fan demanding an autograph or a selfie

OPPORTUNITIES TO FACE OR OVERCOME THIS WOUND

Watching friends with normal lives follow their own paths, and wanting to do the same

Developing a drug habit or other vice that is not sustainable

Having a dream that conflicts with family expectations

Developing depression and anxiety disorders that cause one to contemplate suicide

Having a sibling who is struggling with the pressure and knowing they need an advocate

Watching one's child having difficulty relating to others

GROWING UP IN THE SHADOW OF A SUCCESSFUL SIBLING

EXAMPLES: Growing up with a brother or sister who…
Excelled at a sport
Was gifted in the arts
Succeeded academically
Was a celebrity
Was a prodigy
Was extremely popular or well-liked
Was incredibly beautiful or handsome
Excelled at everything he or she did

BASIC NEEDS OFTEN COMPROMISED BY THIS WOUND: Love and belonging, esteem and recognition, self-actualization

FALSE BELIEFS THAT COULD BE EMBRACED
I'm ugly (or stupid, clumsy, etc.).
I'm not good at anything.
I will never be able to distinguish myself.
I have nothing to offer.
I can't compete, so it's pointless to try.
People will always be more interested in my sibling than in me.
No matter what I do in life, it won't be good enough.
If you want people to love you, you have to stand out.

THE CHARACTER MAY FEAR…
Never being able to distinguish himself
Inadequacy
Failing (and proving their inferiority)
Being loved less than the sibling
Being pitied
Conditional love
Taking risks and ending up worse off than they are now

POSSIBLE RESPONSES AND RESULTS
Pursuing an interest other than the one in which a sibling excels (even if one loves the same things)
Being driven to succeed
Struggling with low self-worth
Needing desperately to distinguish oneself
Always feeling one-upped by the sibling
Friction with the sibling caused by one's inferiority complex
Constantly competing with the sibling out of a desire to beat them at anything

Having low expectations for oneself

Enjoying a sibling's struggles or failures, then feeling guilty about it

Becoming needy out of a desire to gain affection

Adopting negative attention-seeking behaviors (being rebellious, fighting, abusing drugs, etc.)

Confusing the sibling's kindness with pity, and rejecting it

Becoming devious or dishonest in order to appear more successful than one actually is

Undermining one's sibling so he or she will lose favor with others

Rejecting one's sibling as a peer; choosing friends who are part of a different peer group

Becoming subservient to one's sibling; losing one's sense of personal identity

Trying to be just like one's sibling

Being always on the lookout for favoritism, especially with one's parents and relatives

Becoming a people pleaser

Relishing praise and compliments but wondering if they're genuine

Withdrawing from others

Using a sibling's accomplishments to get what one wants (access to a club or group, attention from the opposite sex, etc.)

Purposely adopting positive traits that are different than one's sibling's (being merciful, easygoing, unselfish, etc.)

Healthily distancing oneself from the sibling to cut down on drama and conflict

Determining to take the high ground and support one's sibling rather than tear them down

Seeking to mend the relationship

PERSONALITY TRAITS THAT MAY FORM

Attributes: Ambitious, charming, courteous, disciplined, empathetic, flirtatious, imaginative, independent, pensive, persistent, private, quirky

Flaws: Catty, childish, cynical, devious, frivolous, humorless, insecure, irrational, lazy, needy, oversensitive, rebellious, withdrawn

TRIGGERS THAT MIGHT AGGRAVATE THIS WOUND

One's plans being canceled when a commitment comes up for someone else, highlighting again that one isn't a priority with others

Achieving something great but it being overshadowed by another's accomplishment

Parents missing an important moment in one's life to attend a sibling's event

Discovering that one is being used by a friend to get to one's sibling

As an adult, being constantly overshadowed by a co-worker, parent, or other person

OPPORTUNITIES TO FACE OR OVERCOME THIS WOUND

Discovering that one's sibling is also dealing with identity issues and is wanting to choose a different path but feels unable to do so

One's sibling turning to drugs to cope, and realizing that one can step in and offer support

One's parents blatantly favoring the sibling's children over one's own, causing one to take action

Pursuing a passion despite a lack of giftedness and finding joy, regardless of the outcome

Wanting to be supportive and happy for a partner who has received acclaim

GROWING UP WITH A SIBLING'S DISABILITY OR CHRONIC ILLNESS

EXAMPLES: Getting through childhood can be difficult enough when life isn't overly complicated. But having a sibling with chronic, long-term, or complex issues that require extra financial and physical attention from caregivers can make things much harder. Some examples of these issues include having a sibling with…

A traumatic brain injury

A failing organ in need of a transplant

Cancer

AIDS

Cystic fibrosis, congenital heart problems, muscular dystrophy, cerebral palsy, seizure disorders, and other long-term afflictions

Life-threatening eating disorders

A physical disfigurement (loss of a limb, visible scarring, abnormal growths, etc.)

Blindness, deafness, or muteness

Mental disorders (OCD, depression, schizophrenia, bipolar disorder, etc.)

Developmental disorders (autism spectrum disorders, Down syndrome, Tourette's, etc.)

BASIC NEEDS OFTEN COMPROMISED BY THIS WOUND: Safety and security, love and belonging, esteem and recognition, self-actualization

FALSE BELIEFS THAT COULD BE EMBRACED

My parents love him or her more than me.

It doesn't matter what I do; my sibling will always be more important than me.

This (parents divorcing, being unable to pursue a passion, etc.) is my sibling's fault.

I'm a terrible person for feeling anger (or resentment, frustration, etc.) about this.

Life is not permanent. I could die at any time.

I need to excel in some way so this gift of good health isn't squandered.

The only constant in life is pain. Anything good will be taken from me eventually.

THE CHARACTER MAY FEAR…

The sibling dying

Dying or being struck with the same affliction

That life will never be any different

Never being able to achieve their dreams

Always being loved second best by their parents (or a spouse, their children, etc.)

POSSIBLE RESPONSES AND RESULTS

Avoiding the sibling in public (as a child)

Acting out as a way of getting a parent's attention (when young)

Overachieving as a means of earning a parent's love

Becoming independent out of necessity

Seeking comfort and escape as a youth through overindulging (in food, gaming, etc.)

Developing an eating disorder

Maturing early emotionally

Becoming overly compliant to one's parents so as not to add to their burden

Hiding one's true feelings because one feels guilty about them

Getting upset over little things

Distancing oneself from the family unit

Becoming anxious about oneself or a parent falling ill

Exhibiting hypochondriac tendencies

Rebelling against authority; becoming defiant

Sneaking out to escape one's home and the constant reminders of illness

Acting out whenever the sibling's circumstances interfere with one's plans

Neediness in peer relationships

Blaming all of one's misfortunes on the sibling's illness

Looking to others for love and affection

Seeking connection and love by becoming sexually active at an early age

Refusing to ask for help to avoid being seen as weak

Taking on adult responsibilities to care for one's sibling

Bonding deeply with one's sibling despite hardships

Being fiercely loyal; standing up for one's sibling when others tease or malign them

Empathizing with others who are ill

Engaging in social activism to raise awareness of the sibling's illness

PERSONALITY TRAITS THAT MAY FORM

Attributes: Appreciative, calm, curious, diplomatic, easygoing, generous, gentle, honorable, idealistic, mature, nurturing, passionate, patient

Flaws: Catty, childish, cynical, dishonest, disloyal, frivolous, grumpy, manipulative, martyr, melodramatic, morbid, needy, nervous

TRIGGERS THAT MIGHT AGGRAVATE THIS WOUND

Seeing a parent favoring one child over the other

One's plans being cancelled, even when no one is to blame

Having an important accomplishment or event overshadowed by someone else

Experiencing symptoms that correspond with the sibling's illness or disorder

Favoritism and slights as an adult (e.g., parents always staying at the sibling's house for Christmas)

OPPORTUNITIES TO FACE OR OVERCOME THIS WOUND

Conceiving a child and worrying that he or she will inherit the sibling's affliction

The death of one's sibling

Participating in a charity event and becoming more empathetic toward one's sibling

Having a child develop a condition that requires extra attention and not wanting to make one's other children feel minimized

HAVING A CONTROLLING OR OVERLY STRICT PARENT

EXAMPLES: Being raised by a parent who…
Criticized one's weight and eating habits
Meddled in one's social life, including choosing friends and activities
Manipulated situations to get one to obey or agree with their choices
Ignored emotional pain in order to encourage one to toughen up
Withheld love and affection when one disagreed or didn't behave as expected
Applied harsh punishments for poor academics or rule infractions
Critiqued one's actions and performances so mistakes wouldn't be repeated in the future
Insisted on rigorous practices or instruction in a skill area to increase proficiency
Never admitted to being wrong or not knowing what was best
Was hypocritical, doing things they forbade one to do
Threw away cherished items when they determined it was time for one to move on or let go

BASIC NEEDS OFTEN COMPROMISED BY THIS WOUND: Love and belonging, esteem and recognition, self-actualization

FALSE BELIEFS THAT COULD BE EMBRACED
I'll never be good enough.
I'm a huge disappointment.
My ideas are flawed and shouldn't be trusted.
I need constant structure or my weaknesses will take over.
If I fail at anything, I will prove my parents right.
In order to have value, I have to be the best.
Someone else should make decisions for me because I'll only mess things up.
I can't have kids because I'll ruin them the same way my parents did me.

THE CHARACTER MAY FEAR…
Failing
Being imperfect
Love being withdrawn
Disappointing others; not measuring up
Screwing up something important
Being placed in the spotlight, put in charge, or having to lead
Being shamed and scrutinized
Making a bad choice that will prove their parents right
Expressing their emotions and being vulnerable
Freedom and choices
Becoming a parent and repeating the cycle

POSSIBLE RESPONSES AND RESULTS

Being hard on oneself (via negative self-talk, forcing oneself to work harder to achieve, etc.)

Striving for perfection in all things

Becoming a workaholic

Second-guessing one's decisions (what to wear, do, etc.)

Asking for advice when decisions need to be made; needing reassurance

Struggling with identity issues

Becoming a people pleaser

Making one's achievements known to others in order to be validated

Developing nervous habits, an eating disorder, a stutter, etc.

Choosing partners who resemble one's parent (controlling, narcissistic, inflexible, etc.)

Low self-esteem; seeing oneself as flawed or being devoid of the "right" qualities

Being exceedingly self-critical; berating oneself for mistakes or less-than-optimal results

Exerting control by placing extreme restrictions on one's diet, activities, spending, etc.

Punishing oneself for perceived wrongs by avoiding fun activities, desires, or pleasures

Self-medicating with drugs or alcohol

Finding it difficult to self-advocate

Being uncomfortable when asked what one wants

Feeling personally responsible when things don't go right

Burying one's emotions and feeling shame for having them

Lying to avoid judgment or getting in trouble

Experiencing regret for following a parent's desires and missing out on one's dreams

Blaming one's parents for one's mistakes

Hostility toward one's parents

Being overly strict (repeating the cycle) or lax (overcompensating) with one's children

As an adult, limiting what one shares with one's parents to avoid arguments and judgment

PERSONALITY TRAITS THAT MAY FORM

Attributes: Adaptable, alert, efficient, focused, industrious, loyal, meticulous, obedient, organized, persistent, private, proactive

Flaws: Addictive, cynical, dishonest, evasive, inflexible, inhibited, obsessive, paranoid, perfectionist, rebellious, resentful, stubborn

TRIGGERS THAT MIGHT AGGRAVATE THIS WOUND

Failing in an area where one is expected to succeed

Being paired with a boss, work partner, or mentor who is overly critical

Having one's own children "judged" by their grandparent

Parental gifts that are not-so-subtle hints (a gym membership, a self-help book, etc.)

OPPORTUNITIES TO FACE OR OVERCOME THIS WOUND

Struggling to retain employees at work because one's expectations are set impossibly high

Taking on too much work and responsibility and needing help to avoid catastrophic failure

Needing to care for an elderly parent and not wanting to allow the toxicity into one's home

An addiction escalating to the point where one needs to come to terms with the cause

HAVING PARENTS WHO FAVORED ONE CHILD OVER ANOTHER

EXAMPLES: Being raised by parents who…
Doted on a child because of a special skill, talent, or quality
Put most or all their time into one child's interests and hobbies
Favored birth children over stepchildren (taking them on special trips, buying them gifts, etc.)
Had different rules and privileges for one child because of gender, birth order, etc.
Were more affectionate with one child
Always blamed one, even when a sibling was at fault
Disciplined one more harshly than the other children for the same transgressions
Bonded more with one child because of his or her pleasant disposition
Catered to one child because of an illness or condition
Gave one child more freedom than the other

BASIC NEEDS OFTEN COMPROMISED BY THIS WOUND: Love and belonging, esteem and recognition, self-actualization

FALSE BELIEFS THAT COULD BE EMBRACED
I'll never be as good as my sibling, so why try?
If I try harder to be good, maybe they'll love me just as much.
There must be something wrong with me.
I can't please them; nothing I do is good enough.
Being alone is better than being with people who don't want me.
I will never measure up to those around me.
Love is conditional.
If you aren't first, you're last.
Everything in life is a competition.

THE CHARACTER MAY FEAR…
Being rejected
Competing with others
Being one-upped or outperformed by others
Disappointing people
Making themselves vulnerable
Loving others (since love can be withdrawn)
Failure
Never being able to distinguish themselves

POSSIBLE RESPONSES AND RESULTS
People-pleasing behaviors; doing things for praise
Trying to find a way to stand out and make one's parents proud

Striving for perfection to gain a parent's attention and unconditional love

Seeking negative attention when positive attention is denied

Resentment toward one's sibling

Seeking ways to undermine the sibling

Being drawn to adults (a teacher, a friend's mom, etc.) who show interest or offer praise

Having a strained relationship with one's sibling

Seeing everything as a competition

Being sensitive to even perceived favoritism in all areas of life

Needing frequent reassurance in romantic and work relationships

Difficulty with teamwork and team building; preferring to work alone

Going above and beyond in relationships (via lavishing attention, caretaking, etc.)

Always comparing oneself to one's siblings

A sibling's name being a trigger for anger or resentment

Becoming an overachiever

As an adult, struggling to be happy for the sibling when he or she succeeds

Becoming subservient to aging parents in hopes of being seen in a new light

Accidentally repeating the parent's mistakes with one's own children

Avoiding one's family as an adult

Seeking validation and love from people other than one's parent

Making sure everything is fair when parenting one's own children

Showing love and affection to others without reserve

PERSONALITY TRAITS THAT MAY FORM

Attributes: Ambitious, appreciative, cooperative, diplomatic, empathetic, generous, honorable, humble, independent, introverted, just

Flaws: Confrontational, defensive, disloyal, disrespectful, possessive, rebellious, reckless, rowdy, self-destructive, stubborn, subservient

TRIGGERS THAT MIGHT AGGRAVATE THIS WOUND

As an adult, perceiving a slight (real or imagined) by one's parent

Being a victim of favoritism at work or within a social circle

Being rejected romantically while someone else succeeds

Holidays that bring the family together, making the inequity obvious

Time with one's parent being dominated by conversation about one's sibling

OPPORTUNITIES TO FACE OR OVERCOME THIS WOUND

Experiencing feelings of resentment even after the favoritism has stopped

Being overly competitive (at work, in relationships, etc.) and losing friends or a lover because of it

The constant need for validation causing problems in one's marriage

Recognizing that one is unintentionally favoring one child over another

Growing jealous of the achievements of one's child and feeling insecure as attention is placed on him or her

LIVING IN A DANGEROUS NEIGHBORHOOD

EXAMPLES: Growing up…
In a high crime area
Where neighborhood gangs fight over territory or apply heavy pressure on people to join
In a location stalked by a specific predator (human or otherwise)
Where bombings, minefields, or gun violence are a constant threat
Where militant groups perform routine kidnappings and violence
In an area that has frequent biological or chemical threats
Where extreme poverty gives rise to desperation and fighting over resources
In a prominent drug trafficking location
In an area where one is not only unwelcome but is despised (for one's religious affiliations, race, etc.)
In a place that has been abandoned for political reasons by police or the government

BASIC NEEDS OFTEN COMPROMISED BY THIS WOUND: Physiological needs, safety and security, love and belonging, esteem and recognition, self-actualization

FALSE BELIEFS THAT COULD BE EMBRACED
I can't escape this type of life.
The world doesn't care about people like me.
The only way to survive is to become what I hate.
The only way I can have anything is to take it.
There's no justice in this world.
I can't protect the people I love.
I'm not strong or powerful enough to stand up against the opposition (a group, a gang, etc.).
Nothing I do will change anything.
All these people (of a specific race, affiliation, religion, etc.) are evil, corrupt, or dangerous.
To survive, you must embrace violence.

THE CHARACTER MAY FEAR…
Being hurt or killed
Not being able to protect their family
Being taken advantage of
Losing hope and simply giving in or giving up
Trusting the wrong person
A specific people group, the government, or those in power

POSSIBLE RESPONSES AND RESULTS
Heightened awareness; subconsciously checking one's surroundings for danger
Lying when it's prudent to do so and pretending to be something one is not
Erecting a wall around one's emotions
Being uncommunicative with others
Taking chances or behaving recklessly

Gravitating to or admiring those within one's group who are powerful, respected, and feared
Having a difficult time taking people at their word
Pessimism and negativity
Cynicism due to broken promises, propaganda, and seeing the ugliness in people
Passing one's biases on to one's children
Prioritizing security (e.g., adding locks and alarm systems)
Hiding things to keep them safe
Mistrust of strangers and authority
Making do with less, even if one can afford better, to avoid becoming a target
Pursuing whatever might allow one to escape (education, sports, relocating, etc.)
Formulating and pursuing a plan to escape to a better place
Adopting flexible moral beliefs; doing whatever it takes to survive
Turning a blind eye to one's own safety
Being so focused on day-to-day survival that one doesn't make plans for the future
Becoming highly protective of one's family
Pushing one's children to make better choices
Ensuring one's children stay busy to keep them out of trouble
Returning to the old neighborhood to help improve it (through a rehabilitation project, opening a shelter, etc.)
Mentoring young people from one's former neighborhood

PERSONALITY TRAITS THAT MAY FORM
Attributes: Adaptable, alert, bold, cautious, disciplined, discreet, focused, idealistic, independent, just, loyal, nurturing, observant, persistent, private, proactive, protective, simple, spiritual, thrifty
Flaws: Abrasive, addictive, apathetic, callous, confrontational, controlling, cruel, cynical, dishonest, evasive, fanatical, hostile, impatient, irrational, judgmental, macho, manipulative, nervous, pessimistic, rebellious, reckless, self-destructive, stubborn, suspicious, timid, volatile, worrywart

TRIGGERS THAT MIGHT AGGRAVATE THIS WOUND
Learning that a peaceful neighbor or friend has been claimed by violence
Hearing rumors of a family member hanging out with a gang
The presence of police cars and officers
Learning about the sexual assault of a friend or family member as they walked home
Hearing gun shots or sirens
Being mugged

OPPORTUNITIES TO FACE OR OVERCOME THIS WOUND
Birthing a child and realizing that, if something doesn't change, he or she will face the same difficulties one struggled with growing up
Being victimized by those who are supposed to provide protection (the police, lawmakers, etc.)
Escaping the neighborhood but leaving loved ones behind in the process

LIVING IN AN EMOTIONALLY REPRESSED HOUSEHOLD

NOTES: In this kind of household, one or both parents do not support a child's emotional growth. They use disinterest, avoidance, ridicule, or rejection to invalidate what the child feels and discourage emotional displays. Often the root cause is a mental disorder, an addiction, or a negative coping strategy stemming from a trauma that the parent(s) experienced before the child was born.

BASIC NEEDS OFTEN COMPROMISED BY THIS WOUND: Love and belonging, esteem and recognition, self-actualization

FALSE BELIEFS THAT COULD BE EMBRACED
It's better to keep emotions in than be ridiculed for feeling them.
I am not deserving of love.
No one cares what I think or feel.
Joy is an impossible dream.
It's better to just shut up and toe the line.
What I think and feel doesn't matter because I don't matter.

THE CHARACTER MAY FEAR…
Rejection and abandonment
Attachment and love
Criticism and ridicule
Strong emotions and being overwhelmed by them
That they will never belong
Social situations where they lack the knowledge or experience to navigate them successfully

POSSIBLE RESPONSES AND RESULTS
Wanting to express one's emotions but not knowing how
Resentment toward one's parent(s) for their emotional unavailability
Wondering why one's parents even had children
Having a distant relationship with one's parents
Growing frustrated when someone talks but refuses to listen
Being unable to cry freely
Feeling "different" and disconnected from others
Feeling awkward in one's own skin
Struggling to identify what one is feeling
Having frequent low times when one feels melancholy, sentimental, or sad
Feeling unworthy when people show one love or kindness
Being labeled as uptight because one struggles to relax and have fun
Becoming agreeable as a way of avoiding having to explain one's emotional position
Craving intimacy, affection, and free expression, but feeling unable to give or receive it
Feeling deep shame or embarrassment when strong emotions well up

Keeping secrets

Having well-defined boundaries and keeping people at arm's length

Having few close friends

Not sharing accomplishments or sources of pride with others

Bottling up emotions until they explode

Being unsure of the appropriate emotional response in some situations

Having reserved body language (smaller movements and reactions)

Shutting down and disengaging when high emotions are triggered

Sticking to comfortable routines

Needing and seeking approval (by working hard, going above and beyond, etc.) to feel worthy

Being a follower due to one's lack of identity

Discomfort in social situations that involve engaging with new (or many) people

Overreacting when one feels cornered and unable to safely disengage or deploy coping mechanisms

A profound sense of grief over one's lack of emotional connections, leading to substance abuse

Continuing the cycle with one's children and holding back emotionally

Feeling compassion and empathy but being overwhelmed by both

Becoming overly protective of loved ones and possibly smothering them

A desire to be there for people who need help but not always knowing how

Breaking the cycle and showing one's children emotional support and advocacy

Being a deep thinker

PERSONALITY TRAITS THAT MAY FORM

Attributes: Calm, cooperative, diplomatic, disciplined, gentle, humble, independent, introverted, kind, loyal, merciful, nurturing, pensive

Flaws: Addictive, apathetic, controlling, humorless, inhibited, insecure, irresponsible, needy, nervous, oversensitive, resentful

TRIGGERS THAT MIGHT AGGRAVATE THIS WOUND

Being dismissed by someone

Family holidays and gatherings where one knows the interactions will be superficial

Abrupt changes that throw one off-balance

Achieving something wonderful but feeling awkward about telling anyone about it

Having something bad happen and feeling the void of parental support

Facing a hard decision and needing advice

OPPORTUNITIES TO FACE OR OVERCOME THIS WOUND

A health crisis that raises the desire to try and reconcile with one's parents

Reaching a breaking point and choosing to facilitate healing by cutting off one's parents

Wanting to find love and connection and knowing one must practice self-care first to do so

Recognizing that one is holding back in a promising new relationship

Seeing one's child struggling to express the same emotions one typically represses

LIVING WITH AN ABUSIVE CAREGIVER

NOTES: Abuse in this entry is centered on the physical and psychological sort. (For information on sexual abuse, please see CHILDHOOD SEXUAL ABUSE BY A KNOWN PERSON). Caregivers may be parents, adult family members, adoptive or foster parents, or adults from organizations or institutions that were part of the child's life. When abuse happens at the hand of a trusted caregiver, the aftereffects can be especially traumatic and long lasting. Chronic maltreatment is particularly destructive and can alter the structure of a child's brain during this critical, formative stage.

BASIC NEEDS OFTEN COMPROMISED BY THIS WOUND: Physiological needs, safety and security, love and belonging, esteem and recognition, self-actualization

FALSE BELIEFS THAT COULD BE EMBRACED

No one wants something that's broken.

Dying is the only way to be free of pain.

Being alone is safer.

I am as useless as my parents said I was.

Life will never get better.

People can sense I am a victim and they will always prey on me.

To take my life back, I need to get revenge.

To avoid being the victim, I must become the aggressor.

A system that fails to protect kids cannot be trusted.

THE CHARACTER MAY FEAR...

Rejection and abandonment

Having to rely on other people

Love (because it can be used against you)

People in authority or gatekeepers who have a measure of control over them

The caregiver

Happiness or success, because they can easily be taken away

Being vulnerable and exposed

Being victimized again

People finding out about their past

POSSIBLE RESPONSES AND RESULTS

Depression and anxiety

Developing a psychiatric disorder

High-risk behaviors, such as smoking, drug use, and unprotected sex

Becoming ill or experiencing chronic pain caused by stress

Jumpiness and heightened arousal; being sensitive to the changes in one's environment

Having nightmares or night terrors

PTSD (post-traumatic stress disorder)

Battling low self-esteem and low self-worth

Developing an eating disorder or becoming obese

Escaping or dissociating when people yell or scream

Being unable to recall certain parts of one's childhood

Trust issues that impact one's ability to form friendships and other intimate relationships

Making poor relationship choices (e.g., choosing an abusive partner or a neglectful one)

Viewing the world as a dangerous place

Difficulty coping with stress

Self-mutilation, thoughts of suicide, or suicide attempts

Distorted thinking about possible harm that may befall oneself and loved ones

Feeling powerless when something negative happens

Underestimating one's abilities, talents, and influence

Not trusting one's feelings or instincts

Trying to suppress emotions, which leads to volatile outbursts

Projecting one's feelings about past hurts onto others

Having a difficult time asking for help

Overthinking, worrying, and having thoughts that won't turn off

A deep fear that one might abuse others, especially one's children

Seeking therapy

Becoming a protector or advocate for vulnerable individuals, animals, causes, etc.

Trying to find joy in small things, since large ones can seem impossible

Appreciating the things others take for granted

PERSONALITY TRAITS THAT MAY FORM

Attributes: Appreciative, cautious, courageous, empathetic, generous, independent, just, merciful, nurturing, observant, protective

Flaws: Cruel, dishonest, disrespectful, gullible, hostile, humorless, hypocritical, impulsive, inhibited, irrational, manipulative

TRIGGERS THAT MIGHT AGGRAVATE THIS WOUND

Witnessing an act of violence

Being yelled at, grabbed, or shaken

Hearing the same insults and slurs one's abuser used

Reading a book that contains abuse

Seeing a person who resembles one's attacker in appearance, manner, or habits

OPPORTUNITIES TO FACE OR OVERCOME THIS WOUND

Wanting to have a child but fearing one will continue the dysfunctional parental cycle

Being in a twelve-step program and wanting to make amends for one's poor choices

Becoming suicidal and needing help

Discovering someone else is being abused and wanting to help

Being asked to share one's story and help others

NOT BEING A PRIORITY GROWING UP

NOTES: This wound differs from neglect in that a character's basic needs were provided, but anything that might lead to greater happiness and satisfaction was absent. One's likes and dislikes were of little to no interest, achievements may have gone unnoticed, and a parent's work, hobbies, and desires would have come first. It is also possible that other siblings may have been put before the child; if this was the case, see the HAVING PARENTS WHO FAVORED ONE CHILD OVER ANOTHER entry for additional ideas.

BASIC NEEDS OFTEN COMPROMISED BY THIS WOUND: Love and belonging, esteem and recognition, self-actualization

FALSE BELIEFS THAT COULD BE EMBRACED
The world will never see me, no matter what I do.
Other people should come first because they are more important.
I am a follower, not a leader.
People only notice those who are exceptional.
I shouldn't expect too much out of life.
As long as I help others do what they love, I'll have value.
People walk all over me because I'm weak.
I don't matter, and nothing I do will make any difference.

THE CHARACTER MAY FEAR…
That their needs and desires will never be a priority
Becoming a parent who minimizes their own children, continuing the cycle
Choosing their own path and making a huge mistake
That their life truly has no meaning
Never making a difference, having an impact, or feeling special in any way

POSSIBLE RESPONSES AND RESULTS
Difficulty standing up for oneself
Becoming overly accommodating and being taken advantage of
Being easily intimidated
Bowing out rather than competing with others
Becoming a people pleaser and hating oneself for it
Making choices that will gain a parent's approval
Letting others choose (activities, vacation spots, etc.) and just going along with things
Self-identity struggles
Low self-esteem; focusing on one's weaknesses rather than one's strengths
Being unable to decide what one really wants out of life
Struggling to ask for things that one wants
Appreciating any praise or attention one receives, regardless of who it's from
Being deeply wounded when someone cancels plans or doesn't show up

Difficulty asking others for help due to not wanting to be a burden
Never being the first to make a move in relationships
Choosing partners who are highly assertive or even narcissistic
Feeling that one is a coward for not speaking up
Negative self-talk that sabotages one's boldness
Holding in anger until one explodes
Not sharing one's achievements or good news because doing so makes one feel uncomfortable
Keeping a hobby, interest, or guilty pleasure a secret from others
Hating things one's parents cared deeply about or loved to do
Avoiding places, people, and interests that bring to mind one's low priority in the family
Being surprised when the personal information one disclosed to someone is remembered later
Making secret plans to chase a dream but not following through on it
Enjoying online interaction and relationships because they allow one to feel more confident
Feeling guilty putting time and money into one's own interests if one is also responsible for others
Catering to a child's every desire to avoid being like one's own parents
Seeking help to overcome real or perceived weaknesses via books, courses, or mentors
Always making time for people no matter what
Offering small kindnesses (notes, gifts, favors, etc.) to let people know they are valued
Deep loyalty for close friends who show they care
Making new memories by doing things one didn't get to do growing up
Nurturing one's interests and refusing to feel guilty about doing so
Noticing and memorizing details about others (to show them they matter)
Always keeping one's promises

PERSONALITY TRAITS THAT MAY FORM
Attributes: Ambitious, appreciative, cooperative, courteous, empathetic, friendly, generous, honorable, industrious, kind, loyal, obedient
Flaws: Cowardly, inflexible, insecure, irrational, jealous, judgmental, martyr, needy, obsessive, oversensitive, weak-willed, workaholic

TRIGGERS THAT MIGHT AGGRAVATE THIS WOUND
Conversations with a parent who discusses their own accomplishments, needs, etc.
Asking for something and being turned down for no good reason
A friend or family member failing to come through when one needs help or support
Someone forgetting a promise they made

OPPORTUNITIES TO FACE OR OVERCOME THIS WOUND
Realizing that one is in a domineering relationship and must get out or lose all sense of identity
A health crisis or tragedy where one must become one's own advocate
Wanting to do something altruistic but having to convince people to support the idea
Taking on a leadership role where the well-being of others depends on one's success
Realizing that one's child is self-serving or spoiled because one always put their desires first

WITNESSING VIOLENCE AT A YOUNG AGE

EXAMPLES
Seeing domestic violence
Witnessing a crime, such as a mugging, a brutal fight, or a murder
Being present during a home invasion
Discovering a suicide
Being present during a terrorist attack (and the aftermath)
Witnessing the sexual assault of a sibling or friend, a parent, etc.
Watching a peer or adult torture an animal
Being taken hostage and having to watch captors abuse other victims
Seeing atrocities committed against people of a religion, race, or group
Being present during a horrific traffic accident, including the aftermath
Being present during a firearm mishandling that results in grave injury or death
Being taken from one's family and forced into slavery
Being a child solider
Witnessing police brutality

BASIC NEEDS OFTEN COMPROMISED BY THIS WOUND: Physiological needs, safety and security, love and belonging, esteem and recognition, self-actualization

FALSE BELIEFS THAT COULD BE EMBRACED
If you don't want to be a victim, hit first.
Love can be used against you.
I can't protect anyone because I'm weak.
People respect strength.
The system is broken and can't protect anyone.
The world is a cruel place filled with people who are inherently evil.

THE CHARACTER MAY FEAR…
Becoming a target of violence
That a loved one may be killed
Being abandoned
Isolation
Responsibility
Trusting people and letting them get close
Specific organizations, races, religions, groups, or people that were involved

POSSIBLE RESPONSES AND RESULTS
Anxiety issues
PTSD symptoms (panic attacks, depression, flashbacks, etc.)
Stomachaches or headaches
Pulling away from people; becoming uncommunicative or withdrawn

Needing to be in control (e.g., through manipulating others to get what one wants)

Bed-wetting and behavior problems (if the character is still young)

Solving problems with physical violence

Becoming a juvenile delinquent

Difficulty connecting to other people, especially peers

Distrust or cynicism of authority and police (if one blames the system)

Holes in one's memory

Eyeing unknown situations with mistrust

Resisting change

Adopting biases (e.g., believing that weak people deserve what they get)

Preferring to stay close to home

Becoming safety-conscious

Overreacting to perceived threats

Being desensitized to violence

Growing anxious or mistrustful around strangers

Being hesitant to engage in any situation where one isn't directly involved

Choosing travel destinations carefully

Projecting one's fears about violence onto others, especially one's children

Becoming a helicopter parent

Monitoring the games, shows, and activities one's children are exposed to

Being protective of the people one cares about

Advocating against violence

PERSONALITY TRAITS THAT MAY FORM
Attributes: Alert, analytical, cautious, courageous, empathetic, honorable, just, loyal, nurturing, passionate, responsible, socially aware

Flaws: Antisocial, apathetic, cruel, dishonest, evasive, evil, hostile, impulsive, inflexible, inhibited, insecure, irrational, irresponsible

TRIGGERS THAT MIGHT AGGRAVATE THIS WOUND
Sensory triggers linked to one's trauma (seeing a weapon or bruises, hearing screams, etc.)

Overhearing a news report of a similar violent event that has taken place

One's child being hurt in an accident, in a fight at school, etc.

Visiting one's parents (if one witnessed or was a victim of domestic abuse)

The sight of blood or tears

OPPORTUNITIES TO FACE OR OVERCOME THIS WOUND
Discovering one's child is being bullied or abused

Being trapped in a violent relationship and needing to get out

Being forced into a situation where one must engage in violence to survive or protect another

Assaulting someone and injuring them far more than one meant to

Being victimized and knowing it will continue if one doesn't do something

Traumatic Events

A CHILD DYING ON ONE'S WATCH

NOTES: In most cases of a child dying in one's care—either one's own child or another person's son or daughter—those in charge blame themselves regardless of whether they were at fault or not. But in cases where the caregiver was even accidentally to blame, the weight of responsibility and regret can be crippling. To explore this kind of wound further, this entry will focus on cases where the caregiver may have unintentionally contributed to a child's death but isn't legally liable. For information on losing a son or daughter due to factors completely out of one's control, see THE DEATH OF ONE'S CHILD.

EXAMPLES: A child dying due to…
Them being given food that contained a known allergen
Ingesting poison or medicine that wasn't put away properly
A cord or paper bag causing strangulation
An accidental shooting while playing with a parent's gun
A car backing over them
A maintenance hazard one hadn't gotten around to fixing (a broken railing, etc.)
A house fire that started with one's lit cigarette or a space heater that was left on
A car accident where one was at fault
Drowning while playing with friends in one's pool

BASIC NEEDS OFTEN COMPROMISED BY THIS WOUND: Love and belonging, esteem and recognition, self-actualization

FALSE BELIEFS THAT COULD BE EMBRACED
I can't be responsible for the life of another.
I'm untrustworthy and irresponsible.
I'm a terrible parent.
This wouldn't have happened on someone else's watch.
I don't deserve forgiveness.
I can't keep my loved ones safe.
I am a danger to everyone around me. People are better off without me in their lives.

THE CHARACTER MAY FEAR…
Being responsible for someone else
Rejection by those who are unable to forgive
The judgment of others
Being deemed an unfit parent and having their other children taken away
Whatever caused the child's death (water, driving, heights, etc.)

POSSIBLE RESPONSES AND RESULTS
Falling into a deep depression
Sleeping too much or not at all

Being unable to stop crying, or being emotionally sensitive

Quitting one's job and activities

Shirking one's commitments

Withdrawing emotionally from the other children in one's charge

Avoiding children and places where they gather

Becoming defensive; blaming others out of a need to prove one wasn't responsible

Becoming obsessive or compulsive in an effort to not miss anything again

Being overprotective and overly strict with one's remaining charges

Experiencing panic attacks when those in one's charge are out of sight or unable to be reached

Withdrawing from others out of shame and guilt

Not opening up to others

Becoming a hermit

Contemplating or attempting suicide

Self-medicating

Becoming obsessed with the deceased child; being unable to let go or move forward

Engaging in self-destructive behaviors due to self-loathing

A reluctance to go out, meet people, or make new friends

Moving to a new house, city, or state in an effort to distance oneself from what happened

Creating a memorial

Making a donation of the child's clothing or toys so others may benefit from them

Calling a friend, pastor, therapist, or hotline for help

Attending a group meeting for parents who have lost children

PERSONALITY TRAITS THAT MAY FORM

Attributes: Alert, cautious, cooperative, meticulous, observant, private, proactive, protective, responsible

Flaws: Addictive, callous, cynical, evasive, fussy, humorless, inhibited, insecure, irrational, irresponsible, morbid, needy, nervous

TRIGGERS THAT MIGHT AGGRAVATE THIS WOUND

Being thrust into a situation where one must watch over someone else's child

Having to attend other events (such as a birthday party) with one's surviving charges

Discovering forgotten artwork or gifts from the deceased child

Being in a situation or at a similar place where the event occurred

Mentions of the deceased child's name

OPPORTUNITIES TO FACE OR OVERCOME THIS WOUND

Seeing another adult accidentally endanger a child, and finally accepting that it can happen to anyone

Experiencing fallout (a divorce due to one's inability to cope, a rift in the community, being sued, etc.) and knowing one needs help to process the guilt and pain

Being forgiven by the child's parents and recognizing the need to forgive oneself

A HOUSE FIRE

EXAMPLES: One's home catching fire due to…
Faulty wiring
A lightning strike
A grease fire in the kitchen
Unattended food burning on the stove
Space heaters being left on
A dirty chimney
Careless smokers
A child playing with matches
Flammable liquids igniting
A candle left burning near a curtain
Frayed Christmas tree lights
Arson
Forest fires or wildfires
An elderly family member who suffers from dementia leaving the stove on

BASIC NEEDS OFTEN COMPROMISED BY THIS WOUND: Physiological needs, safety and security

FALSE BELIEFS THAT COULD BE EMBRACED
I can't be trusted with anything important (if one feels at fault).
I can't trust important things to anyone but me (if one is not at fault).
It's better not to get attached to anyone or anything.
I can't ever be truly safe.
If I stay in one place long enough, something bad will inevitably happen.
Through meticulous planning, I can keep something like this from happening again.
I must cling tightly to my loved ones to keep them safe.

THE CHARACTER MAY FEAR…
Fire
Losing irreplaceable heirlooms or sentimental items
Making another huge mistake that has serious consequences
Being responsible for the death of a loved one
Not being able to ensure the safety of loved ones
Their children suffering prolonged trauma from the event

POSSIBLE RESPONSES AND RESULTS
Obsessively checking one's new residence for anything that could cause another fire to start
Moving often, so as not to become attached to a home
Renting rather than owning so someone else will be responsible for the premises
Overreaching one's budget and buying a nicer place in the hopes it will be safer

Only purchasing functional items that can easily be replaced

Disdaining materialism; becoming stingy

Hoarding material items to compensate for what was lost

Avoiding situations that make one responsible for the lives of others, such as hosting sleepovers (if the fire was one's fault)

Withdrawing from others out of guilt or shame

Micromanaging others (if the fault was someone else's)

Smothering loved ones out of a fear of losing them

Going overboard in regard to fire safety (buying only fire-retardant clothing, downloading apps that test the air quality in one's house and send updates via text message, etc.)

Avoiding open flames (candles, a fire in the fireplace, etc.)

Giving up smoking

Always sleeping with the bedroom door open so one will wake immediately if something's wrong

Checking the house and family members throughout the night

Keeping mementos and documents elsewhere (in a safety deposit box, for example)

Adhering to healthy fire-safety practices (changing smoke detector batteries frequently, creating an evacuation plan, etc.)

Joining a fire department as a volunteer

Appreciating one's blessings, knowing they can be taken away without warning

PERSONALITY TRAITS THAT MAY FORM

Attributes: Affectionate, alert, analytical, appreciative, cautious, grateful, meticulous, nurturing, simple, thrifty

Flaws: Apathetic, callous, fussy, humorless, morbid, needy, obsessive, pessimistic, possessive, stingy, ungrateful, withdrawn, worrywart

TRIGGERS THAT MIGHT AGGRAVATE THIS WOUND

Sensory input associated with the fire (the smell of smoke, a fire's crackle, flickering firelight, etc.)

Not being able to find a beloved heirloom, then realizing it must have been lost in the fire

A fire truck screaming by

The sight of fire hazards in someone's home (exposed wiring, cigarettes left burning, etc.)

A fire alarm going off while cooking

Seeing one's child trying to play with matches

A fire breaking out elsewhere that endangers a loved one (e.g., at a child's school or spouse's office)

OPPORTUNITIES TO FACE OR OVERCOME THIS WOUND

Being caught in a building where a fire has started and needing to get oneself and others to safety

A forest fire threatening one's community

A forced evacuation (caused by a flood, earthquake, or other disaster) where one must leave everything behind

Seeing a son or daughter exhibiting abnormal fears related to fire and realizing it's due to one's phobic response to the event

A LIFE-THREATENING ACCIDENT

EXAMPLES
A transportation accident involving a car, boat, train, or plane
A carnival ride malfunction
Ground that gives way (due to snow covering a crevasse, a sink hole, etc.)
Falling through the ice on a lake
An accidental electrocution
Becoming tangled in underwater debris and nearly drowning
Being attacked by a wild animal
A rock-climbing fall due to malfunctioning gear
Falling out a window or off a roof
Construction accidents
A pedestrian or cyclist being run over by a vehicle
Being trampled by animals (a stampede) or people (in a riot, Black Friday insanity, etc.)
Being buried (due to a sand pile collapsing, an avalanche, stepping in quicksand, etc.)

BASIC NEEDS OFTEN COMPROMISED BY THIS WOUND: Physiological needs, safety and security, esteem and recognition, self-actualization

FALSE BELIEFS THAT COULD BE EMBRACED
The world is too dangerous; I'm only safe in my own house.
A boring life is better than being dead.
People only see my scars, not me.
I can never be who I was before this happened to me.
Death is everywhere so why pursue anything permanent (a family, dreams, etc.)?
I could die any time, so why do what's safe?
I can't trust my instincts.
Others should make decisions for me since I'm too stupid to be in charge.

THE CHARACTER MAY FEAR...
Nature, animals, or another element associated with the accident
Being alone or beyond contact
Blood, injuries, and pain
Being stranded
Danger and risk
Not knowing information and details
Making the wrong decision or choice
Travel
Sudden changes, and being caught unprepared

POSSIBLE RESPONSES AND RESULTS
Thinking in terms of the worst-case scenario

Over-planning to the point that it sucks the joy from everything

Sticking close to home; staying in rather than going out

Not wanting to do things alone

Avoiding activities with an element of risk that once brought great satisfaction

Checking in and constantly keeping tabs on loved ones

Checking statistics (safety protocols for an activity, safety ratings for transportation, etc.)

Needing to know the rules before engaging in relationships, activities, travel, etc.

Opposing activities related to the accident and barring one's children from doing them

Reluctance or flat-out refusal to do things that are risky (skydiving, zip-lining, etc.)

Being alert to change (watching the weather, following recall notices for purchases, etc.)

Putting intuition first and leaving if something feels off

A reluctance to leave one's comfort zone

Becoming superstitious about certain things

Voicing one's worries regarding the safety of different activities and situations

Citing possible dangers about products, locales, activities, etc.

Becoming highly reliant on safety technology (home alarms, apps for fact-checking, etc.)

Avoiding spontaneity; needing to assess every situation for possible risks

Going overboard and becoming reckless, almost daring death

Growing anxious if others show worry (being impressionable when fear is involved)

Avoiding serious relationships that could lead to deep attachment

A new interest in what happens after death

Adopting a "safety first" mindset

Learning first aid skills

PERSONALITY TRAITS THAT MAY FORM

Attributes: Alert, analytical, cautious, curious, disciplined, meticulous, nurturing, observant, organized, persuasive, proactive protective

Flaws: Controlling, defensive, gullible, indecisive, inflexible, insecure, irrational, know-it-all, nervous, obsessive, superstitious, timid, worrywart

TRIGGERS THAT MIGHT AGGRAVATE THIS WOUND

A freak accident that happens in one's presence

Witnessing a person who is oblivious to danger (e.g., standing near an open manhole)

A minor accident that causes injury (cutting one's hand on glass, for example)

Media coverage of an accident where someone was hurt or killed

A loved one who experiences a near miss of some kind

OPPORTUNITIES TO FACE OR OVERCOME THIS WOUND

Deteriorating relationships due to one's safety-obsessive tendencies

A survival situation where one must take risks and act quickly

A desire to help someone with much potential recover from an accident

Seeing a loved one brought down by an injury or diagnosis that they refuse to let limit them

Witnessing a role model do great good for others while embracing risk to do it

A LOVED ONE'S SUICIDE

NOTES: A loved one's suicide is a difficult wound to process. Survivors often turn inward, searching for how they could have prevented it, as if they had failed the loved one by missing the signs or not trying hard enough to help. Others try to understand what led to the suicide and if they had somehow contributed to it. The depth of this wound will depend on how well the character copes and the amount to which they bear responsibility in their own mind.

BASIC NEEDS OFTEN COMPROMISED BY THIS WOUND: Safety and security, love and belonging, esteem and recognition

FALSE BELIEFS THAT COULD BE EMBRACED
This is my fault. I should have seen the signs.
If I had been more available (or a better daughter, etc.) he wouldn't have done it.
If she had really loved me she wouldn't have done this.
I'm incapable of true intimacy.
I make life unbearable for others.
I'm good enough when life is easy, but when things get tough, people won't turn to me.

THE CHARACTER MAY FEAR…
Depression, and where it might lead
That they will miss the signs and it will happen again
Never being good enough for their loved ones
Being unable to achieve true intimacy with others
That they're untrustworthy or incapable
That they may succumb to suicide one day just like the family member
Being abandoned by other loved ones
Their children being more susceptible to suicide, since they have now been exposed to it

POSSIBLE RESPONSES AND RESULTS
Withdrawing from family and friends
Lying to others about the cause of the loved one's death
Confusion over how to tell one's children about the suicide
Analyzing interactions with the one who passed to figure out what one missed
Mentally tallying the hurtful things one did to the loved one
Stomachaches and other digestive issues
Losing one's appetite
Sleeplessness due to real or imagined guilt
Maintaining surface relationships as a way of avoiding potential hurt
Becoming overly needy and clingy with loved ones
Becoming hypervigilant with loved ones
Obsessively watching for signs of suicide in others
Panicking if a loved one is feeling low or sad

Growing anxious when a loved one seems to withdraw or grows uncommunicative

Difficulty respecting a loved one's privacy or personal space if they seem vulnerable

Overcompensating (being too strict or lenient, smothering loved ones in an effort to pay closer attention, etc.) for what one feels guilty about

Becoming more nosy; trying to figure out how people are feeling

Trying to make life perfect for others so they'll be happy

Being a "fixer" and annoying people who don't want or need help

Falling into depression

Having suicidal thoughts or attempting suicide

Self-medicating

Trying to improve in the area one felt was lacking (paying more attention, being more obedient, etc.)

Practicing sharing one's feelings freely, and encouraging others to do the same

Seeking therapy or joining a survivor's group

Joining the effort to raise awareness about suicide

Becoming more tuned in to the moods and emotions of others

Mentoring those who are more susceptible to suicide (the elderly, addicts, etc.)

PERSONALITY TRAITS THAT MAY FORM

Attributes: Affectionate, appreciative, nurturing, observant, pensive, private, proactive, responsible, sentimental, supportive

Flaws: Addictive, apathetic, callous, compulsive, confrontational, cynical, fussy, hostile, humorless, inhibited, insecure, irrational, martyr

TRIGGERS THAT MIGHT AGGRAVATE THIS WOUND

Important milestones (the deceased's birthday, a wedding anniversary, the day they would have graduated from college, etc.)

Not hearing from someone when one should have

Commercials and ads for suicide prevention

Witnessing a march for suicide awareness

Attending a family reunion or annual event that the loved one always attended

Encountering the kind of tool or item that was used in the suicide (pills, rope, etc.)

OPPORTUNITIES TO FACE OR OVERCOME THIS WOUND

Seeing depression or suicidal signs in another loved one

Falling into depression and knowing one must seek help

Walking a close friend through the aftermath of a loved one's unexpected suicide

Seeing signs of self-mutilation with a loved one

Losing one's sense of self through trying so hard to be what others need

A friend or family member falling into the same dangerous habits one failed to see with the victim (developing an eating disorder, abusing drugs, etc.)

A child rebelling due to one's clingy attentiveness and smothering tendencies

A MISCARRIAGE OR STILLBIRTH

NOTES: The impact of this wound will have many factors, such as if this is the character's first loss, at what point in the pregnancy it happened, the spiritual beliefs of the parents, the level of support around them, and the circumstances (if any) that led to losing the baby. It should also be noted that this can become a wounding event for both parents, not only the mother.

BASIC NEEDS OFTEN COMPROMISED BY THIS WOUND: Safety and security, esteem and recognition, self-actualization

FALSE BELIEFS THAT COULD BE EMBRACED
This is my punishment for a past transgression (or a known weakness, etc.).
It's my fault; I did something wrong during my pregnancy that killed my child.
There must be a reason I'm not supposed to have kids.
Subconsciously, I caused this by regretting the pregnancy (or wishing the baby away, etc.).
When something good comes along, it will just be taken away from me.
It's better to be childless than to risk this kind of pain again.

THE CHARACTER MAY FEAR…
That it will happen again
Losing their other children through an accident, illness, or negligence
That they will make a bad parent
That there's something intrinsically wrong with her body
Conceiving again
That they will never have a child
Hospitals or things associated with them
That their marriage won't survive

POSSIBLE RESPONSES AND RESULTS
Mentally tracking the "would be" milestones (the one-month mark, the first birthday, when the child would have started kindergarten, etc.)
Possessive behaviors toward one's living children
Blaming oneself or one's partner
Obsessively searching for a reason why it happened
Mixed feelings about sex
Hypochondriac tendencies
Withdrawing from others
Avoiding baby things (the nursery, gifts, baby showers, etc.)
Refusing to redecorate the nursery, even after the decision not to try again has been made
Being drawn to the nursery and the baby's things (rocking a stuffed animal, touching the clothes, etc.)
Pulling away from other couples with babies
Resenting the successful pregnancies of others, then feeling guilty about one's feelings

Becoming depressed

Developing a panic disorder

Becoming more health-conscious, believing this will increase one's chances of future success

Turning one's back on one's faith

Becoming unhealthily obsessed with other peoples' babies

Doubting one's ability to parent

Developing negative thought patterns

Refusing to try to conceive again

Dreading one's birthdays; seeing them as milestones marking another year without a child

Turning to God or faith

Empathizing with and reaching out to others who have suffered the same pain

Looking into adoption

Accepting that fulfillment can be found in other areas beyond parenthood

Filling one's time with meaningful activities

Joining a support group or online chat room for parents who have suffered the same loss

PERSONALITY TRAITS THAT MAY FORM

Attributes: Appreciative, disciplined, empathetic, industrious, inspirational, nurturing, pensive, persistent, private, protective, sensible, spiritual

Flaws: Addictive, controlling, cynical, defensive, humorless, inhibited, irrational, irresponsible, jealous, martyr, morbid, needy, nervous

TRIGGERS THAT MIGHT AGGRAVATE THIS WOUND

The anniversary of the miscarriage or stillbirth

Seeing a friend's child achieve important milestones at the same time one's child would have done so

Being invited to a baby shower or child's birthday party

Friends being unable to meet for lunch because it conflicts with a playgroup meeting

Stores that cater to babies and pregnant mothers

Catching sight of a woman breastfeeding her child in a mall or restaurant

Thoughtless words by a well-meaning friend: *At least you have other children,* etc.

Seeing the decorated nursery that was awaiting one's child

OPPORTUNITIES TO FACE OR OVERCOME THIS WOUND

Becoming pregnant again

Having another miscarriage

Having a close friend who is going through the adoption process, and wondering if one should give up trying to birth a child and go that route

Seeing one's surviving child playing alone, making one question the decision to not try again

Relationship issues with one's partner due to each person processing the trauma differently

A family member or good friend dealing with an unwanted pregnancy and needing one's support

A NATURAL OR MAN-MADE DISASTER

EXAMPLES

Extreme weather, such as an earthquake, hurricane or tropical storm, severe electrical storm, tornado, flood, tsunami, avalanche, heat wave, or ice storm

A volcanic eruption

The meltdown of a nuclear power plant

A chemical attack or accidental gas leak

A viral outbreak

A meteor strike

A rock or mudslide caused by deforestation

Forest fires or other fires started by man

A dam breaking

Industrial waste leaks creating widespread contamination

Devastating droughts and famines

BASIC NEEDS OFTEN COMPROMISED BY THIS WOUND: Physiological needs, safety and security, love and belonging

FALSE BELIEFS THAT COULD BE EMBRACED

God is punishing me (or humanity, my community, etc.).

Control is only an illusion.

We can never be truly safe.

I am justified to do whatever I must to stay safe.

Those in power must be brought down before they get us all killed.

The only one who can protect my family is me.

The only way to stay safe is to be prepared for anything and everything.

When you need them most, people let you down.

Nature is dangerous and should be avoided.

Question everything. Trust no one.

THE CHARACTER MAY FEAR...

Certain places associated with the disaster (snowy mountains, storm shelters, etc.)

Seasons or weather phenomena (temperature, precipitation, etc.) tied to the event

Populated areas and large groups of people

Natural areas

Getting sick or being injured (and therefore being helpless)

Running out of food, water, or medicine

The government or people in power

Climate change

POSSIBLE RESPONSES AND RESULTS

Researching the event to try and understand it

Keeping a stockpile of supplies, just in case

Formulating an evacuation plan

Questioning what one is told by one's government and media

Checking with multiple news sources rather than relying on one

Being jaded by the lack of compassion one experienced during the event

Being uncomfortable when one's children stay with other people or are too far away

Moving to another area to avoid a specific danger

Experiencing night terrors

Difficulty relaxing and enjoying the little things

PTSD symptoms (panic attacks, insomnia, flashbacks, delusions, etc.)

Hoarding tendencies

Becoming a hypochondriac

A tendency to think about the worst-case scenario

Being unable to sleep during certain types of weather

Altering one's property to account for emergencies (putting up fences, installing a well, etc.)

Doomsday prepping activities

Becoming a conspiracy theorist (if the disaster was man-made)

Joining online groups that align with one's beliefs or help prepare for the future

Learning how to become self-sufficient in case one has to survive on one's own

Making one's health more of a priority

Staying in better contact with one's family

PERSONALITY TRAITS THAT MAY FORM

Attributes: Adaptable, alert, disciplined, efficient, focused, independent, industrious, inspirational, loyal, nature-focused, observant

Flaws: Antisocial, apathetic, inhibited, insecure, irrational, materialistic, needy, obsessive, paranoid, pessimistic, selfish, stingy

TRIGGERS THAT MIGHT AGGRAVATE THIS WOUND

Symbols of industry (if a man-made disaster was the event) like factories or smoke stacks

Reminders of hardship, such as an empty cupboard

A tree that has fallen down in a storm

TV news reports of disasters in other countries

The anniversary of the event

The sound of sirens or other emergency vehicles

Smells associated with the event (smoke, gas or chemical smells, ozone, etc.)

OPPORTUNITIES TO FACE OR OVERCOME THIS WOUND

Another emergency event or disaster

Facing an emergency where one must rely on others (including police) for help

Being in a position of hardship and having others show compassion and a willingness to help

Seeing someone be merciful and generous instead of taking advantage or ignoring the need

Being given an opportunity to make a difference for others or join a cause for a better future

A PARENT'S DIVORCE

NOTES: The intensity of this wound will have several factors: the circumstances of the divorce; the personality, age, and adaptability of the character when the trauma took place (especially if it was during formative years); and the changes that will result, which could include a new financial reality, having to move, custody arrangements, alterations to one's support structure, and one's relationship with each parent moving forward.

While there are short-term and long-term effects from divorce, this entry will highlight its repercussions on adult or near-adult characters, covering the long-range impacts.

BASIC NEEDS OFTEN COMPROMISED BY THIS WOUND: Safety and security, love and belonging

FALSE BELIEFS THAT COULD BE EMBRACED
Children strain relationships; that's why my parents divorced.
There's no such thing as a long-term relationship.
If I love someone completely, I'll end up hurt.
Marriage is for suckers.
Everyone keeps secrets, so I can't trust anyone completely.
Keeping the peace means keeping your mouth shut.
There's always something better out there.

THE CHARACTER MAY FEAR...
Being abandoned
Not being a priority
Instability (financial, emotional, etc.)
Infidelity
Rejection or betrayal
Being discarded for something better
Failing in their own marriage
Having children and failing them
Committed relationships

POSSIBLE RESPONSES AND RESULTS
Resisting or avoiding long-term relationships
Making excuses for not committing
Poor relationship choices
Becoming overly attached to people or purposely avoiding attachment
A strained relationship with one or both parents
Being generally critical of one's parents and their choices
Resentment due to one's childhood not being what it should have been
Struggling to fully trust a partner or spouse

Tending to walk away from conflict rather than work through it

Giving one's children the support one lacked, even to one's own detriment

Feeling insecure often and needing reassurance, praise, or positive reinforcement

Monitoring situations carefully for change

Worrying about finances more so than may be normal

Having trouble letting go (of the past or of things in general)

Fearing to be responsible for others

Being territorial or possessive (of people, personal spaces, one's role and job, etc.)

Finding it difficult to forgive people

Being a people pleaser or manipulator (depending on what worked as a child to get attention)

Being easily overwhelmed by change

Becoming angry and reactive when things don't go as planned

Feeling threatened by competition

Fierce independence; a reluctance to ask for help

Feeling guilty when something doesn't go right, as if one is somehow to blame

Feeling overly responsible for the happiness of others

Holding onto friendships and relationships too tightly, possibly smothering others

Cautioning one's children against getting their hopes up in uncertain situations

Being reluctant to try something new

Disliking surprises

Having a deep sense of ownership for one's things

Taking pride in what one has built (a safe home, a family, a career, etc.) despite setbacks

Understanding that if one is always in control, others will miss the chance to learn and grow

PERSONALITY TRAITS THAT MAY FORM

Attributes: Affectionate, analytical, cautious, charming, discreet, empathetic, independent, industrious, just, loyal, mature

Flaws: Confrontational, controlling, defensive, evasive, hypocritical, impatient, insecure, jealous, judgmental, manipulative

TRIGGERS THAT MIGHT AGGRAVATE THIS WOUND

Spousal arguments

Visiting one's parent(s) over the holidays

A parent announcing their intent to remarry

The suspicion that one's partner is keeping a secret

Family reunions, weddings, funerals, or other events where family gathers

OPPORTUNITIES TO FACE OR OVERCOME THIS WOUND

Marriage or personal counseling

Wanting to get married but being afraid to do so

Learning that one is going to be a parent for the first time

Staying in a failed marriage for the kids' sake but realizing it's still harming them

A SCHOOL SHOOTING

NOTES: A school shooting is a wound that impacts people differently. Students, teachers, and support staff are primary victims, as they are the closest to the situation, while parents (of children within the school, of victims, and even of the shooter) can also be traumatized. This carries through to first responders, city leaders, the media, and the community, who may all be affected by the atrocity. If you choose this wound, think about how your character's personality, role, and closeness to the situation will cause different behaviors and feelings to crop up. The timeline is also important to keep in mind, as some responses are more immediate while others will become long-term behaviors and reactions.

BASIC NEEDS OFTEN COMPROMISED BY THIS WOUND: Safety and security, love and belonging, esteem and recognition

FALSE BELIEFS THAT COULD BE EMBRACED

This is my fault. I should have done something to stop it.
I can't keep my loved ones safe.
I could die at any moment.
You can never really know a person.
People can turn on you at any minute.
Violence is everywhere.
My life can end at any moment, so why try to make something meaningful?
The world is an evil place.

THE CHARACTER MAY FEAR…

Dying
Guns and violence
Loving people only to lose them
Strangers (if the shooter was unknown to the character)
Freezing up or making a mistake at a critical moment
Placing trust in others (especially for their own welfare or the welfare of loved ones)
Being in crowds or in populated places
That another school attack will happen

POSSIBLE RESPONSES AND RESULTS

Difficulty concentrating
Emotions that quickly escalate to extremes
Self-medicating with drugs or alcohol
Feeling guilty for being alive when others are not
Struggling with one's faith (if one is religious)
Becoming hypervigilant (e.g., watching for possible dangers and threats)
Over-reacting or under-reacting in times of stress
Suffering from prolonged stress (headaches, stomach problems, aches that don't abate, etc.)

Having nightmares where one is murdered or one is helpless to save someone else
Waking in a panicked state (with a racing heart, disorientation, etc.)
Needing to know where loved ones are at all times
Panic attacks and overwhelming fears
Struggling to enjoy the little things in life
PTSD (anxiety, depression, sleeplessness, nightmares, night terrors, flashbacks, etc.)
Taking life very seriously or not seriously enough
Feeling guilty for laughing, having fun, or enjoying something trivial
Worrying that moving on is dishonoring those who died
Clinging to loved ones
Refusing to talk about the event
Obsessively researching in hopes of trying to make sense of what happened
Critiquing one's actions out of guilt for not saving others
Seeking to protect oneself (obtaining a weapons permit, carrying a knife, etc.)
Becoming an anti-gun advocate
Trust issues; being uncomfortable around people one does not know well
Anxiety at being home alone or being separated from family members
Becoming risk-averse and less spontaneous
Wanting to talk about what happened to process one's emotions
Going to group or individual counseling
Writing about one's experiences and feelings

PERSONALITY TRAITS THAT MAY FORM
Attributes: Alert, analytical, cautious, disciplined, empathetic, loyal, merciful, nurturing, perceptive, protective, responsible
Flaws: Antisocial, controlling, humorless, impulsive, insecure, irrational, needy, obsessive, paranoid, scatterbrained

TRIGGERS THAT MIGHT AGGRAVATE THIS WOUND
Loud noises, like car backfires, explosions, or firecrackers
Symbols that act as triggers, such as seeing the same sneakers or ball cap that the shooter wore
A friend or family member being present at a random act of violence
Having to go to the hospital
The wail of emergency vehicle sirens
Running into the family members of those who died

OPPORTUNITIES TO FACE OR OVERCOME THIS WOUND
Attending vigils and reconnecting with other victims
Homeschooling one's children, then realizing one is making decisions based on fear
Encountering violence again and having to act to save oneself and others
Seeing a friend struggling with the trauma and wanting to help them through it

A TERMINAL ILLNESS DIAGNOSIS

NOTES: A terminal illness cannot be cured; for these patients, treatment options will, at best, prolong life rather than save it. While some patients do outlive their doctor's best guesses for life expectancy, patients are considered terminal when they are given six months or less to live.

BASIC NEEDS OFTEN COMPROMISED BY THIS WOUND: Physiological needs, safety and security, esteem and recognition, self-actualization

FALSE BELIEFS THAT COULD BE EMBRACED

This diagnosis is a mistake, and I'm going to be fine.

God won't let me die because I'm a good person.

God is cruel to force me to experience such a painful or premature death.

I deserve this (because of something I did, not being good enough, etc.).

I am a burden to the people around me.

If I had money and power, I wouldn't be dying.

THE CHARACTER MAY FEAR…

Death

Pain

The pity of others

Wasting away slowly while friends and family watch

Saying and doing things they can't control because of medication and the advancing disease

Being remembered as ill and weak rather than strong and capable

Their identity becoming all about the illness

Whatever comes after death (judgment, that it's different from what they believe, nothingness, etc.)

POSSIBLE RESPONSES AND RESULTS

Uncontrolled crying and sadness

Growing quiet around other people

Needing breaks from people and normal activities

Depression

Self-medicating with alcohol and drugs

Being unable to get out of bed

Sleeping constantly or suffering from insomnia

Appearing to give up (having poor hygiene, pulling away from loved ones, ignoring pets, etc.)

Refusing to acknowledge one's illness or go to the doctor

Paranoia that leads to analyzing one's appearance for signs of the advancing illness

Having to stop certain routines (workouts, healthy eating, cleaning, etc.) as the disease progresses

Refusing to talk about finances, creating a will, or other end-of-life concerns

A manic need to take risks to feel alive

Throwing oneself into work to avoid having time to think

Spending money recklessly

Choosing aggressive treatment options regardless of their effectiveness

Investigating fringe treatments and procedures in hopes of finding a cure

Rebelling against the diagnosis through poor choices (having unprotected sex, binge drinking and partying, visiting unsafe locations, etc.)

Disengaging one's filter and saying what one really thinks, even if it hurts others

Denying one's illness by rationalizing symptoms: *I didn't get enough sleep,* or *Must have been something I ate.*

Refusing offers of help because one refuses to be seen as weak

Lying to concerned people about one's diet, sleep habits, medication routines, etc.

Talking about the illness as if it's temporary: *When I feel better, we should take the kids to Disneyland,* or *Maybe I'll get back into hiking once I'm myself again.*

Thoughts often turning to suicide

Displaying frustration and impatience as one grows more limited in what one can do

Seeking out second opinions

Researching one's diagnosis to better understand what is to come

Looking into pain management options and how to slow the illness if possible

PERSONALITY TRAITS THAT MAY FORM

Because this wound is more immediate and has less time to fester, the character will not experience significant personality shifts. Instead, traits (especially those which help facilitate denial) that are already part of the character's personality may become more pronounced. For instance, a character may grow more private, or they may become more spontaneous, reckless, pensive, or uninhibited if it helps them cope with this wound.

TRIGGERS THAT MIGHT AGGRAVATE THIS WOUND

Seeing a travel ad for a place one always wished to go but will never be able to visit now

Driving past a church or other symbol of God

Annual holidays (Christmas, a birthday, etc.) that one may never see again

Visiting a doctor or a hospital for a treatment or procedure

Discussions about a will or one's end-of-life requests

The birth of a child within one's family

Wanting to start a book that is part of a series one wouldn't be able to finish

Planning a last vacation

OPPORTUNITIES TO FACE OR OVERCOME THIS WOUND

Seeing an estranged family member and wanting to mend that fence before dying

Having a big regret that is all-consuming and seeing an opportunity to deal with it

Accepting one's diagnosis and seeking to enjoy one's remaining time

Being able to right a wrong if one can move past one's anger

Having a dream or goal and wanting to achieve it

A TERRORIST ATTACK

EXAMPLES
A bomb detonation
A chemical attack, such as gas being released in a subway system or a building's filtration unit
A violent situation resulting in people being taken hostage
A biological attack, such as poisoning a water supply or releasing an airborne virus
An attack on an embassy during a hostile takeover
Cyber-terrorism or eco-terrorism
A nuclear threat or deployment of nuclear force

BASIC NEEDS OFTEN COMPROMISED BY THIS WOUND: Physiological needs, safety and security, esteem and recognition

FALSE BELIEFS THAT COULD BE EMBRACED
I don't deserve to live when so many good people died.
I should have done something to prevent this.
I am not safe anywhere.
I can't keep my family safe.
The police only care about the rich and powerful, and the rest of us have to fend for ourselves.
Sooner or later, the terrorists will win, so why try to build anything good for the future?
It would be wrong to bring a child into this messed-up world.
Only revenge will fill this need inside of me.
Anyone of that religion (or race, belief, etc.) is untrustworthy and possibly dangerous.

THE CHARACTER MAY FEAR...
Places where lots of people converge (subways, airports, train stations, malls, etc.)
Death
Freezing up when it really matters
Being subject to pain and torture
People of an ethnicity, religion, or belief associated with the attackers
Being in an enclosed space—especially one that has a lot of people, like an airplane
Strangers and crowds
Intolerance (believing it to be the root source of the ordeal)

POSSIBLE RESPONSES AND RESULTS
Stockpiling weapons, food, and water
Refusing to travel
PTSD, anxiety, and depression
Vocalizing hate against those one believes is responsible
Avoiding large venues (stadiums, concert halls, fairgrounds, etc.)
Feeling survivor's guilt; questioning why one is alive when others are not

Becoming highly protective of family members, especially children

Staying up-to-date on current events

Avoiding situations where one will have to interact with strangers

Looking for patterns in the news that forecast what may happen in order to protect oneself

Being more susceptible to propaganda and fear-mongering

Questioning the motives of others

Not openly wearing religious or national symbols if one is worried about persecution

Growing anxious in potentially violent situations (protests, rallies, strikes, etc.)

A heightened sensitivity to changes in one's environment

Experiencing chest pain, headaches, and other medical ailments as the body reacts to stress

Difficulty returning to day-to-day life after the event

Struggling to enjoy the little things

Expressing one's anger in violent ways

Creating caches of survival necessities

Having a disaster or evacuation plan for one's family

Difficulty eating or sleeping

Feeling restless, like one should be doing more

Donating blood on a regular basis

Creating or visiting a memorial for those who died in the event

Returning to the church if one was not a regular attender

Educating oneself on the happening and events leading up to it to understand it better

Seeking ways to volunteer or help protect one's community

PERSONALITY TRAITS THAT MAY FORM

Attributes: Alert, analytical, cautious, intelligent, loyal, organized, patriotic, perceptive, proactive, protective, responsible, socially aware, wise

Flaws: Apathetic, callous, confrontational, controlling, fanatical, hostile, impatient, irrational, judgmental, nervous, obsessive

TRIGGERS THAT MIGHT AGGRAVATE THIS WOUND

Fire drills and evacuation procedures

Violent movies or news reports

Media coverage of marches, protests, and riots

Passing the site of the terrorist attack

The sight of blood

OPPORTUNITIES TO FACE OR OVERCOME THIS WOUND

Being caught in a natural disaster and having to flee to get one's family to safety

Being in a bank or store robbery and having to think clearly to survive

Experiencing a gas leak or fire within a building and being responsible for getting others out

Being the first to arrive after a terrible car accident and needing to help in order to save lives

BEING HUMILIATED BY OTHERS

EXAMPLES

A teacher singling out a student in front of others
Having one's reputation damaged (due to sex videos surfacing, a rant being recorded, etc.)
A shameful secret, closely guarded, being shared with peers or the public
A messy job firing that was not handled with respect or dignity
Being falsely accused of a terrible or taboo crime
College fraternity, sorority, or sports-related hazing
One's infidelity becoming public when a vengeful spouse posts about it on social media
Vicious rumors or truths being shared, causing shame or embarrassment
A rival smearing one's reputation by revealing embarrassing information
Someone who wasn't ready to reveal his or her sexual preference being outed publicly
Bullying that involves humiliating acts

BASIC NEEDS OFTEN COMPROMISED BY THIS WOUND: Safety and security, love and belonging, esteem and recognition, self-actualization

FALSE BELIEFS THAT COULD BE EMBRACED

I will never be able to achieve anything because people will judge me based on what happened.
It doesn't matter that I'm innocent; people will always wonder about me.
I am defective and weak. I will always be a target.
I don't deserve happiness after what I did.
I will never fit in or be understood.
If anyone finds out about my past, my life will be over.
Don't trust anyone to have your back because they won't.

THE CHARACTER MAY FEAR…

Being recorded (via video, an audio recording, etc.)
Being exploited
Trusting the wrong person
Public opinion or the gossip wheel
The person who caused the humiliation
Other important secrets becoming known
Being abandoned by loved ones to face shame and humiliation alone

POSSIBLE RESPONSES AND RESULTS

Developing social anxiety
Self-medicating with drugs, alcohol, or food
Pulling away from friends out of embarrassment
Making excuses to avoid social events
Feeling anxiety when the phone rings or email alerts chime

Trying to change one's appearance to fly under the public's radar

Not returning to the place where the humiliation took place (quitting one's job, changing schools, leaving politics or the limelight, etc.)

Mistrusting new people; not taking them at their word

Not taking care of oneself (out of shame, humiliation, depression, etc.)

Assuming that everyone knows about what happened, though it may only be a few people

Being afraid to go out; worrying one will be recognized

Fearing that other mistakes will be brought to light

Walking into a room and feeling watched, as if everyone is staring

Mulling over the humiliating things that were said, wondering if they might be true

Second-guessing one's decisions and actions

Reading into the motives of others; thinking the worst of people

Clinging to the loyal people in one's life

Losing interest in hobbies and activities

Narrowing one's friendship group to only a few trusted people

Avoiding social media; closing one's accounts

Using the incident to draw attention to a problem or bias in society in hopes of changing it

Getting a pet to fill the void (because it is non-judgmental and loves unconditionally)

PERSONALITY TRAITS THAT MAY FORM

Attributes: Cautious, courageous, discreet, honest, honorable, inspirational, merciful, objective, persuasive, private, tolerant, uninhibited

Flaws: Addictive, confrontational, cowardly, defensive, dishonest, foolish, gullible, martyr, melodramatic, paranoid, resentful, self-destructive

TRIGGERS THAT MIGHT AGGRAVATE THIS WOUND

Running into the person who was the cause of one's humiliation

Being at a location that is similar to where the humiliating event took place

Seeing someone being ripped apart or having their secrets outed on social media

Overhearing unkind gossip about a co-worker

Being recognized by a stranger (because of a video or media coverage, etc.)

Making a potential new friend who brings up what happened

OPPORTUNITIES TO FACE OR OVERCOME THIS WOUND

Wanting to enter a trusting relationship but struggling with how to be vulnerable again

A relationship evolving to the point where one becomes afraid the other person will find out about the humiliating event

Overhearing someone being pressured into doing something that will hurt them if it goes sideways

Wanting to chase a dream that requires disclosing one's past to gatekeepers

Having to testify in a lawsuit against the person or company that caused the humiliation

Witnessing the person who caused one's humiliation doing the same thing to someone else

BEING TORTURED

EXAMPLES: Survivors who were…
Tortured for information (POWs, politically-motivated kidnappings, etc.)
Captured by a serial killer or sadistic individual
Living with a violent cult, family, or other group
Targeted by a terror group, including "pack mentality" peers who embrace sadistic bullying
Accused of political or religious crimes
Persecuted for being in the ethnic or religious minority
Captured journalists
Human rights defenders and health professionals in volatile countries
Members of an opposing criminal group (e.g., the mafia)

BASIC NEEDS OFTEN COMPROMISED BY THIS WOUND: Physiological needs, safety and security, esteem and recognition, self-actualization

FALSE BELIEFS THAT COULD BE EMBRACED
I can't trust anyone.
I am broken and defective because of what was done to me.
I can never live a normal life.
People can't cope with life's ugliness. If they find out what happened to me, they'll leave.
God abandoned me.
I can't control what happens to me. I am helpless.
I am only safe inside my comfort zone.
It's better to bury what happened than try to move past it.

THE CHARACTER MAY FEAR…
Being held against their will
Yelling, arguing, or any situation that could escalate to violence
Fire, water, electricity, or specific implements used in the torture
Being touched
Isolation
Having their breathing or movements restricted
People in authority (if the torturers held power or station)
Sex and intimacy
Being alone, or alternatively, being with people or in crowds

POSSIBLE RESPONSES AND RESULTS
Being startled by sudden movements
Difficulty assigning certainty to anything because one still believes that control is an illusion
Negative self-thoughts
Paying close attention to one's intuition (e.g., quickly identifying potential threats)
Being confused about one's self-worth

Staying inside or close to home when one feels overwhelmed or unsafe

Feeling "apart" from other people (an isolation that comes from one's experience)

Analyzing the behavior of others; second-guessing their motives

Difficulty enjoying life as one used to

Needing space; feeling uncomfortable when people get too close without invitation

Developing an eating disorder

Being prone to an upset stomach, joint pain, and frequent sickness

Hoarding food and resources (if they were associated with one's ordeal)

Thinking about the same thing obsessively, especially when it is tied to a negative emotion

Having to talk oneself down when anxiety causes a racing heart and restricted breathing

Worries that can escalate quickly to anxiety or develop into paranoia

Developing PTSD (depression, insomnia, night terrors, panic attacks, flashbacks, etc.)

Feeling overwhelmed by basic tasks, such as cooking, cleaning, and organizing

Thoughts of suicide

Difficulty with relationships and connecting to people

Trust issues and a fear of vulnerability

Intense feelings of shame that continue to be present

Struggling with criticism, no matter how well-intentioned

Self-soothing behaviors (stroking one's forearm, cuddling with a pet, reading a book, wrapping oneself in a blanket, eating a sweet treat, etc.)

Journaling, writing poetry, or penning letters to one's captors to express emotions

PERSONALITY TRAITS THAT MAY FORM

Attributes: Alert, analytical, appreciative, cautious, courageous, gentle, introverted, kind, loyal, merciful, sentimental, socially aware

Flaws: Antisocial, compulsive, controlling, cynical, defensive, fanatical, forgetful, humorless, inhibited, insecure, paranoid, pessimistic

TRIGGERS THAT MIGHT AGGRAVATE THIS WOUND

Reading a story where the character experiences trauma similar to one's experience

Being accidentally locked inside a room

Nightmares or daytime flashbacks

Power outages; being alone in the dark

Violence or the threat of violence resulting from intolerance, hatred, and persecution

Being touched, especially if it happens unexpectedly

OPPORTUNITIES TO FACE OR OVERCOME THIS WOUND

Being caught in a hostage situation and having to stay calm to survive

Having goals and dreams that are within reach if one can stay optimistic and focused

Meeting someone special and wanting a life with them

Discovering that one is pregnant

Wanting to mentor other survivors and be a role model to give them hope

BEING TRAPPED IN A COLLAPSED BUILDING

EXAMPLES: Being trapped in a building that collapses due to…
The floor or ceiling unexpectedly giving way
A tornado's destructive winds
The building supports shifting after an earthquake
It being condemned
A house fire
An explosion caused by a gas line breach
Age and decay
A terrorist attack
Bombs being dropped in an air raid
A sinkhole opening under the house and causing it to crumble

BASIC NEEDS OFTEN COMPROMISED BY THIS WOUND: Physiological needs, safety and security

FALSE BELIEFS THAT COULD BE EMBRACED
Life could end at any second, so why waste it being responsible and sensible?
I am not safe anywhere.
I need to eradicate all sin from my life or this will happen again (if one is prone to extreme religious ideology).
I cheated death once. It won't happen again.
Planning for the future is a waste of time.
People are incompetent and not to be trusted (if the collapse was due to human error).
I should have died instead (if loved ones perished in the collapse).

THE CHARACTER MAY FEAR…
The dark (being in basements, parking garages, tunnels, etc.)
Death by smothering
Being unable to move; not being in control of their body
Squandering a second chance at life by not reaching their full potential
A loved one being the victim of a random accident

POSSIBLE RESPONSES AND RESULTS
Avoiding buildings that remind one of the event
Refusing to enter a basement or below-ground apartment
Keeping tabs on the weather (if it played a part in causing the original collapse)
Always keeping one's phone fully charged
Panicking when one is in an MRI machine or other enclosed space
Refusing to enter an elevator
Struggling with survivor's guilt (if others died in the event)
Suggesting activities with friends that are outdoors or in wide-open spaces

Feeling safer outside than inside

Carrying an inhaler for panic attacks and anxiety

Refusing to live in a home with a basement

Leaving doors and windows open when one is inside

Parking in a lot or at the curb rather than in a garage

Keeping blinds or curtains open so one can see outside

Feeling claustrophobic in rooms without windows

Taking the stairs whenever possible

Changing careers to something that allows one to be outside or on the ground floor of a building

Carrying emergency supplies (a flashlight, water, power bar, etc.) in a purse or backpack

Always needing to know where one's family members are; frequently checking in via texts or calls

Overseeing the building of a new house so one can be sure it's safe

Studying building structure so one can identify signs of stress

Recognizing the gift of a second chance and reordering one's priorities

Living life to the fullest, since no one knows when it will end

Making sure family members and friends know how much they're loved

Showing gratitude to one's rescuers

PERSONALITY TRAITS THAT MAY FORM

Attributes: Alert, appreciative, cautious, generous, humble, inspirational, kind, nurturing, protective, spiritual, uninhibited, unselfish

Flaws: Compulsive, cowardly, fanatical, humorless, inhibited, martyr, paranoid, pessimistic, withdrawn, worrywart

TRIGGERS THAT MIGHT AGGRAVATE THIS WOUND

Watching live television or online reports of a building collapse with victims trapped inside

Finding oneself in an enclosed space

Deciding to face one's fears and overcome them, but failing

Being in a building with creaking walls (in an old house, for instance, or during a windstorm)

The power going out

Building demolitions taking place in one's neighborhood or near one's work

A loud storm that shakes the building one is in

The sensation of not being able to breathe (breathing dusty air, being compressed in a tight spot, a lover's weight pressing down on one during times of intimacy, etc.)

Being stuck in a long tunnel during gridlock traffic

OPPORTUNITIES TO FACE OR OVERCOME THIS WOUND

Facing a job where one is forced to go underground (e.g., in a subway tunnel)

Having to enter a tight space (such as a crawlspace or vent) to rescue a pet or fix something

Going on a vacation excursion that requires one to enter a cave or navigate a tight passage

Working as a mechanic and having to face the tight spaces beneath trucks to do repairs

A scenario hinting that one may have survived the ordeal for a reason (being an organ-donor match for a sibling, successfully administering CPR to someone, saving a child from being abducted, etc.)

BEING TRAPPED WITH A DEAD BODY

EXAMPLES
In the aftermath of a plane crash
After a car accident, when a passenger is deceased and one is disabled and awaiting rescue
Being kidnapped and tossed into a trunk with another victim who is deceased
Being held somewhere with other prisoners who have died
Being abandoned in a hospital with dead patients because of a sudden mass evacuation
Being the only survivor in a collapsed building and needing rescue
A child being left in an apartment with a parent who overdosed or died suddenly
Being put in a room with a dead body as a form of twisted punishment
Being in a hostage situation where some of the hostages have been killed but not removed

BASIC NEEDS OFTEN COMPROMISED BY THIS WOUND: Safety and security, esteem and recognition, self-actualization

FALSE BELIEFS THAT COULD BE EMBRACED
This was my fault and this is my punishment.
I should be the one who is dead.
I could have prevented this, but I didn't.
I should have fought harder; this happened because I am weak.
I can't ever be who I was before.
To honor the dead I must succeed for them.
No one will miss me when I'm gone.
The only way to atone for this is to make it up to the victim's family.

THE CHARACTER MAY FEAR...
Corpses (e.g., in body bags on the roadside following a fatal accident)
Death and what happens afterward
Dying alone
The pain of grief
Their death not mattering to anyone
Dying and their body not being found
Having their body and movements restricted
Connecting with people who will one day die

POSSIBLE RESPONSES AND RESULTS
PTSD (difficulty sleeping, insomnia, night terrors, anxiety, etc.)
Developing phobias (e.g., a fear of driving if one was trapped with a dead person after an accident)
A short temper; becoming angry at small things
Experiencing fatigue
Self-medicating with alcohol or drugs
Thoughts that circle death

Becoming superstitious and adhering to certain rituals

Lessened emotional responses to events and people; having numbed emotions

Struggling to fit back into one's life after the event

Pulling away from family and friends or clinging to them

Struggling with ambition or enthusiasm about the future

Flashing back to disturbing images

Avoiding places, people, and events that remind one of the trauma

Being more attuned to death (noticing a dying rose on a bush, dead bugs on a windowsill, etc.)

Not wanting to talk about the experience despite needing to

Using anger to keep people from asking questions

Becoming distracted and having difficulty staying focused on tasks

Becoming risk-averse

Increased anxiety

Being unable to watch shows and movies that contain dead bodies

Becoming light-headed at the sight of blood

Sensitivity to the smells or textures associated with one's trauma

Developing a morbid outlook on life

Seeking distractions for comfort (promiscuous sex, bingeing, gambling, partying, etc.)

Implementing and strictly observing safety protocols

Cherishing and appreciating loved ones and working to show it better

Becoming protective of others, especially immediate family members

PERSONALITY TRAITS THAT MAY FORM

Attributes: Alert, cautious, discreet, focused, introverted, kind, nurturing, observant, private, proactive, protective, sentimental, spiritual

Flaws: Abrasive, addictive, controlling, impatient, impulsive, inattentive, inhibited, irrational, morbid, needy, nervous, scatterbrained

TRIGGERS THAT MIGHT AGGRAVATE THIS WOUND

Waking from a nightmare or having a flashback

Watching television and being exposed to a situation similar to one's wounding event

The sight of dead animals or other things that were once alive

Returning to places that are tied to one's trauma

Funerals

Situations tied to the trauma (e.g., having to get on a plane after surviving a crash)

OPPORTUNITIES TO FACE OR OVERCOME THIS WOUND

Being isolated with a gravely injured person and needing to keep them alive until help arrives

Seeing an opportunity to support a family member during treatment for a terminal illness

Being in a scenario where one must master fear to stay alive (e.g., a hostage situation)

Experiencing a life-or-death situation with a child and needing to stay calm for their sake

Being willing to do anything to help a loved one survive, even facing one's worst fears about death

DIVORCING ONE'S SPOUSE

NOTES: In the case of divorce, the character's behavior and ability to cope will vary depending on the reason for the marriage breakdown and whether it was a mutual choice or not. Taking the time to brainstorm the backstory leading to this event (infidelity, growing apart, financial issues, a sexual identity shift, a child's death, etc.) will help you better determine the turbulent emotions your character may be feeling and the actions and behaviors that will result.

BASIC NEEDS OFTEN COMPROMISED BY THIS WOUND: Physiological needs, safety and security, esteem and recognition

FALSE BELIEFS THAT COULD BE EMBRACED
I am unworthy of being loved.
All men (or women) cheat.
I'm just a meal ticket.
All women (or men) are gold-diggers.
Someone younger and better will always come along to replace me.
True commitment is a myth.
Only stupid people allow themselves to be vulnerable.
Love and happiness are mutually exclusive.
I was a fool for thinking love lasts forever. People are too selfish to commit.

THE CHARACTER MAY FEAR…
Getting old
Intimacy and vulnerability; being open with someone else
Commitment
Rejection
Betrayal
Being alone forever
Making a mistake with a relationship again
Trusting the wrong person

POSSIBLE RESPONSES AND RESULTS
A negative outlook; pessimism about the future
A tendency to generalize: *All men lie, they'll say anything to get what they want,* etc.
Transference: *My boss is just like my ex-husband, expecting me to sacrifice my plans for his.*
Resentment when good things (a new job, house, relationship, etc.) happen to the ex-partner
Fantasizing about exacting revenge
Anger that one can't shake
Falling apart when one is alone
Feeling overwhelmed at trying to manage everything on one's own
Viewing one's flaws in an unfair light (e.g., focusing on signs of aging, weight gain, etc.)

Believing one is somehow defective

Falling apart over small mishaps, like the dog getting into the trash and making a mess

Becoming jaded regarding relationships

Talking bad about one's ex to others

Worrying about money and resenting one's current financial position

Sending the ex-spouse angry messages or texts

Questioning one's children to gather information about the ex-partner

Saying things in front of one's kids that cast the spouse in a bad light

Refusing to help the spouse (e.g., if he or she has plans and needs to swap weekends)

Over-sensitivity; believing one's ex is pushing buttons on purpose

Feeling like one is being watched or followed (if the marriage was violent)

Paranoia that a volatile ex is causing misfortunes

Possessiveness (following one's ex, driving past their house, etc.)

Using one's children as a way to see the ex (if one wants closure or reconciliation)

Reckless behavior, such as having a one-night stand with a much younger person

Buying small gifts or taking trips to try and feel better about oneself

Competing as a parent with the ex (buying better gifts, taking the kids on a trip, etc.)

Changing one's appearance (wearing different clothing, growing a beard, etc.)

Gaining or losing a considerable amount of weight

Starting up old habits, like taking up smoking again

Becoming flirtatious or promiscuous

Buying a pet for a companion

PERSONALITY TRAITS THAT MAY FORM

Attributes: Adaptable, adventurous, flirtatious, happy, independent, industrious, loyal, nurturing, observant, pensive

Flaws: Callous, childish, confrontational, controlling, dishonest, gossipy, hostile, impatient, impulsive, inhibited, insecure, jealous

TRIGGERS THAT MIGHT AGGRAVATE THIS WOUND

Being contacted by one's in-laws

Bumping into the ex at a friend's place or the grocery store

One's kids asking questions about the divorce

Dining at a restaurant that used to be a favorite when one was married

Learning that one's spouse is dating

Having to drop off one's kids at the ex's for the weekend

Being asked on a date

OPPORTUNITIES TO FACE OR OVERCOME THIS WOUND

Being attracted to someone new and wanting to start a relationship

One's spouse reaching a relationship milestone, such as a girlfriend moving in

Having to unite with the ex to address a disciplinary problem with one's child

The ex helping one through hardship, like a cancer diagnosis or the death of a parent

GETTING LOST IN A NATURAL ENVIRONMENT

EXAMPLES: Being lost and alone for an extended period of time…
In the woods
In the mountains
In a desert
While hiking or camping
On the ocean

BASIC NEEDS OFTEN COMPROMISED BY THIS WOUND: Physiological needs, safety and security, esteem and recognition

FALSE BELIEFS THAT COULD BE EMBRACED
I am incompetent.
I can't trust my instincts.
I need others to rescue me.
To never be helpless again, I must prepare for everything.
When I take chances, I risk death.
If I am in charge of others, I will fail them.
Nothing I do matters because everything is determined by fate.
Nature is unpredictable and should be avoided.

THE CHARACTER MAY FEAR…
The specific landscape in which they were lost
Death by exposure or starvation
Being alone or isolated
Specific weather they may have experienced (e.g., snowstorms)
Venturing too far from home
New places or trying new things

POSSIBLE RESPONSES AND RESULTS
Rarely leaving one's home
Growing anxious if one's environment becomes too quiet, too dark, etc.
Avoiding places like the one where one was lost
Becoming obsessed with places like the one where one was lost
Hoarding food, blankets, or whatever else would have staved off suffering during one's trial
Being thrifty with resources
Developing a general mistrust for nature; expecting hidden danger to be present
Becoming dependent on others
Needing an abundance of technology to feel safe (internet service, a cell or satellite phone, a radio, a police scanner, etc.)
Never going anywhere alone
Becoming addicted to social media so one is always connected with others

Avoiding new places and experiences—especially those that require travel

Refusing to accept help from others

Relocating to a place where one feels more secure

Needing to be in control of everything

No longer adhering to social norms due to the lengthy amount of time spent alone (ignoring personal space, undressing in public, not bathing, etc.)

Difficulty being spontaneous

Being a downer during group activities and outings because one is so risk-averse

Deliberately putting oneself in those places as a way of facing one's fears

Educating oneself on survival skills

Working to become more independent and skilled

Planning ahead for emergencies (keeping a survival kit in the car, buying freeze-dried foods for an emergency stash, etc.)

Appreciating small comforts

Needing less materially than one did before the event

PERSONALITY TRAITS THAT MAY FORM

Attributes: Adaptable, alert, cautious, independent, observant, optimistic, patient, persistent, resourceful, sensible

Flaws: Controlling, defensive, selfish, superstitious, temperamental, timid, uncommunicative, uncooperative, withdrawn, worrywart

TRIGGERS THAT MIGHT AGGRAVATE THIS WOUND

Getting lost, even in a safe place (while trying to find a new doctor's office or visiting a friend in a different town, for instance)

Knowing that a loved one will be entering the same place where one was lost

Losing cell phone service while traveling

Extreme storms or weather that could lead to one being cut off from others

Current events hinting at a coming war or apocalypse that could create a survival situation again

Not having enough to eat or drink

OPPORTUNITIES TO FACE OR OVERCOME THIS WOUND

Being asked to go to a place similar to the area where one was lost (winning a cruise through work, a child needing a chaperone on a camping trip, etc.)

Developing a disorder (such as agoraphobia) from one's ordeal

A family member or friend who becomes lost and needs to be found and rescued

Having children who wish to bond through experiencing the outdoors and wanting to provide this for them

A child's growing resentment when one consistently denies them the opportunity to do certain things (go on campouts, sail on a friend's boat, etc.)

GIVING UP A CHILD FOR ADOPTION

NOTES: The process for adoption has changed over the years, so if your character has given up a child, carefully research the time period when it occurred. Depending on the date and location, the adoption may have been closed regardless of what the mother wished, she may have been coerced or forced into giving up her baby, or the type of adoption (open, semi-open, or closed) may have been her choice.

The level of pain this wound creates will likely depend on the reason for the adoption: to give one's child a better life, because one was unable to care for a baby, due to a rape or unwanted pregnancy, if the adoption was required due to an incarceration, or something else. So dig into your character's backstory as to why they made this choice.

BASIC NEEDS OFTEN COMPROMISED BY THIS WOUND: Love and belonging, esteem and recognition, self-actualization

FALSE BELIEFS THAT COULD BE EMBRACED
I would have been a terrible mother and my child is better off.
My child must hate me, so I should stay away.
My child will never forgive me for giving him or her up.
My child must hate me, and with good reason.
My child will never believe how much I wanted her, so I shouldn't try to explain.
I gave up my child, so I deserve to be alone.

THE CHARACTER MAY FEAR...
Meeting their child and disappointing him or her
Facing a daughter or son's anger at being given up
Never knowing what happened to the child
Family members discovering the adoption (if it was a secret)
That the child is being mistreated, needs help, is sick, etc.
Being rejected by family members for giving up the child
The child may show up at the door one day
The child will never seek them out

POSSIBLE RESPONSES AND RESULTS
Feeling guilt and regret at giving up one's child
An inability to move past the event
Breaking down and crying when one thinks about the child
Angry outbursts that result from bottled-up feelings
Self-medicating with alcohol or sedatives
Feeling guilty when others discuss their own children and the trials of rearing them
Wondering what one's child looks like
Looking into the mirror and trying to imagine which features the child might share

Daydreaming about having a relationship with the child

Struggling to care about day-to-day activities, like laundry, shopping, and work

Anger at those who withheld support when the decision was made

Anger at the birth father (for his abandonment, getting one pregnant, etc.)

Alternating between jealousy of the adoptive parents and wishing them well for the child's sake

Buying small gifts for one's child and hiding them away

Depression around the child's birthday and the day one gave him or her up

Thoughts of suicide and feelings of low self-worth

Searching social media or other public records to try and find one's child

Seeking to discover the child's current identity

Writing letters to one's child and then hiding or destroying them so they cannot be found

Dreams (positive and negative ones) that involve the child

A deep sense of loss that never abates

Imagining the child on important holidays (blowing out candles on a birthday, etc.)

Adopting another child or starting a family in hopes of easing the pain

Learning to practice self-care and self-forgiveness

PERSONALITY TRAITS THAT MAY FORM

Attributes: Affectionate, bold, idealistic, imaginative, loyal, nurturing, persistent, private, protective, resourceful, sentimental, unselfish

Flaws: Cowardly, defensive, disorganized, impatient, impulsive, insecure, jealous, obsessive, resentful, self-destructive, subservient

TRIGGERS THAT MIGHT AGGRAVATE THIS WOUND

Running into the birth father

Birthdays and holidays

Having to buy baby gifts for other new parents

Discovering that a family member has chosen to terminate a pregnancy or adopt a child

Seeing a boy or girl that looks the way one imagines the relinquished child might look

Being in a restaurant or airplane where a crying baby is present

TV commercials featuring babies

Movies about adoption

The relinquished child's eighteenth birthday (when he or she can request birth documents)

OPPORTUNITIES TO FACE OR OVERCOME THIS WOUND

A pregnancy

Being contacted by the relinquished child

One's family or spouse finding out about the child that was given up

Being diagnosed with an illness where a familial donor is needed

The desire to start a family

A rekindled relationship with the birth father

HAVING AN ABORTION

NOTES: The decision to have an abortion is never an easy one. Often this choice is the result of failed contraceptives, fetal birth defects, a pregnancy that is the product of rape or incest, an inability to care for and support a child, the pregnancy being unwanted, and when the mother, child, or both risk mortal danger if the pregnancy continues.

This wound can effect both parents, but because it is the female's body and she typically has ingrained maternal feelings regarding childbearing, this trauma impacts women more often than men. How a character deals with this event will depend on the circumstances, level of support, whether one was coerced into getting an abortion, one's personal and spiritual beliefs, if violence or abuse was involved, and whether there was a legitimate threat to the mother or baby's life.

BASIC NEEDS OFTEN COMPROMISED BY THIS WOUND: Love and belonging, esteem and recognition

FALSE BELIEFS THAT COULD BE EMBRACED
I should have resisted the pressure. I am a terrible person for failing to protect my child.
I should never have children as I am clearly unfit to be a parent.
Because of what I did, I deserve the bad things that happen to me.
If people discover what I did, they will shun me.
Some secrets should never be told, no matter how much they hurt.
Family only supports you in good times, not bad.
Hard times reveal the truth: love is conditional.

THE CHARACTER MAY FEAR...
Condemnation from the church
That others will discover she had an abortion
Getting pregnant again
Being judged by God
Being judged by loved ones
That she may not be able to have children when the time is right

POSSIBLE RESPONSES AND RESULTS
Feeling emotional numbness at times
Periods of sadness and depression
Suppressing one's grief, especially when the abortion is a secret
Sleeplessness and nightmares
Self-medicating with alcohol or drugs
Avoiding people and places with children, especially babies
Confusion and mixed emotions (relief that the crisis is over, grief at the loss, regret, etc.)
Having a difficult time pursuing new romantic relationships

Developing an eating disorder

Sexual dysfunction (a loss of pleasure, pain during intercourse, frigidity, avoiding sex, etc.)

Suicidal thoughts, or acting on one's suicidal thoughts

Crying as feelings of grief or shame hit

Isolating oneself; pulling away from family, friends, and one's partner

Putting on a false front to pretend one is fine

Difficulty bonding with one's other children out of guilt

Finding it difficult to relax or enjoy the little things

Becoming a workaholic

Feeling guilty when putting one's desires before others

Trying to be a "super-parent" to one's surviving children

An obsession with what one's child would have looked like had he or she been born

Anger at people who pushed for the abortion or contributed to the situation that led to it

Being plagued with doubt about important decisions

Avoiding pregnancy, even if one wishes to be a parent

Believing one is being punished when bad things happen

Opening up about one's abortion to someone trustworthy

Going to a therapist to process one's emotions

Becoming a strong pro-life supporter or advocate for a woman's right to choose

PERSONALITY TRAITS THAT MAY FORM

Attributes: Ambitious, analytical, discreet, empathetic, gentle, industrious, introverted, merciful, nurturing, protective, sentimental

Flaws: Abrasive, addictive, defensive, forgetful, humorless, impulsive, insecure, judgmental, martyr, obsessive

TRIGGERS THAT MIGHT AGGRAVATE THIS WOUND

The baby's due date

Passing a playground filled with children

Being invited to a baby shower

When abortion issues become hot topics in the media

Discovering that a friend is pregnant

Seeing another mother neglect her child

Seeing new mothers interact with their newborns

Seeing an ultrasound image of someone's baby

OPPORTUNITIES TO FACE OR OVERCOME THIS WOUND

Discovering one is pregnant

Wanting to start a family

Not wanting a friend who is considering abortion to go through it alone

Trying to get pregnant but being unable to do so

Being advised by a doctor to terminate a new pregnancy due to health problems

One's daughter getting pregnant as a teen and needing advice about what to do

HAVING TO KILL TO SURVIVE

EXAMPLES

A forced initiation into a gang

Killing to escape confinement or torture

A parent protecting a child or himself from a stranger

A parent protecting a child or herself from a violent spouse

A child protecting a loved one

Having to kill in battle (as a soldier) or as part of one's job (a bank guard, police officer, etc.)

Being forced to kill someone as part of a sadistic game or situation

Killing to protect one's vital resources in dire circumstances

Killing to obtain vital resources (food, water, weapons) for one's family

A child being forced to become a soldier

BASIC NEEDS OFTEN COMPROMISED BY THIS WOUND: Safety and security, love and belonging, esteem and recognition

FALSE BELIEFS THAT COULD BE EMBRACED

I am a violent and dangerous person. A monster.

I did the unthinkable and so I am capable of anything.

I will suffer damnation for what I've done.

No one will ever trust me again.

People look at me differently now.

It doesn't matter what I do, people will only see me as a killer.

If you take a life, you don't deserve to have one yourself.

The world is an evil place.

THE CHARACTER MAY FEAR...

What they are capable of

Passing violent tendencies on to their children

People finding out about what happened

Loved ones leaving if they discover what happened

Retribution or consequences (being arrested, the victim's loved ones taking vengeance, their children being removed from the home, etc.)

A specific people group or organization associated with the event

Being judged for what they did

POSSIBLE RESPONSES AND RESULTS

Self-loathing due to guilt or shame

Becoming hardened

Pulling away from loved ones

Struggling with anxiety when people argue or fight

PTSD symptoms (depression, anxiety, flashbacks, nightmares, etc.)

Worrying that one chose the violent option instead of considering others
Having to know where one's loved ones are at all times (if retribution is a possibility)
Difficulty building trust and friendships
Reluctance to share personal information
Being unable to be spontaneous
Reliving the killing over and over in one's mind
Self-medicating as a way of dealing with the guilt or shame
Becoming angry
Fearing one's own anger and what one is capable of
Experiencing broken sleep or insomnia
Assuming the worst; having a pessimistic outlook
A lack of faith in society and the good of people
Difficulty relaxing or enjoying the little things
Constantly noticing dangers and threats
Being deceptive; lying easily to keep one's actions hidden
Turning to or away from religion
Building an arsenal for self-protection
Increasing the security protocol for one's home and family
Venturing into new relationships slowly and with caution
Seeking to make amends to balance the scales (even if one's guilt is unfounded)
Becoming a pacifist; avoiding all conflict and friction

PERSONALITY TRAITS THAT MAY FORM

Attributes: Alert, appreciative, cautious, courageous, decisive, diplomatic, disciplined, independent, protective, resourceful, socially aware

Flaws: Addictive, antisocial, controlling, cynical, defensive, impatient, inflexible, irrational, needy, paranoid, pessimistic, prejudiced

TRIGGERS THAT MIGHT AGGRAVATE THIS WOUND

Movies or TV shows depicting physical violence
Nightmares where one relives the event
A fistfight breaking out nearby
An argument that escalates into yelling and screaming
Specific sensory details from one's experience, such as the roughness of a length of wood
One's children playacting violent situations (e.g., a pretend game of heroes and villains)
Running into the victim's loved ones

OPPORTUNITIES TO FACE OR OVERCOME THIS WOUND

Being faced with a life-or-death situation where the life of another is in one's hands
Discovering later that one misread the situation and the death wasn't necessary
Being judged, tried, or maligned for the action, even if it was done in self-defense
Noticing a change in the way one's child or spouse behaves in one's presence

LOSING A LOVED ONE TO A RANDOM ACT OF VIOLENCE

EXAMPLES
A sibling being hit by stray bullets in a drive-by shooting or gang war
A spouse being killed in a robbery
A child or spouse dying in a school shooting
A loved one being jumped by hopped-up addicts
Friends or family being killed in a terrorist attack
A loved one stepping in to break up a fight and being stabbed or shot
One's partner being fatally wounded after a mugging
A family member being killed due to a case of mistaken identity
One's child being run over as criminals leave a scene or flee from police
One's parent (a police officer, swat team or bomb squad member, etc.) dying in the line of duty

BASIC NEEDS OFTEN COMPROMISED BY THIS WOUND: Safety and security, love and belonging, esteem and recognition, self-actualization

FALSE BELIEFS THAT COULD BE EMBRACED
I should have been able to prevent it.
I am a terrible spouse (or parent, person, etc.) for not protecting my loved one.
It's better to not love anyone than to love and have someone taken from you.
The system is broken. There is no protection or justice for people like us (those sharing the victim's race, gender, religious affiliation, etc.).
Evil always wins.
It's only a matter of time before what you love is taken from you.
It's stupid to plan for the future when bad things will happen no matter what you do.

THE CHARACTER MAY FEAR...
Being alone
Losing another loved one to violence
Not being in control
Having to raise their children alone (if a spouse was killed)
Specific situations connected with the death (e.g., being afraid to drive if the loved one was carjacked)
People who resemble the killer (those of a certain ethnicity or gender, with facial scars, etc.)
Trusting someone and endangering a loved one as a result

POSSIBLE RESPONSES AND RESULTS
Crying bouts and depression
Engaging in displays of anger to release emotion at whoever was responsible
Talking to the deceased loved one when times are hard or the hurt is especially difficult
Smelling the loved one's clothing or pillow in hopes of catching their scent
Going through photos and mementos

Becoming safety-obsessed; worrying about the welfare of remaining loved ones
Obsessively locking and checking one's door and window locks
Repeatedly checking in with loved ones (via texts, looking in as a child sleeps, etc.)
Carrying a weapon
Always having a cell phone fully charged and handy
Avoiding crowded areas or strange people
Forcing remaining family members to adhere to safety protocols
Being aloof; having a hard time letting people in (especially if a partner was killed)
Frequently visiting a grave site or the area where the loved one died
Drinking or self-medicating
Becoming obsessed with bringing the perpetrators to justice
Rejecting one's faith or rededicating oneself to it
Becoming prejudiced against the kind of people associated with the loved one's death
Joining a support group
Adhering to a specific routine that one deems to be safe
Becoming alert and more aware of one's surroundings
Making the most of every opportunity with remaining loved ones
Being more affectionate with loved ones than one was before
Dedicating oneself to effecting change (through speaking to raise awareness, financially supporting an advocacy group, etc.)

PERSONALITY TRAITS THAT MAY FORM
Attributes: Appreciative, decisive, empathetic, generous, hospitable, introverted, just, loyal, merciful, observant, passionate, pensive
Flaws: Addictive, antisocial, confrontational, hostile, humorless, impulsive, indecisive, inflexible, irrational, needy, nervous, obsessive

TRIGGERS THAT MIGHT AGGRAVATE THIS WOUND
Hearing gunshots, sirens, tires squealing, or other sounds associated with the violent crime
Violent movie trailers and video game ads
Waking up from a nightmare where the event was replayed
Finding an old text or picture on one's phone
A child coming home with a scrape or other visible injury

OPPORTUNITIES TO FACE OR OVERCOME THIS WOUND
Learning that the responsible person has victimized someone else
A scenario that causes worry for the safety of another loved one
One's neighborhood growing increasingly dangerous
Desiring justice so badly that one must take action
Finding out the perpetrator is being let go because of a technicality or police screw-up
Learning that a family member has ties to the responsible party (they're friends, co-workers, etc.)

THE DEATH OF ONE'S CHILD

NOTES: Though a son or daughter's death can take many forms, one factor that can greatly affect resulting outcomes is whether or not the parent was responsible. When a child dies and there was nothing the parent could do, they'll still often blame themselves to a certain degree. The depth of this wound (and therefore the fallout from avoiding dealing with it in a healthy way) will depend on how keenly the parent feels responsible for their child's death. To explore this kind of wound further, this entry will focus on the death of a child for which the parent was technically not to blame. (For information on a wounding event where the person in charge of the child was even accidentally or incidentally at fault, see A CHILD DYING ON ONE'S WATCH.)

EXAMPLES: One's child dying…
From a terminal illness
In a car accident
In a natural disaster
From a freak accident during a sporting event (e.g., suffering a fatal head injury)
Due to an undiagnosed condition (a serious allergy, bleeding out due to hemophilia, etc.)
From being hit by a car while walking home from the bus stop
While lost in a natural environment
From a dangerous activity one had forbidden them to do (e.g., climbing on the roof)
Of Sudden Infant Death Syndrome (SIDS)
In utero, during birth, or shortly thereafter

BASIC NEEDS OFTEN COMPROMISED BY THIS WOUND: Love and belonging, safety and security, self-actualization

FALSE BELIEFS THAT COULD BE EMBRACED
I can't keep my loved ones safe.
I am to blame for my child's death (even when one was not responsible).
I don't deserve forgiveness.
God did this to punish me (for whatever imagined or irrational transgression creates guilt).
If I am not a mother (or father), I am nothing.
Nothing is worth risking this pain of loss again.
Danger is everywhere. I have to be prepared or I'll lose someone else.
Letting others care for my child is reckless. I will make sure she stays safe.

THE CHARACTER MAY FEAR…
That they will never feel whole
Being alone for the rest of their life
Forgetting what the child looked like or sounded like
Losing another loved one (a spouse, sibling, child, etc.)
Specific situations that led to the child's death

POSSIBLE RESPONSES AND RESULTS

Spending a lot of time in the child's room

Looking for someone to blame, even if there is no one

Watching old videos or going through old pictures

Struggling to care about other people and their problems

Friction with a spouse over grieving processes (one wanting to purge the child's things, the other wanting to keep everything, etc.)

Adopting superstitions or rituals to better protect one's other children

Mistaking other children for one's child due to a similar look or mannerism

Vivid dreaming that can be emotionally painful

Developing an anxiety disorder

Pulling away from people

Wanting to live in the past and avoid the present

Turning away from one's faith

Talking aloud to the deceased child, especially to apologize for failing them

Avoiding kids, especially those the same age as one's deceased child

Refusing to participate in special holidays because doing so hurts

Researching to better understand the circumstances that led to the child's death

Carrying a memento of one's child at all times (a bracelet, a picture or favorite key chain, etc.)

Moving to a new home that doesn't have so many painful memories

Returning to one's faith or finding faith

Creating and maintaining a memorial at the place where one's child died

PERSONALITY TRAITS THAT MAY FORM

Attributes: Appreciative, empathetic, gentle, industrious, inspirational, nurturing, pensive, persistent, private, proactive, protective, spiritual, unselfish

Flaws: Addictive, controlling, cynical, humorless, irrational, irresponsible, jealous, martyr, morbid, needy, nervous, obsessive, oversensitive, perfectionist

TRIGGERS THAT MIGHT AGGRAVATE THIS WOUND

The mention of the child's name

When people are clearly avoiding mentioning the child at all

When another person asks how many children one has

Being around children the same age as one's child

Attending a baby shower, birthday party, or coming-of-age event, like a graduation

OPPORTUNITIES TO FACE OR OVERCOME THIS WOUND

The desire to have another child

Discovering one is pregnant before one has fully processed the death

Deteriorating relationships with one's other children because they feel neglected

Wanting to help a surviving child process their sibling's death but being unable to do so because of one's own grief

WATCHING SOMEONE DIE

EXAMPLES

Trying (and failing) to help a passenger in the aftermath of a car accident

Witnessing a friend's hit and run as she crosses the street

Losing a loved one to a drowning or boating accident on a family vacation

Offering end-of-life comfort (e.g., after a fatal fall)

Finding someone alive after a natural disaster but being too late to save him or her

Being helpless to stop a violent act such as a mugging or hate crime beating

Witnessing someone die in a random accident, like being electrocuted by faulty wiring or being involved in a fatal motorcycle accident

Being unable to reach a person who is trapped by fire (seeing them on a high-rise balcony with nowhere to go or being unable to reach the building floor they're trapped on)

A child experiencing a fatal accident during a sporting game or practice

BASIC NEEDS OFTEN COMPROMISED BY THIS WOUND: Love and belonging, esteem and recognition, self-actualization

FALSE BELIEFS THAT COULD BE EMBRACED

I failed when I was needed most.

I should have died, not them.

Anyone I love will be taken from me.

I'm toxic to the people around me (if blame comes into play).

Loving someone will only end in pain.

I could die at any moment, so why plan for the future?

Danger is everywhere and I can never let down my guard.

THE CHARACTER MAY FEAR...

Abandonment through death

Dying and abandoning those in their care

Becoming too emotionally connected to people

Circumstances and other factors associated with the cause of death (guns, fire, heights, driving in the rain, etc.)

Causing loved ones harm (if real or imaginary self-blame is a factor)

Failing someone when they desperately need help

Being responsible for others

Danger and risk

POSSIBLE RESPONSES AND RESULTS

Suffering from PTSD

Depression

Obsessing about the victim to the point that others are marginalized

Being unable to sleep

Avoiding people who were present at the time of death

Becoming clingy with remaining loved ones

Becoming overprotective of family and obsessing over their whereabouts

Refusing to allow one's children to do activities that could be risky

Becoming safety conscious to the extreme

Always worrying about possible dangers

Needing to plan and negate all risks before committing to an action or decision

Avoiding anything spontaneous; becoming very risk-averse

Behaving in self-destructive ways or being reckless (to prove one is not worthy of living)

Avoiding future responsibility for the welfare of others

Distancing oneself from friends and family

Scaling back one's relationships so they are surface-level rather than deep

Throwing oneself into work or other activities to avoid dealing with grief

Seeking justice, vengeance, or restitution for the death (investigating, raising public awareness, suing involved parties, etc.)

Attending a survivor's support group meeting

Processing the deceased's things (donating items, distributing things to loved ones, etc.)

Creating a scholarship in the deceased's name

Weaning oneself off medication or sleeping pills that have been used as a coping mechanism

PERSONALITY TRAITS THAT MAY FORM

Attributes: affectionate, alert, cautious, focused, independent, nurturing, observant, organized, proactive, sensible, wise

Flaws: Indecisive, perfectionist, resentful, self-destructive, temperamental, timid, uncommunicative, withdrawn, worrywart

TRIGGERS THAT MIGHT AGGRAVATE THIS WOUND

Witnessing one's children acting in a foolhardy way

Sensory input from the event (e.g., antiseptic smells reminding one of hospital visits)

A loved one being injured or hospitalized

Visiting the scene of the accident

Witnessing another "close call" type accident

Internet videos that show accidents, close calls, and foolhardy behavior just for entertainment

OPPORTUNITIES TO FACE OR OVERCOME THIS WOUND

Having responsibility thrust upon oneself in some way, such as a sister dying and being the only relative left to care for her son

Discovering who was responsible for the death, but police are unmotivated or unable to enact justice

Uncovering a fault associated with the person's death (an equipment malfunction, a structure was not built to code, etc.)

Being a single parent or a sole provider and having to be strong for others

APPENDIX A: WOUND FLOWCHART

Figuring out a character's wounding event can be daunting for an author. Not only is it an important piece of the backstory puzzle to identify, it's also the first in a series of dominoes that will threaten the character's very foundation. As the author, it's important to know all of these pieces so the character will be believable and can be written consistently. To better understand which elements will need to be researched and the cause-and-effect relationships between them, use the following flowchart as a handy reference.

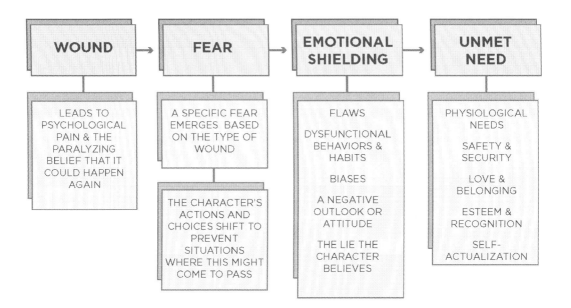

APPENDIX B: CHARACTER ARC PROGRESSION TOOL

Once you have a basic understanding of how the wound will impact a character, you'll need to know how those aftereffects should play into his or her arc. This graphic provides an overview of how everything fits together. You can find a blank copy on the next page, which can be printed out and filled in for different characters.

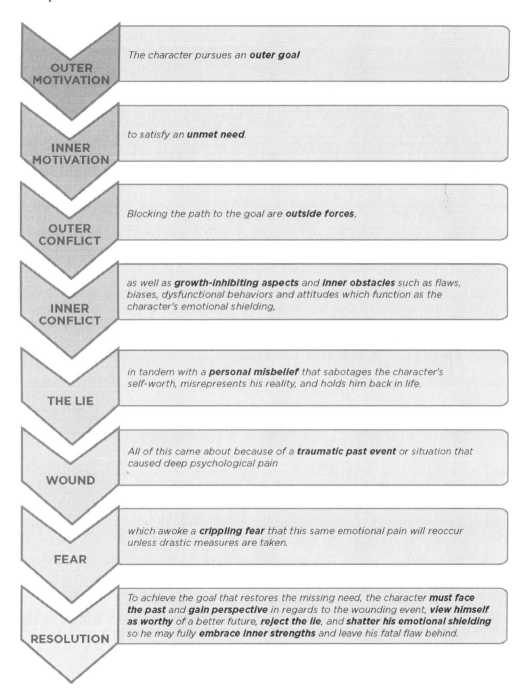

OUTER MOTIVATION — *The character pursues an **outer goal***

INNER MOTIVATION — *to satisfy an **unmet need**.*

OUTER CONFLICT — *Blocking the path to the goal are **outside forces**,*

INNER CONFLICT — *as well as **growth-inhibiting aspects** and **inner obstacles** such as flaws, biases, dysfunctional behaviors and attitudes which function as the character's emotional shielding,*

THE LIE — *in tandem with a **personal misbelief** that sabotages the character's self-worth, misrepresents his reality, and holds him back in life.*

WOUND — *All of this came about because of a **traumatic past event** or situation that caused deep psychological pain*

FEAR — *which awoke a **crippling fear** that this same emotional pain will reoccur unless drastic measures are taken.*

RESOLUTION — *To achieve the goal that restores the missing need, the character **must face the past** and **gain perspective** in regards to the wounding event, **view himself as worthy** of a better future, **reject the lie**, and **shatter his emotional shielding** so he may fully **embrace inner strengths** and leave his fatal flaw behind.*

APPENDIX B: CHARACTER ARC PROGRESSION TOOL

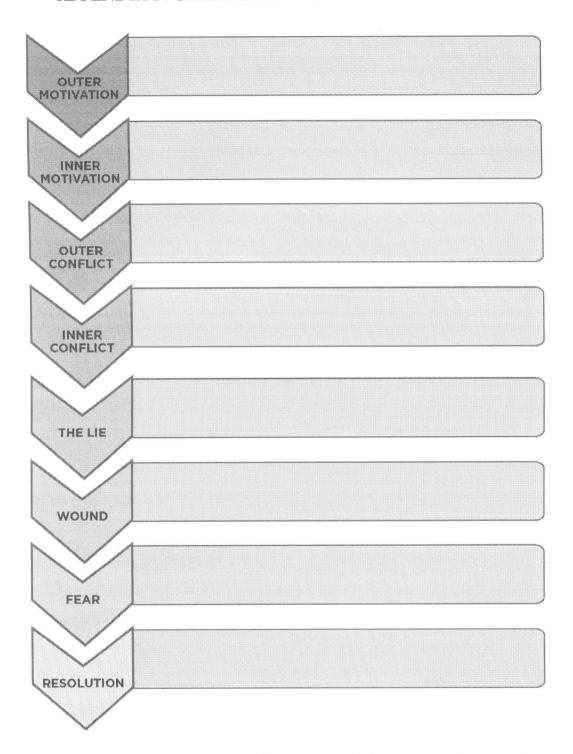

A printable version of this tool is available at www.writershelpingwriters.net/writing-tools.

APPENDIX C: WOUNDING EXAMPLES
FROM POPULAR STORIES

An author may not always reveal all the details behind a wounding experience, and so some of the inner turmoil left in the trauma's wake is only hinted at. In particular, the resulting fears and lies from a wound are rarely stated outright; however, this allows readers to get involved and use their imaginations to visualize the aftereffects. To help you see how the pieces can fit together successfully, we've profiled some popular characters and their wounding events. If any of the elements are implied rather than clearly defined (such as the lie, for instance), it won't be included here; still, these examples should help you see how the wound can lead to a greater fear, what emotional shielding might be donned, and the unmet need that will play a large role in the character's present story.

Jack Torrance (*The Shining*)

<u>Wound</u>: Growing up with an abusive and alcoholic parent

<u>Fear</u>: That he will be just like his dad

<u>Emotional Shielding</u>: Jack is a recovering alcoholic with rage issues who struggles to banish the demons of his past. Though he recognizes his long-dead father's negative influence over him, he doesn't fully refute the resulting insecurities and self-doubt, which undermine his efforts to become a better parent and husband.

<u>Unmet Need</u>: Ultimately, Jack is lacking Esteem and Recognition because he doesn't respect himself. He knows his father's words are toxic, but his inability to separate himself from them makes him second-guess himself and his capabilities. Though he finds redemption in the end, the insecurity resulting from his wound eventually leads to his physical demise.

Will Hunting (*Good Will Hunting*)

<u>Wound</u>: Being abandoned by his birth parents and living in a series of abusive foster homes

<u>Fear</u>: Being rejected or abandoned again

<u>Emotional Shielding</u>: Will is a classic underachiever, purposely ignoring his potential and sticking with the only people in his life he knows he can trust. He has anger issues, is cocky, and lashes out when threatened. Though he seeks out romantic relationships, he sabotages them before they get too serious.

<u>Unmet Need</u>: In part, Will is missing Love and Belonging; he has friends, but his pursuit of Skylar shows that friendship isn't enough to satisfy him. However, his biggest unmet need—the one at the root of his inability to obtain the belonging he desires—is that of Esteem and Recognition. Like many abuse survivors, he blames himself in part for the violence he suffered growing up. He also likely fears that because his parents rejected him, there's something in him that will make others reject him too. Once he faces the possibility that he wasn't responsible for the traumatic events from his past, he's able to accept himself for who he is: someone with value and potential who is worthy of being loved.

Marlin (*Finding Nemo*)

Wound: The violent loss of his wife and children

Fear: That he will lose his remaining son, too

Emotional Shielding: Marlin was the definition of a helicopter parent before anyone knew what it was. He assumes the worst about the world, constantly hovers over Nemo, and allows his son to make few important decisions for himself. He also lives in constant fear, believing that everything and everyone poses a threat and cannot be trusted.

Unmet Need: With the loss of his wife and children, Marlin's Safety and Security has gone out the window. Ironically, his over-the-top efforts to protect his son drive him further away, putting Nemo in danger and creating exactly the kind of nightmare situation Marlin most wants to avoid.

Zack Mayo (*An Officer and a Gentleman*)

Wound: Finding his mother after she committed suicide, then being sent to live with a father who was too busy drinking and whoring to raise him properly

Fear: That he will never truly belong anywhere

Emotional Shielding: Mayo has grown up with a caregiver who told him he didn't want to be a father. As such, he's pretty much raised himself and is now completely self-reliant. He doesn't work well with others, is self-serving, and has understandable issues with authority. While he has friends, they are secondary to his own needs and him getting what he wants.

Unmet Need: Mayo's decision to enter Aviation Officer Candidate School seems like a strange one for an independent character who is uncooperative and doesn't like taking orders. But his real reason for pursuing this particular goal is that he needs Love and Belonging; he wants to belong and be part of a group—something he's never been able to do before.

General Woundwort (*Watership Down*)

Wound: Witnessing the death of his siblings at the hand of a farmer and seeing his mother killed by a fox

Fear: That he will be victimized by those more powerful than him

Emotional Shielding: Forced to raise himself alone in the wild, Woundwort has become shrewd, savage, and controlling, forcibly taking over every community he's encountered. Anyone questioning or threatening his authority must be dealt with immediately. This is where we find him in *Watership Down*, viciously ruling his warren with an iron thumb without a shred of mercy for anyone.

Unmet Need: While his need isn't stated outright, readers can assume that Woundwort's behavior springs from a missing Safety and Security need. The fear of succumbing to his family's fate has driven him to adopt the goals, behaviors, personality traits, and habits that have made him one of literature's most memorable villains.

APPENDIX D: BACKSTORY WOUND PROFILE TOOL

The person who hurt your character in the past: _____
_____
_____

What happened (the wounding event or situation): _____
_____
_____

Where it happened: _____

It was a ☐ single   ☐ ongoing   ☐ repeated event.

Factors that made the situation more difficult:

☐ Personality   ☐ Physical Proximity   ☐ Responsibility   ☐ Support   ☐ Recurrence
☐ Justice   ☐ Compounding Events   ☐ Invasiveness   ☐ Emotional proximity ☐ Emotional State

Details: _____
_____
_____

Fallout resulting from this experience (flaws, behaviors, sensitivities, relationship issues, insecurities, etc.):
_____
_____

Negative life lessons this situation taught the character:_____
_____
_____

Trust issues that developed:_____
_____

Ways the character's self-worth was damaged: _____
_____
_____

The fear that emerged:_____
_____

Flaws that developed to keep people and painful situations at a distance: _____
_____

Biases that developed due to this experience: _____
_____

Negative attitudes or outlooks that resulted: _____
_____

The lie the character now believes (that contributes to self-blame, self-worth, disillusionment, etc.): _____
_____

Emotions the character now avoids: _____
_____

Triggers for this wound: _____
_____

A printable version of this tool is available at www.writershelpingwriters.net/writing-tools.

RECOMMENDED READING

Understanding a character's inner landscape allows you to effectively show what drives him or her throughout the story. To read further on character motivation, wounds, and how these play out within character arc, try these excellent books.

Creating Character Arcs: The Masterful Author's Guide to Uniting Story Structure helps you look deeper into the story beats that create realistic and compelling character arcs. (K.M. Weiland)

Writing the Heart of Your Story: The Secret to Crafting an Unforgettable Novel will teach you how to mine the heart of your plot, characters, themes, and so much more. To write a book that targets the heart of readers, you need to know the heart of your story. (C. S. Lakin)

Story Genius will take you step-by-step from the first glimmer of an idea to an expansive, multilayered cause-and-effect blueprint—including fully realized scenes. (Lisa Cron)

Writing Screenplays That Sell, New Twentieth Anniversary Edition teaches all writers to think deeply about their characters' motivations, story structure, and the art of selling. (Michael Hauge)

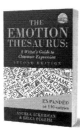   

  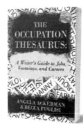 

PRAISE FOR...

THE EMOTION THESAURUS

"One of the challenges a fiction writer faces, especially when prolific, is coming up with fresh ways to describe emotions. This handy compendium fills that need. It is both a reference and a brainstorming tool, and one of the resources I'll be turning to most often as I write my own books."

~ James Scott Bell, International Thriller Writers Award Winner

THE POSITIVE AND NEGATIVE TRAIT THESAURUSES

"In these brilliantly conceived, superbly organized and astonishingly thorough volumes, Angela Ackerman and Becca Puglisi have created an invaluable resource for writers and storytellers. Whether you are searching for new and unique ways to add and define characters, or brainstorming methods for revealing those characters without resorting to clichés, it is hard to imagine two more powerful tools for adding depth and dimension to your screenplays, novels or plays."

~ Michael Hauge, Hollywood script consultant and author of *Writing Screenplays That Sell*

THE URBAN AND RURAL SETTING THESAURUSES

"The one thing I always appreciate about Ackerman and Puglisi's Thesauri series is how comprehensive they are. They never stop at just the obvious, and they always over-deliver. Their Setting Thesauri are no different, offering not just the obvious notes of the various settings they've covered, but going into easy-to-miss details like smells and tastes. They even offer to jumpstart the brainstorming with categories on potential sources of conflict."

~ K.M. Weiland, best-selling author of *Creating Character Arcs* and *Structuring Your Novel*

THE EMOTIONAL WOUND THESAURUS

"This is far more than a brilliant, thorough, insightful, and unique thesaurus. This is the best primer on story—and what REALLY hooks and holds readers—that I have ever read."

~ Lisa Cron, TEDx Speaker and best-selling author of *Wired For Story* and *Story Genius*

THE OCCUPATION THESAURUS

"Each and every thesaurus these authors produce is spectacular. *The Occupation Thesaurus* is no different. Full of inspiration, teachings, and knowledge that are guaranteed to take your writing to the next level, it's a must. You need this book on your craft shelf."

~ Sacha Black, bestselling author of *Anatomy of Prose*

ADD WRITERS HELPING WRITERS° TO YOUR TOOLKIT!

Over a decade of articles are waiting to help you grow your writing skills, navigate publishing and marketing, and assist you on your career path. And if you'd like to stay informed about forthcoming books, discover unique writing resources, and access even more practical writing tips, sign up for our newsletter onsite (https://writershelpingwriters.net/subscribe-to-our-newsletter/).

Writers, are you ready for a game-changer?

In a flooded market, exceptional novels rise above the rest, and to get noticed, authors must bring their A-game. One Stop for Writers gives creatives an edge with powerful, one-of-a-kind story and character resources, helping them deliver fresh, compelling fiction that readers crave.

Brought to you by the minds behind *The Occupation Thesaurus*, One Stop is home to the largest show-don't-tell description database available anywhere and contains an innovative toolkit that makes storytelling almost criminally easy. A fan favorite is the hyper-intelligent Character Builder, which helps you explore a character's deepest layers to uncover their desires, fears, motivations, and needs that drive the story. It will even create an accurate Character Arc Blueprint for you, making it easier to marry the plot to your character's internal journey. And the site's story structure maps, timelines, worldbuilding surveys, generators, and tutorials give you what you need when you need it. So forget about staring at the screen wondering what to write. Those days are over, friend.

If you think it's time someone made writing easier, join us at https://www.onestopforwriters.com and give our **two-week free trial** a spin. If you choose to subscribe, use the code **ONESTOPFORWRITERS** for a one-time discount of 25% off any plan*. We're Writers Helping Writers, remember?

See you at One Stop!
Becca Puglisi & Angela Ackerman

*For full details and conditions, see our Coupon Redemption guidelines at https://onestopforwriters.com/coupon

Printed in Great Britain
by Amazon